The Forgotten Zionist

The Life of Solomon (Sioma) Yankelevitch Jacobi

The Forgotten Zionist

The Life of Solomon (Sioma) Yankelevitch Jacobi

Rodney Benjamin and David Cebon

gefen publishing house

JERUSALEM ◆ NEW YORK

Cover Design: Michal Cohen
Typesetting: Irit Nachum

ISBN: 9781791846251

1 3 5 7 9 8 6 4 2

Gefen Publishing House Ltd.
6 Hatzvi Street
Jerusalem 94386, Israel
972-2-538-0247
orders@gefenpublishing.com

Gefen Books
11 Edison Place
Springfield, NJ 07081
516-593-1234
orders@gefenpublishing.com

www.gefenpublishing.com

Printed in Israel　　　　　　　　　　　　　　*Send for our free catalogue*

Library of Congress Cataloging-in-Publication Data

Benjamin, Rodney, 1930–
The life of Solomon (Sioma) Yankelevitch Jacobi / Rodney Benjamin and David Cebon.
p. cm.
Includes bibliographical references.
ISBN 978-965-229-571-2
1. Jacobi, Shlomo, 1917–   2. Revisionist Zionists—Biography.
3. Revisionist Zionism—History.   4. Jews—England—Biography.
5. Jews—Ukraine—Biography.   6. Revisionist Zionism—Palestine—History.
7. New Zionist Organization. I. Cebon, David. II. Title.
DS151.J24B46 2012
320.54095694092–dc23
[B]
2012006448

Contents

Foreword   vii

Preface   xi

1   There Was a Man   1

2   The Early Years   7

3   Jewish Self-Defense in Odessa   21

4   Palestine on Both Sides of the Jordan   41

5   Palestine and Then to England   57

6   The Birth of the Revisionist Movement   67

7   ORT-OZE and Emigdirect – The 1928 Journey   85

8   Marriage   99

9   Melbourne, China, Melbourne, South Africa   113

10 South Africa   121

11 To London – The Revisionist Split   129

12   Michael Haskel and the Stavsky Affair   145

13   The Jordania Experiment   155

14   London, 1933 and 1934   159

15   Jabotinsky, Ben-Gurion, Jacobi, and the New Zionist Organization   173

16   Back to the NZO   183

17   Af Al Pi – Clandestine Immigration in Spite of the British Restrictions   195

18   Postscript   213

Selected Bibliography   221

Index   225

Foreword

The coming to power of the government of Menahem Begin in Israel in June 1977 stimulated a new interest in the history of the Revisionist movement within Zionism, of which Begin was a prominent member. There had already appeared in 1956 a major biography of the founder of Revisionist Zionism, Vladimir Jabotinsky, by his close associate Joseph Schechtman, entitled *Rebel and Statesman: The Vladimir Jabotinsky Story*.[1] Among the works now published are a comprehensive biography of Begin by Eitan Haber, *Menachem Begin: The Legend and the Man*;[2] Shmuel Katz's biography of Jabotinsky, *Lone Wolf: A Biography of Vladimir (Ze'ev) Jabotinsky*;[3] the study of the second cadre of Revisionist ideologues – the circle of young men who associated themselves with Jabotinsky and the Revisionist movement in Palestine in the 1920s and 1930s – under the title *Jewish Radical Right: Revisionist Zionism and Its Ideological Legacy*[4] by Eran Kaplan; and a new English translation of Jabotinsky's novel describing Jewish life in Odessa, *The Five: A Novel of Jewish Life in Turn-of-the-Century Odessa*.[5] In addition, a government commission investigated the disputed question of whether members of the Revisionist movement were

---

1 New York: T. Yoseloff, 1956.
2 New York: Delacorte Press, 1978.
3 New York: Barricade Books, 1996.
4 Madison, WI: University of Wisconsin Press, 1995.
5 New York: Cornell University Press, 2005.

responsible for the assassination of Histadrut leader Haim Arlosoroff in Tel Aviv in June 1933.

Yet in all these works, as well as in the *Encyclopedia Judaica* and in the *YIVO Encyclopedia of Jews in Eastern Europe,* there is almost no mention of one of Jabotinsky's closest associates and friends, Solomon (Sioma) Jacobi. There is thus all the more reason to welcome this well-researched and comprehensive biography, based on approximately five hundred letters between Jacobi and Jabotinsky, which form an invaluable new source for the history of Revisionist Zionism.

Solomon Jacobi was born in Berdichev, one of the largest Jewish centers in Ukraine, which in 1897 had a Jewish population of nearly forty-two thousand (80 percent of the total population). Between 1908 and 1919 he lived in Odessa, and also studied engineering in St. Petersburg in 1917 and 1918. The Russian civil war saw a major outbreak of anti-Jewish violence mainly in Ukraine. It is uncertain how many people died in the pogroms; the most reliable estimates vary from fifty thousand to one hundred thousand. These estimates do not include the many more who were wounded or, in the case of women, raped, while as many as two hundred thousand children were orphaned. There were also many affected by psychological disorders.

One Jewish response was to form self-defense groups, most of which were organized under the auspices of the Jewish Ministry of the Ukrainian Directorate, the Ukrainian government which sought to establish its independence in these years. These groups did not possess a centralized command, which greatly impeded the effectiveness of locally established units. Some "Self-Help" committees organized local militias, which were often useless against the pogroms organized by the stronger forces of the Directory and the White Army. However, they were fairly effective against less organized attacks. It remains a moot point whether the earlier creation of a coordinated system of Jewish self-defense could have limited the scale of the pogrom wave. Jacobi, then a young man in his early twenties, played a key role in the defense unit established in Odessa, which was the scene of much violent conflict in these years.

Jacobi's experience in organizing the self-defense unit in Odessa convinced him of the importance of military force in advancing the Zionist cause. This, together with the reputation he had established there, brought him into contact with Vladimir Jabotinsky, with whom he shared a common background in Odessa. They became lifelong friends, as is well-documented by the correspondence in this volume.

Jacobi then moved to England, where he was able to qualify as a civil engineer in 1925. His commitment to completing his studies meant that he could not attend the founding conference of the Union of Zionist-Revisionists, which took place in Paris in 1925. Nevertheless, Jabotinsky invited him to work on the group's journal, *Rasswyet*. He was a signatory of the Revisionist manifesto signed in Paris in the same year and accompanied Jabotinsky on his speaking tour in the United States in 1926.

In the following years, he worked as a fundraiser for ORT-OZE, which enabled him to travel widely and also to win some support for Revisionist Zionism. He visited Egypt, India, Australia, the USA, China, and South Africa. It was in Australia that he met his wife, Edna, who was his devoted supporter throughout his life and beyond.

Relations between the Revisionists and the World Zionist Organization deteriorated. In 1935, the Revisionists decided to secede from the World Zionist Organization and form their own organization, the New Zionist Organization (NZO). Jacobi became more active in the organization. Already in 1933, he had played a role in organizing the defence of Abba Ahimeir and Zevi Rosenblatt, members of Betar, the Revisionist youth movement, who were accused of the murder of Arlosoroff. In 1934, Jabotinsky appointed Jacobi to run the movement's London office. He did so with some success for the next five years. Then, in 1939, Jabotinsky asked him to move to Warsaw to take charge of Revisionist activities there. This was an important responsibility because Warsaw was a center for illegal Jewish emigration to Palestine. Jabotinsky and the NZO had established close links not only with the government, particularly the Consular Section of the Ministry of Foreign Affairs, which was eager to facilitate Jewish emigration, but also with the General Staff and Military Intelligence. The meetings, which began in early 1936 and continued until the outbreak of the war, led to a series of covert agreements to facilitate

Jewish immigration to Palestine and provide training and weapons for the Irgun Zvai Leummi (National Military Organization, known popularly as the Irgun), the paramilitary force established by the NZO. This military assistance was on a smaller scale than has sometimes been claimed, and some of the arms purchased in Poland never reached Palestine because of organizational obstacles. The Polish government also supported Jabotinsky's claim for a Jewish state on both sides of the Jordan River and pressed the British authorities to facilitate immigration to Palestine.

The outbreak of the war and the Nazi occupation of Warsaw forced Jacobi to move to Romania, where he continued his important work. The strain and effort took its toll and in November 1939 he collapsed with a brain tumor and died at the tragically early age of forty-two. His death was followed by that of Jabotinsky himself in August of the following year. How different might the fate of the Jewish people have been had these two great leaders not been removed from the scene at the start of the worst tragedy in Jewish history. All the more reason, therefore, to welcome this biography of Solomon Jacobi, the forgotten Zionist.

Professor Antony Polonsky
Albert Abramson Professor of Holocaust Studies, Brandeis University
September 2011

PREFACE

Over their twenty-year friendship Solomon (Sioma) Yankelevitch Jacobi and Vladimir Jabotinsky exchanged some five hundred letters. Jacobi's letters to Jabotinsky began "Dear V. E." and Jabotinsky's responses began "Dear S. L."

Both men spoke and wrote fluently in a number of languages. Jacobi's surviving letters to Jabotinsky were written in English, and where they are directly quoted in this work they have been reproduced exactly as written. Likewise for his letters to his wife Edna, which were all written in English. Many of Jabotinsky's letters to Jacobi have survived in the Jabotinsky archives. They had been translated into Hebrew and a selection of them was translated into English and edited for inclusion in this book.

Jabotinsky did write a number of letters and speeches in English, notably his graveside oration at Jacobi's funeral and his letter to Michael Haskell after Jacobi's death. Where the originals are in Jabotinsky's English they have not been edited.

The authors wish to thank warmly all those who have assisted them in their research and in translating letters and documents. Without their generous help, writing this book would not have been possible. Nina Praslova translated boxes of original documents and newspaper and journal articles from Russian and provided an invaluable wealth of background information on Russia in the late nineteenth and early twentieth centuries. Danielle Charak translated newspaper articles from Yiddish newspapers, and Efrat Weiss was responsible for translating many of the letters from Hebrew that are used in this work. In Kiev, Berdichev, and Odessa we were welcomed and assisted by members of the Jewish communities in each place.

We relied on Solomon Jacobi's wife, Edna, for her marvelous store of taped recollections; and we remain indebted to, and grateful for, the assistance and support of their daughters, Naomi and Carmel. In Israel we were helped by Ludmilla Epstein as well as Amira Stern and other members of their staff at the Jabotinsky Institute in our searches of the institute's archives. We are also grateful to the late Shmuel Katz, who allowed the taping of his memories of Solomon Jacobi, and to the late William Pearl for his recollections of the prewar period.

Suzanne Zyngier was of inestimable value in assisting with the editing.

CHAPTER 1

THERE WAS A MAN

Solomon Jacobi was born in Berdichev, a small town in the Ukraine, in 1897 and died in Paris in 1939.[1] From 1908 until 1919 he lived in Odessa except for a short period in 1917 and 1918, when he attended university in St. Petersburg to study engineering. His studies were interrupted by the Russian Revolution and he returned to Odessa.

He lived through the cauldron that was Russia during the first quarter of the twentieth century. He was witness to the effects of World War I, the Russian Revolution, and the renewed pogroms in the Ukraine that followed in the turbulence of the power struggles from 1917 to 1921. As the *American Jewish Year Book* reported, this was the atmosphere in 1919:

> In the Ukraine…political chaos prevails, and the very existence of the Jewish population is in jeopardy…. The latest reports from reputable sources place the number of Jews who have lost their lives in Ukrainian riots and pogroms at upwards of one hundred twenty thousand.[2]

---

1   The chapter title is derived from the article written by A. Ramba, *Herut*, November 2, 1965, on the occasion of the anniversary of Jacobi's death.

2   "Events in 5679: June 1, 1918, to May 31, 1919," *American Jewish Year Book*, vol. 21 (New York: American Jewish Committee, 1920), 170.

While he was still a university student, Jacobi was distinguished by his personal bravery and charismatic leadership ability. Vladimir Jabotinsky eulogized him thus:

> When he was twenty years old Jacobi was the founder and commander-in-chief of the Jewish Defence Corps which protected the Jews of Odessa throughout 1918 and 1919.... During those years the rest of the Ukraine swam in Jewish blood.... Perhaps 160,000 Jews were murdered.... Every city and town had its pogrom...except Odessa with its 140,000 Jews...where there was not one serious disturbance throughout the whole civil war...and that was due to the Jewish Defence Corps commanded by Jacobi.[3]

In 1919, he was arrested by the Red Army when it captured Odessa, and condemned to death when he refused to disclose where the defense force's weapons were hidden.

Released when the White Army recaptured the city, he made his way to Palestine. If childhood and youth are father to the man, then Jacobi's experiences of the entrenched anti-Semitism of his childhood home, his own demonstration that well-organized armed resistance could be successful against those forces, and his experiences of the injustices perpetrated during the Bolshevik seizure of power in Russia – both generally and particularly against Jews – were to influence the course of his life. At the age of twenty-two he was a committed Zionist who believed in active self-defense and mistrusted the power of the proletariat.

Soon after his arrival in Palestine, he met Vladimir Jabotinsky (1880–1940). It was the start of a comradeship and of a shared view of Zionism: Jews must have their own country in what had been the biblical Land of Israel. Jabotinsky's experience as a commissioned officer in the British army during the war and Jacobi's civil defense command in Odessa created an additional bond between the two men. Jews, they were convinced, had to acquire the skills and arms necessary to defend themselves.

Although Jabotinsky was nearly twenty years older than Jacobi, the

---

3   Vladimir Jabotinsky, graveside oration at Jacobi's funeral. Private collection.

friendship between the two men and their families continued throughout the rest of Jacobi's life. Jabotinsky was best man at Jacobi's wedding and gave the eulogy at his funeral. He referred to Jacobi's children as his grandchildren.

Between the years 1924 and 1939, Jabotinsky wrote more than 350 letters to Jacobi. Much of this biography is based on this correspondence. The original letters were written in Russian, Hebrew, Yiddish, English, French, and German. Both men spoke and wrote fluently in all those languages. There is internal evidence from the 1924 letters that they had kept in touch since 1920. There are letters that Jabotinsky wrote to Jacobi's wife, Edna, and postcards that he wrote to the Jacobi children. A lesser number of letters from Jacobi to Jabotinsky have survived. They are all in English and date from 1933. There are many photographs of the families together.

Determined to complete his qualifications as an engineer, Jacobi went to England in 1920 where in 1925 he graduated with first-class honors in civil engineering. Some years later, he was naturalized as a British citizen. England would be his home until his death. After Jacobi graduated, Jabotinsky invited him to Paris to work for the newly created Revisionist group. Jacobi was a signatory to the Revisionist manifesto signed in Paris in 1925. He worked with Jabotinsky for a year, including accompanying him on the failed tour of the USA in 1926. In that year, Jacobi decided that in order to earn a living he should return to England and start a career as an engineer. In the difficult English economic climate of the time he was unable to find satisfactory professional employment.

Since his arrival in England, Jacobi had been involved with local groups that sought to assist the Jews of eastern Europe and the Ukraine. In 1927 he found employment as a fundraiser in ORT-OZE[4] and Emigdirect.[5]

---

4   ORT, a Jewish occupational retraining organization, stands for Obshestvo remeslenofo zemledelcheskofo truda, the Society for Trades and Agricultural Labor. OZE was founded as the Society for the Protection of the Health of the Jewish Population (Obshchestvo okhraneniia zdorov'ia evreiskogo naseleniia; later, Obschestvo zdravookhraneniia evreev, or OZE).
5   Emigdirect was founded by the Jewish Emigration Conference in Prague in 1921 to organize Jewish emigration from Europe. In 1935 it merged with ORT.

For six years Jacobi traveled the world on this mission with great success, from Egypt through India and what was then known as the East Indies, Australia, the USA, China, South Africa, and in the UK.

In 1934, Jabotinsky appointed Jacobi to run the Revisionist movement's London office. Jacobi worked for the Revisionist movement in London for the next five years, but in 1939 Jabotinsky asked Jacobi to move to Warsaw to take charge of the Revisionist organizations that were engaged in rescuing Jews from eastern Europe. He led this program, moving between Prague, Athens, Bucharest, Paris, and London, arranging documents and papers, getting permission for Jews to cross frontiers, and chartering and provisioning ships that would run the British blockade of Palestine. In November 1939 he was in Bucharest in the course of this mission when he collapsed with what was eventually diagnosed as a brain tumor. He was rushed to Paris for surgery but died on the operating table.

A recent entry on the Betar[6] website contained the following tribute to Sioma:

> The person responsible for Aliyah Bet[7] on behalf of the Betar directorate was engineer Shlomo Jacobi, who embodied a combination of excellent education and practical skills. Jacobi was the living force of the enterprise and all his efforts were invested in its success. He traveled through the European continent, and it seemed, at times, as if he could be encountered at the same time in London and Paris, Warsaw and Bucharest, Prague and Zurich – anywhere in which matters pertaining to the Aliyah required his attention. He would rally public opinion, win the hearts of influential individuals – allies as well as opponents – and persuade them to support Aliyah Bet. He would meet with both government officials and representatives of refugee committees.

---

6   The Jewish youth movement Betar was founded in Riga, Latvia, in 1923. Over the next two decades, it grew in importance into an integral part of the Revisionist movement.

7   This was the dangerous Jewish "national sport" of running the British blockade of Palestine.

Jacobi died in Paris on Thursday, November 16, 1939. Because it was difficult to arrange shipping his body back to England during wartime, his funeral could not be conducted in accordance with the customary Jewish practice of burial within twenty-four hours. He was buried more than a week later, on Friday, November 24, in the London Jewish Cemetery at Willesden. His widow, Edna, had a tombstone erected on the grave that was inscribed only with the words "Solomon Y. Jacobi, 1897–1939."

Years later, when Edna was asked why she did not include any details of his family or his life in the inscriptions, she answered that he was so well known at the time that no other record was necessary. At the time, Jacobi was chairman of the Executive of the New Zionist Organization, a director of Aliyah Bank, the repository of that organization's funds, and a member of the executive of ORT-OZE.

In that last capacity, he had contact with the international leaders of world Jewry, including Albert Einstein, Lord Rothschild, Lord Marley, and the chief rabbi of the British Empire; and in his travels on behalf of those charities he had met the leaders of Jewish communities in the USA, Australia, South Africa, China, India, and Singapore.

In his position as head of the Political Commission of the Revisionist movement in London, it had been Jacobi's responsibility to lobby the members of both houses of the British parliament, including the leading political figures Winston Churchill, with whom he had much contact, and Lord Wedgwood. This work also entailed gaining the support of the leaders of British Jewry, many of whom were anti-Zionist, and the pro-Zionist members of influential non-Jewish British society.

Jacobi had been managing director of Jordania Society Limited, a Jewish mutual life insurance company that was backed by the British Royal Exchange Assurance Company. Jordania was formed with the intention of using its available funds for investment in Palestine. Jacobi was also a director of a South African gold mining company that he had floated on the London Stock Exchange on behalf of its principal shareholder, Michael Haskel, a South African Jew who financed the Revisionist movement for some years.

On three occasions he conducted negotiations with David Ben-Gurion, the leader of the left-wing Zionist movement and the first prime minister of Israel. The meetings were held in attempts to heal the rift between the two Zionist organizations. The first meeting was with Jabotinsky and Ben-Gurion in Jacobi's home in London. Two later meetings were between Ben-Gurion and Jacobi only. Neither the first nor the last meeting was successful. At the second meeting the two men reached an agreement, but the terms were rejected in a referendum of the rank-and-file members of Ben-Gurion's party.

It is little wonder that Jacobi's widow, Edna, felt that he was so well known to a wide circle of Zionists, the Jewish community generally, and to a number of non-Jewish leaders of the British political scene that only his name needed to be inscribed on his tombstone.

Jacobi was at the pinnacle of his career when he died at the age of forty-two. Despite his widow's belief that his identity was known so widely within and outside the Jewish community, twenty-five years later the Israeli newspaper *Herut*[8] published a tribute to the man written by the paper's editor. The opening paragraph read, "I feel the emotional need to resurrect the memory of a man, S. Y. Jacobi, to whom many of us owe our lives, albeit unknowingly. The younger generation has never heard of his name, and even among the older generation, only a few know his name."

In 1990, Jacobi's family erected an additional stone on his grave inscribed with the names of his wife, his two daughters, and his eight grandchildren. Space did not allow for the inclusion of the names of his many great-grandchildren.

---

8   *Herut* was the organ of the Herut political party, which Menachem Begin established in 1948. In 1977, Begin became Israel's sixth prime minister, serving in that position until 1983. Herut merged into the Likud in 1973.

CHAPTER 2

THE EARLY YEARS

Sioma was born on May 22, 1897, in Berdichev, some 190 kilometers southwest of Kiev. The date on his birth certificate is that of the pre-revolutionary Russian calendar, which equates to the Western calendar as June 4, the day on which his family celebrated his birthday.

Both of Sioma's parents were born in nearby Ukrainian towns. His father, Leib Alterovich Yankelevitch, was born in 1872 in Snitovka, and his mother, Suria-Genia (Sarah) Berovna, was born a year later in Rogashev. They were married on February 14, 1895, in the Ukrainian town of Novograd-Volinsk, and went to live in Berdichev. An unconfirmed family history relates that their marriage was arranged when they were still children and that they were first cousins.

It is not known whether Leib had moved to Berdichev before his marriage. On an internal Russian passport issued when he was forty years old, Leib was described as being of medium height with light brown hair. His occupation was described as a merchant. Another family story tells of his being involved in the timber industry, but there is no surviving documentary evidence to confirm this. There are two existing photographs of him. One is when he was, perhaps, in his thirties. He is wearing a three-piece suit with a fashionable handkerchief peeking out of his breast pocket. His hairline is just starting to recede and there is no sign of grey. He wears glasses, a bow tie and a small toothbrush moustache. His clothes and general appearance indicate that he was not an observant Jew and that he belonged to the successful middle class, perhaps even of moderate wealth. In the second photograph he is in the family group at Sioma's wedding. Although he would have been fifty-seven years old, he appears much the same as in the earlier photograph. He has a full head of hair and still wears a bow tie over a neatly tailored suit.

Leib's appearance is in contrast to that of his parents, Sioma's grandparents. In photographs taken when they were perhaps in middle age, Leib's father is dressed in the usual garb of observant Jews of his generation in a black shapeless jacket and a black round cap that sits on the top of his head. He wears a long white beard. Leib's mother is also dressed as an observant woman. She wears a black dress with a high, closed neckline, and her face is showing from under a black cape that covers her head. The only relief from her sombre attire is three shiny buttons, perhaps of a precious metal, down the front of her dress.

There are two surviving photographs of Sioma's mother, who was known as Sarah. One is in the group at Sioma's wedding when she was fifty-six years old, and the other is a studio shot taken when she was older. In both photographs she is wearing modern but quite severe-looking clothing, with a matching unsmiling expression. One granddaughter remembers her as a stern, domineering woman who kept a strictly kosher home and attended synagogue every Saturday without fail. Her religious observance was not followed by any of her children.

In a photograph of Sarah's parents – Sioma's grandparents on his mother's side – her father is wearing a small fur cap and black clothing in the observant Jewish tradition with his white beard reaching down his chest. Her mother is also traditionally dressed, wearing a black scarf that covers her head and shoulders, leaving only her face for the camera.

All the indications are that Sioma's parents had abandoned the strictly observant life of his grandparents and were part of the "enlightened" generation of Russian Jews of the late nineteenth century.

Leib and Sarah had five children, all of whom were born in Berdichev.

Their firstborn, a daughter named Ira-Asaya, died at the age of seven in 1903. Sioma was born in 1897. A daughter, Mamuya-Dina (called Manya) was born in 1899 and twin boys, Simha and Mordechai, were born in 1904.

Sioma was ten years old when his parents decided to move the family to Odessa. Probably the move was made, at least in part, to enable Sioma and his siblings to have a good high-school education, which was not available in Berdichev.

To understand Jewish life in the Ukraine means tracking back through the late nineteenth century and the first half of the twentieth. The easiest way to visit Berdichev today is to drive the 190 kilometers on a two-lane road from Kiev. Although it does not fall within the time frame of this book, no Jew can visit Kiev without visiting Babi Yar, the site of the German massacre of Kiev's entire Jewish population – between thirty-three thousand and one hundred thousand men, women and children – on September 29 and 30, 1941. The massacre at Babi Yar, which was the culmination of a century of the killing of Jews, was the destruction of Jewish life in the Ukraine.

Babi Yar is now a park that lies within the environs of the city. In 1941 it was a deep ravine on its outskirts. Kiev had been occupied by the German army on September 24, 1941, after a catastrophic defeat of the four Soviet armies that were defending the city.

Just four days later, the victorious Germans spread pamphlets in the Jewish areas of the city that read:

> All Jews of the city of Kiev and its environs must appear on Monday, September 29, by 8:00 a.m. on the corner…near the cemetery. You are to take your documents, money, valuables, warm clothes, linen, etc. Whoever of the Jews does not obey this order…will be shot.

A German soldier later gave testimony that when the Jews arrived at Babi Yar, "The Ukrainians led them…where they were forced to remove… all their clothing…anyone who hesitated was kicked or pushed by the Ukrainians to keep them moving." The commander of the German soldiers wrote two days later: "Thanks to the special talent of our organization, the Jews still believed to the very last moment before being murdered that indeed all that was happening was that they were being resettled."

Naked, the Jewish men, women, and children were lined up on the edge of the ravine and mown down by machine guns. Gypsies and the inmates of psychiatric hospitals followed. How many in total? No one will ever know. Bodies were burned, skeletons pounded into powder, and the ravine filled in.

In 1961 Yevgeni Yevtushenko wrote his poem "Babi Yar." Two stanzas of the poem read:

> Wild grasses rustle over Babi Yar,
> The trees look ominous, like judges,
> Here, all things scream silently, and, baring my head,
> slowly I feel myself turning gray.
>
> And I, myself, am one massive, soundless scream
> Above the thousand and thousand buried here, interred,
> I am every old man here shot dead,
> I am every child here shot dead.

Today all that can be seen is a long depression in the ground where the steep ravine had been. The Russian government refused to acknowledge the site of the massacre for many years. It was not until 1976 that a sculpture was commissioned to mark the place. It bears the inscription "Monument to Soviet citizens and POWs shot by the Germans at Babi Yar." It is a typically Stalinist massive heroic bronze sculpture erected on the end of a long concrete block wall near where the ravine once existed. Even in 1976 there was no mention of the Jews who had been killed. It was not until 1991, fifty years after the massacre, that a monument commemorating the murdered Jews was allowed. It is a moving small bronze piece of a little girl, hands reaching out in supplication. At her side is a broken doll. It stands on a small concrete plinth in the large park that now surrounds Babi Yar, some distance away from the site of the killing field.

The road from Kiev to Berdichev winds through a succession of small mixed farms and villages. It is a closely settled area. The Ukraine has long been famous as a major producer of grain, but the wheat fields of Ukraine lie elsewhere.

From the sixteenth to the eighteenth centuries, Berdichev was in Polish territory. In 1732, the Polish hereditary owners of the area gave a charter to a guild of Jewish tailors in the town. In 1762, the Polish king decreed that Berdichev could hold commercial fairs. At the time its population was only fifteen hundred, of whom some twelve hundred were Jewish. Trade as a fair town brought an increase to the population that was largely Jewish. In 1791, the area of Poland in which Berdichev then lay was ceded to Russia. In that year, Catherine the Great established the Pale of Settlement.[1] An enormous area stretching from the Black Sea in the south and touching on the Baltic Sea in the north, it included most of the territory that now forms part of modern Poland, the Baltic States, and the Ukraine. Jews were required to live within the Pale to restrict their influence over Russian commerce.

Berdichev grew to be the fourth largest city in the Ukraine and a major commercial center. The 1897 Russian census reported that 97 percent of Jews in the Ukraine spoke Yiddish as their mother tongue and that they constituted 80 percent of the population. Jews lived in towns. In 1914, the total population of Berdichev was more than eighty thousand and some 80 to 90 percent were Jewish. It was said that the town's non-Jews needed a working knowledge of Yiddish to obtain employment.

In the eighteenth century, Berdichev was the leading center of Hasidism[2] and the home of several noted rabbis. At the time it was second only to Warsaw as the largest Jewish city in eastern Europe. It was home to the most famous rabbi of his time, Rabbi Levi Yitzhak (1740–1809), who was known as a scholar and a mystic throughout the Jewish communities of Poland and Russia. Today the most active sign of the presence of a Jewish community in Berdichev is that its elderly members are building

---

1   The word *pale* in this sense derives from the word *paling*, as in a fence paling. It was used to mean a confined area. The term *the English Pale* was used in the fourteenth century to define that part of Ireland where English rule was effective. "Beyond the pale" came to mean "beyond the bounds of civilized behavior."

2   A movement that began as a religious and spiritual revival in eastern Europe during the eighteenth century.

a memorial to Levi Yitzhak among the ruins of the old and otherwise neglected Jewish cemetery of the town.

During the second half of the nineteenth century, Berdichev lost some of its Jewish population to the prosperous cities of Odessa and Warsaw. Despite the strength of the Hasidic movement in Berdichev, business and employment opportunities, together with the modern movements such as the Bund[3] and Haskalah,[4] were attracting Jews to move to those larger cities. In Berdichev the old Jewish culture remained largely unaffected by the changes.

Vasily Grossman, the celebrated Russian Jewish war correspondent of World War II, was born in Berdichev. He ridiculed the shtetl atmosphere that still prevailed into the twentieth century. He wrote to his father that he regretted that his mother still lived in "the terrible Berdichev environment" and felt "oppressed by that lousy rotten town" whenever he visited her. When Grossman died, a letter was found in his shirt pocket. It was from his mother, the last letter that she wrote to him before she was killed by the Germans, one among the thirty thousand Jews of Berdichev who were murdered after the invasion.

Before World War II, the town was a hub of railway lines leading north, south, east, and west. The most impressive building in Berdichev is its nineteenth-century railway station. The substantial Gynlopyat River flows through the town. Its imposing monument to those who fell in World War II is surmounted by a Russian tank. In the city park, there is a small plaque that commemorates the Berdichev Jews who were slaughtered.

In the wake of the initially successful German invasion of Russia in World War II, Hitler flew into Berdichev on August 4, 1941, as part of an inspection tour of the conquered territory. One of his staff recorded in his diary, "Ghastly town. Open coffins. Executions. Many Jews. Ancient cottages." The "many Jews" did not survive long under the German occupation. SS troops and Ukrainian militiamen set about killing Jews

---

3   The Jewish socialist party that embraced Yiddish and secular Jewish nationalism and opposed Zionism.
4   "Enlightenment," meaning "modernization," which involved the acquisition of Western culture, including dress and behavior.

throughout the area. One SS operational report discovered after the war, dated September 19, 1941, stated that on that day in Berdichev, 627 Jewish men and 875 Jewish women were slaughtered. They were all, said the record in some bizarre effort of justification, over twelve years of age.[5]

The two-story building that was the largest synagogue in town is now a glass factory. Instead of the single synagogue that exists for the few Jews who live in the town today, there were eighty places of worship.

Throughout his later life, Sioma always gave Odessa as his birth place. He gave it in all his many newspaper interviews throughout the world and even on official documents, including his application for British naturalization. His naturalization certificate consequently gave Odessa as his place of birth. His children were told that Odessa was his birthplace, although his wife told an interviewer many years later that she believed he was born in a small town in the Ukraine near Odessa. Why he persisted in the Odessa story is not clear. Perhaps because of the Crimean War of the 1850s, immortalized by Tennyson's poem "The Charge of the Light Brigade" and the deeds of Florence Nightingale, the cities of the Crimean Peninsula were known throughout the British world. Odessa would be accepted without question, rather than the unknown, shtetl-like town of Berdichev.

Sioma started school at Odessa school number 254 in 1908, a private gymnasium whose headmaster was Mr. I. R. Rappoport. The school still exists today but it has no records of that period. The family lived in an apartment close by at 45 Bazarnya Street. The building, a two-story apartment block in khaki-colored sandstone, still stands. Built around an open courtyard in the French manner, the entry to the courtyard is through a single door from the street. It is not known in which apartment they lived.

Only three years before the Jacobis moved to Odessa it had been the site of a particularly vicious pogrom. The city was a major center of the

---

5   See Yitzhak Arad, Shmuel Krakowski, and Shmuel Spector, *The Einsatzgrupen Reports: Selections from the Dispatches of the Nazi Death Squads* (Jerusalem: Yad Vashem, 1989), for details of the murders.

failed Russian revolution in 1905. During the course of the battles for the city, a pogrom ensued during which some eight hundred Jews were killed and five thousand injured, and Jewish property looted and destroyed. Stories and signs of this recent pogrom must have been an influence on the character of a sensitive ten-year-old.

Sioma seems to have coped well with this new environment and succeeded scholastically. Despite the restrictions on the number of Jews admitted to tertiary education at the time, he was admitted to the University of Novorossiysk at its campus in Odessa in 1915 as a student in the Physico-Mathematical faculty in the Department of Natural Sciences.

Russian Odessa is only two centuries old. In the distant past, it had been a minor Ottoman settlement. In the eighteenth century it had been turned into a fortress and naval port, known as Khadzhi-Be, for the Ottoman Empire. In 1789 it was captured for Catherine the Great of Russia by a Neapolitan mercenary, José de Ribas. He renamed it Odessa after a nearby Greek trading post, Odessus, which had been founded in the sixth century BCE. De Ribas proceeded to build a new city with the help of a Dutch architect. Few Russians moved in and it was settled by people from the surrounding countries – Greeks, Romanians, Bulgarians, Jews from the Ukraine, and a number of Frenchmen. The last group had followed a French nobleman, Duc Richelieu, who was appointed governor in 1803. Richelieu's statue still stands at the top of the steps that lead down from the city to the seaport. He actively sought to add more Jewish settlers in the hope that they would create a prosperous trading center.

A *hevra kadisha* (Jewish burial society) was founded in 1795, and the first synagogue was built three years later. Richelieu developed the city as a port with duty-free status and an administrative center. The architecture and layout were developed by French émigrés and the city still has discernible French overtones. The hotels and restaurants on the boulevard overlooking the sea have an air of a French Riviera town, and even the current police uniforms bear a resemblance to those of a gendarme. It was more than twenty-five years after the founding of the city that a Russian was appointed governor of the town.

In its early days there was an added exotic tinge to the city. Alexander

Pushkin, the great Russian poet, was exiled there from St. Petersburg in 1823 for suspected anti-state activities.

Pushkin wrote in *Eugene Onegin*:

> I lived then in Odessa.
> There the skies are always clear.
> The tongues of Golden Italy
> Resound happily across the pavement.

But it was not all sunshine for Pushkin. His exile was supervised by the governor, Vorontsov, but he did not endear himself to his mentor when he was found to have seduced Madame Vorontsov. As punishment, he was sent to confinement in his father's country estate in 1824.

By the 1880s Odessa was second only to St. Petersburg as the largest port in the Russian empire. It was the base of the Russian Black Sea Fleet. Mark Twain commented during a visit that it looked like an American city. But Twain was exercising his sense of humor with that remark. He went on:

> [F]ine, broad streets, and straight as well…a familiar *new* look about the houses and every thing; yea, and a driving smothering cloud of dust that was so like a message from our own dear native land that we could hardly refrain from shedding a few grateful tears and execrations in the old time-honored American way. Look up the street or down the street, this way or that way, we saw only America! There was not one thing to remind us that we were in Russia.[6]

A census in 1897 counted 140,000 Jews in Odessa. They were 35 percent of the population. The census included an analysis of the languages spoken in the city. Only half the people spoke Russian and 5 percent spoke Ukrainian. Nearly a third of the population spoke Yiddish while Greek, Turkish, and several Balkan languages made up the cosmopolitan balance. The city was now an important commercial center of the Russian

---

6   Mark Twain, *The Innocents Abroad* (New York: Harper's, 1869), 306–7.

empire. The Baltic ports were closed in winter. Odessa was Russia's only all-seasons port through which Ukrainian grain could reach western Europe and which could receive imports from the rest of the world. It was a university city; the University of Novorossiysk had a large campus at the end of the imposing Alexandrovsky Prospect.

From the 1880s until the 1920s Odessa overtook Berdichev as the city with the second largest Jewish population in Europe. Odessa had attracted young Jews from traditional backgrounds who longed for European nineteenth-century enlightenment. Orthodox Jews regarded the city as a dangerous and demoralizing center for freethinkers. In 1904 the total population of Odessa was half a million; the number of Jews in the city had increased to some 165,000. This compared to 200,000 Russians with a mix of Turks, French, Greeks, and Armenians making up the balance.

Vladimir Jabotinsky was born in Odessa in 1880 and grew up there. He wrote of his youth that the concept of being Jewish did not exist for the group with whom he mixed. Although his friends recognized that they were Jews and most of the young men went out only with Jewish girls, religion played a minor part in their lives. It was a cosmopolitan place where Jewish orthodoxy was theoretically dominant, but Jewish children could grow up being conscious of their Judaism with no meaningful knowledge of the religion. Jabotinsky's father had died when Vladimir was only six, and although his mother was an observant Jew, Vladimir went to synagogue only once a year, on the anniversary of his father's death. He described the joys of his childhood and youth "in light-hearted Odessa."

Jabotinsky wrote a novel, *The Five*, in 1935.[7] Set in Odessa, it is a story of the five children of a Russified Jewish family from the turn of the nineteenth century to the Revolution. The family, which lives in a cosmopolitan setting, attends operas and balls where the ability to dance the quadrille and the waltz is a social requirement. The novel also tells of boating and swimming in the Black Sea, including a scene in which one of the daughters goes skinny-dipping at midnight.

7　First published in Paris in 1936, it has since been published in New York in 1947, and subsequently in Jerusalem, Odessa, and Moscow.

A nineteenth-century historian of the city remarked on the absence of traditional Jewish communal structure. Russian was widely spoken in the community, and many economic opportunities were open to Jews in such a culturally vibrant port city. It was said that some 90 percent of Jewish shops were open on the Sabbath.[8]

This picture of life in the city is in marked contrast to the one painted by another Odessa-born Jew, Isaac Babel, in four stories that he wrote under the title *Tales of Odessa*.[9] These stories center around a Jewish organized-crime figure, the "King" of Odessa, and his gang who operated in a milieu of small-time merchants and shopkeepers in the poorest area of Jewish Odessa. There was little enlightenment in this stratum of Jewish life in the city.

The Jabotinsky family lived in the same street as the Jacobis, but as Vladimir left Odessa for Switzerland in 1898 and returned as a young adult in 1901, it is unlikely that Vladimir and Sioma knew one another.

Despite his upbringing in a strictly kosher family home, Sioma was not an observant Jew as an adult. He kept the major Jewish holidays of Passover, the New Year, the Day of Atonement, and the rituals of mourning for close members of his family. It is probable that his youth resembled that of Jewish society in Odessa as portrayed in Jabotinsky's novel, although his school days and entry to the university must have been influenced by the repressive laws enacted against Russian Jews by Alexander III.

Shortly after Alexander II was assassinated in March 1881, there was an outbreak of more than 250 pogroms, many of them in the Ukraine. The long-held view that these horrific disturbances were orchestrated by the authorities in order to prevent a possible outbreak of revolutionary violence early in the reign of the new tsar has recently been revised. Recent studies suggest that the pogroms were more the result of the abolition of serfdom, which exacerbated a long history of antagonism toward Jews because of their commercial success. Local authorities could not have curbed the

---

8   S. J. Zipperstein, *The Jews of Odessa: A Cultural History, 1794–1881* (Palo Alto, CA: Stanford University Press, 1985).

9   The stories, which were first published in 1916 in a St. Petersburg monthly edited by Maxim Gorky, were published in book form in 1935.

violence even if they had wished to do so. The government's response was to lessen opportunities for Jewish economic activity and education. The prevailing view of the Jews was that their economic activity, combined with their so-called tribal seclusion and religious fanaticism, could only be curbed by government restrictions on their activities. In May 1882, the so-called "May Laws" were introduced as a supposedly temporary measure, but remained in force for more than thirty years and were made harsher as time went on. Under these laws, the number of Jewish students was restricted to 10 percent of the total number in a public school, and limits were placed on the number of Jewish doctors and lawyers. Some areas within the Pale on the Crimean Peninsula were forbidden to Jews, and they were not allowed to move from place to place without permission.

From a young age, Sioma was active in the Zionist movement. In later years he was quoted as saying that he had been one of eighteen students who were imprisoned for fourteen days for daring to listen to a report on Palestine. By the time they were released, they were all ardent Zionists.

Generally, life was so harsh for Jews in the Ukraine that it is estimated that between 1881 and 1920 more than two million Jews fled to the United States. A small number went to Palestine in 1882 in what has been called the First Aliyah.[10] Palestine had been under Ottoman rule since the sixteenth century. In the 1880s, Russian authorities were quite eager to help Jews emigrate. The Russian government of the time felt that if Jews chose to leave to go to Palestine, why stand in their way? They allowed a formal organization, which became known as the Odessa Committee, to be set up in 1890 that would assist Russian Jews to immigrate to Palestine and help them to buy land and settle there. In the year of its formation, it helped to establish the villages of Rehovot and Hadera in Palestine. At its peak it had over four thousand members, most of whom joined the Zionist Organization after 1897. As it continued its work until 1913, this active group of Zionists was part of Sioma's childhood.

As a university student Sioma was active in the Central Council of the Zionist Federation of Odessa. In November 1922, when he was living in

---

10 *Aliyah* is defined as immigration to Palestine with the intention of settling there.

London, Sioma applied for a permit to travel to Palestine. In answer to the question that asked of any previous residence in Palestine, part of his answer was "Before the War in the colony of Judea." There are no other references in his records to such a visit. It is possible that as a student he may have visited one of the settlements of Russian Jews that had been established during and since the 1880s. The phrase "the colony of Judea" is interesting. It does not appear to have been in current usage at the time. It was the name used by the Romans for the biblical land of the Jews, and it included all the land west of the Jordan to the sea, including what is now known as the West Bank, and it went further east to include a substantial part of what is now Jordan.

Sioma turned eighteen the year that he was admitted to Novorossiysk University. If he had not been a student, he would have been called up into the Russian army. The Russian system did not call up university students if they enrolled in the army reserve. In a CV that Sioma compiled in the early 1930s, he wrote that he served in both the 49th Infantry Regiment and the 13th Regiment of Fusiliers of the Russian army.

Two documents survive that relate to this service. The first was issued by the Odessa military hospital on June 21, 1917. It discharged him from the army because of a congenital heart defect that had resulted in an enlarged heart. The discharge form lists him as a private in Division 49 of the Reserve Regiment. It seems that he had served as a volunteer in the Fusiliers before his service with the unit from which he was discharged. A question on his discharge form read, "State the Outcome (recovered, released temporarily or permanently from service)." The answer was "Discharged from the service without ever enlisting." The second document, which was issued by the administration of the military commander of Odessa on June 28, 1917, gave Sioma's rank as a private in the volunteers and stated that he was due to be called up in 1918.

At university, Sioma had transferred from Natural Science to the Medical Faculty, but he now sought a career as an engineer. He was accepted to the foremost school of engineering in Russia, the Institute of Railway Engineers in Petersburg. It is now known as the Railway University.

CHAPTER 3

JEWISH SELF-DEFENSE IN ODESSA

Odessa of the nineteenth and early twentieth centuries has been described as the most pogrom-prone city in Russia. Major pogroms took place in 1821, 1859, 1871, and 1881.Their primary purpose seems to have been attacks on Jewish homes and businesses. In the 1871 pogrom, 863 houses and 552 businesses were damaged or destroyed. Six people were killed and twenty-one wounded. During this period, pogroms throughout the Ukraine were common. At the turn of the century, the Russian government encouraged anti-Semitism as part of its attempts to divert general unrest. The Ukrainian peasants' custom of attacking Jews went back to the seventeenth century, when they were led by the notorious self-appointed Cossack leader Bogdan Chmielnicki.[1] Two hundred years later, Cossack and Ukrainian peasants needed little encouragement to carry out attacks on Jews and their property in the province's small villages and towns. But now the object of these forays was not just to destroy Jewish property, but to kill Jews.

---

1   Bogdan or Bohdan Chmielnicki (c. 1595–1657) is known for the massacres he and his supporters perpetrated on the Jewish people during the Cossack uprising that took place from 1648 to 1656.

In several places Jews decided to offer organized resistance. The Bund[2] was the first group to attempt Jewish self-defense. It was put to the test in April 1903 when a local anti-Semitic newspaper agitated for a pogrom in the town of Kishniev. Forty-seven Jews were killed and more than four hundred were injured. An estimated one thousand Jewish homes were destroyed. The Jewish self-defense force that had been formed in the town was armed only with crude weapons and no firearms. It was said their efforts probably served to inflame their attackers. It was the worst pogrom of the new century.

As a result of this disaster, the Bund and the Zionist movement combined in several towns to form an armed militia for self-defense. Five months later, the combined forces met to repulse a pogrom in the town of Gomel. Half the population of Gomel was Jewish. In what was later described as a battle, rather than the intended pogrom, "only" ten Jews and eight of the attackers were killed. This success moved Jewish communities throughout Russia to organize similar self-defense groups.

Results in other cities were less successful. As mentioned in the previous chapter, during the First Russian Revolution of 1905, Odessa suffered its worst pogrom. The city was one of the major centers of the workers' and sailors' revolt against the tsar. The revolt in Odessa was made famous by the Eisenstein film *The Battleship Potemkin*, with its horrific scene of the massacre on the steps leading from the city to the waterfront. The Potemkin steps that lead down from the promenade overlooking the harbor are still crowded with visitors. What Eisenstein did not include in his film was the aftermath of the failed rebellion. More than three hundred Jews, including an estimated fifty members of an embryonic self-defense force, were killed in the pogrom that followed.

---

2   The Bund, a Jewish social democratic labor organization, was founded in Russia in 1897 and joined the international socialist movement a year later. Its aim was to fight for the rights of Jewish workers in their countries of residence. The Bund was anti-Zionist. It saw Zionism as a bourgeois movement of escape rather than standing up for Jewish workers' rights in the countries where they lived. Bundists regarded Yiddish as the Jewish national language.

Jabotinsky was in Odessa in 1905. He had gone in 1898 to study in western Europe, where he became a foreign correspondent for Odessa newspapers. He returned to Odessa in 1901, and the Kishniev pogrom in 1903 confirmed his Zionist views. He could see no future for Jews in Russia.

There are differing accounts of Jabotinsky's reaction to the 1905 pogrom in Odessa. Two biographies state that he began raising funds from the Jewish community to buy arms for self-defense. Others have written that he was actively involved in the self-defense group, but his biographers do not record this. In 1905, the self-defense groups in Odessa had been organized into cells of ten men armed only with revolvers. These cells were positioned throughout the city with no coordination between them. This form of self-defense failed to halt the killing and destruction of property. As a result of this experience Jabotinsky wrote about Jewish self-defense in disparaging terms. "One can hardly speak about self-defense in earnest when one compares the number of Jews killed with the deaths of the perpetrators."

Generally speaking, pogroms were a secondary phenomenon of social unrest. There were ninety-nine pogroms recorded in the Ukraine from 1917 to the end of 1918. From January 1919 to December 1921, the number of recorded pogroms totalled a further 1,190. An attempt to form a Jewish military union failed because of internal dissension. A comparatively small number of Jews joined the Ukrainian Communist Party. They were only 13.6 percent of the membership in 1922.

In the turmoil of the civil wars, the foreign invasions, and the independence movements that took place in the Ukraine from 1917 to 1920, rule of the city of Odessa changed hands twelve times. A succession of military forces tried to exercise control over this important seaport. These armies and militias included local Bolsheviks, Ukrainian separatist forces, the German army of occupation, the Red Army, the White Army, and a French invasion to support the White Army, until the Red Army finally captured the city for the Soviet government. In the short interregnums between these battles, local authorities endeavored to restore some order.

Anarchy ruled in the Ukraine during those four years. The largely defenseless three million Jews who lived in the territory were considered fair game by the organized armies, roaming bands of deserters, and groups of Ukrainians and Cossacks. It is not known how many Jews were killed. Estimates range from sixty thousand to nearly three times that number. In later years Sioma, who used authenticated data whenever it was available to illustrate his arguments, cited 896 pogroms (although he noted that Soviet sources published a figure of 1,236) from October 1917 to December 1919. Sioma used the figures of one hundred thousand deaths, eighty-six thousand disabled, and three hundred thousand children orphaned. The precise figures will never be known.

In Abba Eban's book, *My People: The History of the Jews*,[3] there is a chilling photograph with the following caption: "On August 10, 1919…Cossacks unashamedly display the corpses of Jews that they have murdered." Four armed Cossacks squat behind the bodies of seven Jewish men laid out in a row. The corpses are wrapped in their prayer shawls. The photograph is in the style of one used by hunting parties to show off their kill of wild animals.

By contrast, from 1917 onward there was an active and well-organized Jewish self-defense force in Odessa.

There are three surviving original documents relating to Sioma's involvement with the Jewish self-defense force in Odessa. One, in Russian, dated April 2, 1919, certifies that he was head of the Organizational Committee of Jewish Self-Defense Forces of the City of Odessa from November 1917 to April 1, 1919. Another document in his scrapbook, in Hebrew, written in ink on a piece of flimsy paper, is a letter of introduction, in a "To whom it may concern" style from the Odessa Zionist Histadrut. It states that Sioma was an activist in all the work of the Central Council of the Zionist Federation of Odessa and that he was the organizer of Jewish self-defense in Odessa. The letter asks the reader to "please give Yankelevitch Jacobi all the assistance that you can in his work in Eretz Israel." It is dated November 24, 1919.

---

3   Abba Eban, *My People: The Story of the Jews* (New York: Behrman House, 1968), 350.

In fact, between November 1917 and November 1919, Sioma was in Petersburg for several months.

In March 1917 the tsar abdicated, and administration was assumed by a provisional government in St. Petersburg. Power struggles took place throughout Russia. In June 1917, the Ukraine proclaimed its independence. Odessa was a naval base and the only major all-weather port in Russia. The Russian ports on the Baltic Sea were icebound during the winter months. Several groups sought control of Odessa in order to gain the upper hand in the power vacuum created by the civil war and several foreign invasions.

Looking back on that period, Sioma published a series of articles in the Yiddish New York newspaper *Tog* in October 1927. The articles were entitled "Odessa during the Times of the Pogroms." His description of the situation in Odessa in 1917 follows, in edited excerpts of an English translation of the published Yiddish story:

> Although the provisional government[4] was nominally running the country, in the Ukraine there were a number of secessionist groups struggling for power in competition with revolutionary and counterrevolutionary movements. In the absence of central control of Odessa from Petersburg or from Kiev, the old Municipal Duma and the local military council were nominally running the city. They were challenged in December 1917 by an external group known as the Rumcherod.[5] The Rumcherod, although it assumed power, was ineffective as a controlling body for Odessa, and the population was really left to its own resources. This situation lasted for only the months of December 1917 and January 1918. But during this period there were reports that spread quickly throughout the Odessa Jewish community of pogroms in neighboring towns and cities. The names of the victims were listed in the Jewish quarter

---

4   The short-lived administrative body, sometimes known as the Kerensky government, that took power after the abdication of the tsar in March 1917. The Bolsheviks took over the government in October 1917.

5   This was the central committee of the Soviets for the Romanian front, the Black Sea Fleet, and the Odessa military district. It functioned in the area from May 1917 to May 1918.

of the town. It was considered to be very dangerous for Jews to go out at night in Odessa for fear of this violence spreading to the city.

The papers were full of the violence and looting committed by groups of armed army deserters. Their slogan was "Everything is permissible – that is what freedom is for." At this time of disruption of civil order in the Ukraine it was common for Bolshevik soldiers to imprison and execute numbers of "bourgeois hostages."

Because there was no umbrella group for the Jewish community in Odessa, and because of the uncertainty of the times since the start of the Revolution, in August 1917 twelve Jewish organizations met in an empty warehouse. They were brought together on the initiative of the Maccabi sports group and the Zionist youth group Hehaver. Because of the state of anarchy in the province, the meeting was called to discuss the need to form a Jewish self-defense force in Odessa.

The other organizations attending the meeting represented the left-leaning Zionist Zeirei Zion, two Labor parties, Poalei Zion and the Radical Poalei Zion Party, the Jewish Democratic Party, and the United Jewish Socialist Party. Two organizations were not represented – the Jewish People's Party, which was a party of rich Jews, and the Socialist party, the Bund. The People's Party declared that they would not take part in the work of the committee because the defense of the Jewish population should be the responsibility of the authorities and not a separate national organization. The Bund, on the other hand, announced that they would not join because a Jewish self-defense force should be solely to defend the Jewish population, not Jewish private property. The self-defense organization was formed without the representatives of those two parties. Two months later they both agreed to join.

A committee was formed bearing the title of the United Committee of Jewish Democratic Organizations to Fight the Pogroms. This was shortened to an acronym, *Okoyed*. An executive was chosen that included the author of this article.

There is a studio photograph of seventeen men who are the representatives of the eight Jewish parties. Sioma is seated in the center of the middle row, in the place usually given to the leader of the group. He is wearing the uniform that was worn by all university students in Russia. Most of the others in the photograph are in civilian clothes, six are in military uniform, and two others in student uniforms. If this photograph was taken in 1917, Sioma was just twenty years old. His appearance in the photograph is that of a very young man. Most of the others appear to be in their late twenties or thirties. There are several older men. None of them appears to be armed.

This photograph has been reproduced on several occasions. In a book on the history of Russian Zionism, it is captioned, "The leadership of the self-defense Hebrew fighting unit in Odessa in 1918." Each man is named. Sioma is "Sioma Yankelevitch [Jacobi], the organizer of the *druzhina*."[6] Several others in the photograph would join the Revisionists in later years.

Sioma's narrative continued:

> There was no shortage of volunteers to serve with the group, but we had no arms and no money. Our approach to the military commander of Odessa offering our services and requesting arms was rejected. So the committee set about raising funds from the community. The money collected was only enough to buy ten revolvers and about twenty rifles.
>
> Mob violence broke out soon afterwards. The lack of a strong government in the city allowed what was called an outbreak of "drunken excesses." Groups of soldiers and sailors would break down the doors of wine cellars and get drunk. They would be joined by a mob and it was feared that riots would follow and that these could develop into pogroms. The city commander sent in whatever forces he had available but rather than restoring order they joined in the drinking.

---

6   Military force.

Okoyed set up its headquarters in a vacant warehouse. It had advertised its phone numbers in the newspapers asking for people to contact us wherever there was violence against Jews, or anyone else, in the city. We were successful in preventing several attacks and robberies and we became quite popular both with the Jewish community and the citizens at large. As a consequence our funds and our stock of weapons began to grow.

Within *Okoyed* there were two views of how it should be organized. One view was that it should repeat the organization that was established in 1905. Ten groups of ten volunteers would be formed under an overall command. The command would call several groups together from time to time for training. There was to be a committee to raise funds to buy and distribute arms. It was to be a clandestine group devised to suit tsarist days when such a body could only exist illegally.

The other view of organization, which was the one that I supported, wanted a military-style organization, a fighting unit that would operate under military discipline. It would have a permanent membership and would be ready for immediate response when the need arose. Those supporting this view believed that only a permanent organization was capable of instilling discipline among its members and of getting them to believe in themselves. We had found that the *pogromtchikes*[7] were cowards when they found that looting and assaults would not go unanswered, and that any attempts at violence could cost them their lives.

It was finally agreed that the permanent fighting group concept would be adopted. An apartment was rented which would be a base for a group of former soldiers. At its head would be an officer who would be responsible for creating a true fighting unit. Around this permanent unit would be reserve units in the style of the 1905 groups. It was decided that rather than having a committee of

---

7   Wild pogromists who killed, plundered, and destroyed Jewish property.

three to run the fighting unit there should be only one person as chairman. The unit commander, his adjutant, and its members all fell under the control of the chairman. I was given the honor of being that person, a position that I filled until February 1919 when Senator Gruzenberg[8] was elected in my place. The permanent unit composed of ex-soldiers, almost all Georgian cavalry, was established in the rented apartment.

News was reaching us of assaults on Jews from a number of other parts of the Odessa region. We organized two groups of thirty men that were sent to two of the trouble spots where they quickly restored order. It was a message to the peasants in the area that the Jewish community was not defenseless. Our efforts were acknowledged by the provisional government, the workers' council, and the local Ukrainian boss.

With the breakdown of civil order in Odessa the real power fell into the hands of the crews of two Russian naval ships, the *Almaz* and the *Sinop*, anchored in the harbor. To a man the crew members were Bolsheviks. The name *Almaz* became the euphemism for the murder of those who opposed the Revolution. To be "sent to the *Almaz*" was to be taken to the Odessa harbor, tied to a heavy rock, and dumped in the sea.

One night I was called by my unit to tell me that the sailors had captured some seventy members of the bourgeoisie, including a number of Jews. It was rumored that they had been "sent to the *Almaz*," but the next day we established that they had been taken to the city prison.

This situation was complicated by the appearance of another group of sailors dubbed the *Simferopoltses*. They had arrived from the capital of Crimea, Simferopol, where they had executed a number of the local intelligentsia and the bourgeoisie. When they

---

8   Oscar Gruzenberg (1866–1940), a lawyer who achieved fame by his successful defense in the ritual murder trial of Mendel Beilis in 1911 in Kiev. He was appointed a senator in the Kerensky government. There is a Gruzenberg Street in Tel Aviv.

arrived in Odessa they made it plain that they would adopt the same approach. We were particularly concerned as the Odessa council of workers' deputies included a number of Jews.

We went to the man on the Odessa council who was nominally in charge of law and order in the city, and pointed out to him that the lives of those in the prison were at risk from the Simferopoltses. We asked the councilman to give us arms and let us defend the prison. He referred it to the council, who agreed that we should take over guarding the prison but would not give us any arms.

Our concern was that the Simferopoltses would combine with the sailors from the *Almaz* and the *Sinop* and that a pogrom might be the result. Such a group that included tough, well-armed sailors would pose a threat that we might not be able to meet.

It was decided that we should enlist the help of another armed group in Odessa, the Anarchists. They were quite independent and owed no allegiance to any other faction. The Anarchists remained strong throughout this troubled period. They were well armed with grenades, bombs, and guns. They had trucks that were used as transport. They raided warehouses and shops to satisfy their needs. On one such occasion we had confronted the Anarchists, who were carrying out a raid, and persuaded them to withdraw. Several of the leading Anarchists were Jews and thereafter there seemed to be an agreement not to confront each other.

Despite the chaotic situation in Odessa, Sioma felt that the *Okoyed* was strong enough for him to go to Petersburg, where he could achieve an ambition to become a student at the Institute of Railway Engineers. In Sioma's scrapbook there is a receipt for fifty rubles issued by the institute on August 31, 1917. It acknowledged payment for attendance at lectures for the first half of the academic year. In Russia this runs from September to December. It is possible that he felt that the provisional government would introduce stable democracy in Russia, but in fact he had made his way to Petersburg in time to witness the October 1917 Revolution.

In December 1923, Sioma wrote a short piece for an English

student magazine[9] in which he described the effects of the revolution on educational institutions in Petersburg.

> Before two months had elapsed after the Bolsheviks came to power, the Commissar of Public Knowledge issued a decree dismissing all the Provosts, Principals, and Wardens of the High Schools and Universities. In their place Executive Committees were appointed composed of members selected by the Commissar. In the University where I was a student the Committee consisted of three members, all of whom were Bolsheviks. They were a young lecturer, a student, and one of the porters. Life in the university became unbearable. No other course was left than to go south. It was neither an easy nor a safe journey, but most of us managed it.

Sioma did manage the journey. He arrived back in Odessa in December 1917.

In November 1917 the Ukraine had declared itself a republic as part of Russia, but in January 1918 it proclaimed itself an independent republic. The struggle for power in the city of Odessa, which at first was between local Bolsheviks and Ukrainian forces, had begun. In this climate, pogroms were now widespread in the Ukraine and the threat to the Jewish population in Odessa was very real. Sioma resumed command of the Jewish self-defense force.

There is another surviving photograph of the Jewish self-defense unit that was taken at this time. Other than Sioma, no one in this photograph appeared in the first studio photograph referred to earlier. There are forty-five men in this photograph, which was taken in the open air against a stone and brick wall. Again Sioma is sitting in the center of the seated row in the position of leader. He is dressed in the same university uniform, but on this occasion he is wearing a cap. The cap has a badge on it which has been identified as the badge of the Institute of Railway Engineers. All the

---

9   While he was a student at Loughborough College in England, he wrote an article entitled "The Exile" for the student magazine, *The Limit*. Sioma wrote that he was one of the known fifty-one Russian students who had fled to England to continue their studies. They were, they thought, in temporary exile.

others in the photograph are wearing army uniforms. Most carry rifles with fixed bayonets. Several have swords but no guns. One has a bugle; one is brandishing a hand grenade and another, a larger grenade. A number wear fully loaded ammunition bandoliers. At the front of the group a young man kneels at a machine gun that has a fully loaded ammunition belt.

Sioma's story printed in *Tog* continued:

> During the period when the provisional government ruled in Petrograd the Odessa *Duma* [city council] had remained loyal to the government. But immediately following the October Revolution in Petrograd the government in Odessa declared in favor of the Bolsheviks. During the following six months there was a continuing struggle between the Bolsheviks in the city and marauding bands of Ukrainians who were known as Haydemakes.[10] In January 1918 a battle for supremacy broke out between these forces. There was open warfare in the center of the city. The Jewish self-defense unit remained neutral. It was determined to remain an apolitical force that existed to protect the Jewish community, although both sides sought their assistance. The leader of the Jewish unit [Sioma himself] obtained a letter from the Ukrainian command that the unit was neutral and must not be disarmed. Despite this agreement a 300-strong group of Haydemakes attacked and broke into one of the Jewish unit's command posts and overpowered the 35 Jews in the post, who were taken prisoner.
>
> How to get to the Haydemakes to obtain the release of the captives? A frontal assault was out of the question because we were greatly outnumbered, 150 of our unit against several thousand Haydemakes. We were advised that a neutral center had been established in a hotel in the city where there was contact between the Haydemakes and the Bolsheviks. Two other of our committee and I put on Red Cross armbands and made our way to the hotel. From there an officer of our group and I were allowed to enter

---

10   Translates roughly as "the attackers."

the central telephone exchange, which was under the control of the Bolsheviks. We were allowed to telephone the Haydemakes' headquarters. Introducing myself as the chairman of the committee of the Jewish unit, I threatened to mobilize the entire Jewish population of Odessa to oppose the Ukrainians unless they released our fighters. It was agreed that they would meet us to negotiate the matter that night.

I determined that I would negotiate this by myself. That night, ignoring the curfew, I went unarmed, to show my good faith, to the Bolshevik headquarters. The Red Guard had won a major battle that day and I was told that the Haydemakes were coming to make terms that night. They did arrive and after those negotiations were completed I introduced myself to the Ukrainian leaders. One of them responded that the attack on our post and the capture of our men had been a mistake and that the captives would be released in the morning.

But the next day fighting between the Ukrainians and the Bolsheviks erupted again and our men had not been released by early afternoon. I decide to go myself to the Ukrainian headquarters in a Red Cross vehicle. But we were shot at and one of the nurses was killed. We were forced to turn back. So we decided to muster the rest of our unit to force our way into the Haydemakes' stronghold. But just then all of our captured fighters turned up. Their story was that the Bolsheviks had attacked the barracks where they had been held, and in the confusion that followed they had overpowered their guard, seized all the available weapons at the barracks, and escaped.

The Bolsheviks were now in control of Odessa. They retained their rule until the German army marched in and occupied the city on March 13, 1918.[11]

---

11 A cease-fire between Russia and Germany was followed by negotiations at Brest-Litovsk in December 1917. No agreement was reached, and Germany resumed hostilities against a now virtually defenseless Russia. The Bolshevik government signed the Treaty of Brest-Litovsk in March 1918. Under its terms, Russia ceded

Sioma's story in the *Tog* continued:

> When the Germans captured Odessa they decided to disarm all national units that existed in the town. But the local government felt that it should retain a loyal fighting collective and convinced the Germans to leave the Jewish fighting unit as a militia reserve. We welcomed this, but felt that we should take precautions to preserve part of our now considerable stock of armaments. Although we handed over 22 grenade launchers and 1,000 rifles to the Germans, we kept eight grenade launchers, 300 rifles, and a supply of ammunition. We smuggled the arms that we did not hand over through the German patrols and buried them on the outskirts of town. The arms were carefully protected from rust, and different groups of our force were used to bury small quantities of arms in a number of places. Only one other officer and I knew the whereabouts of all the sites where the arms were buried.
>
> The Germans controlled the city without any civil disturbances until they withdrew after the German capitulation to the Western Allies in November 1918.

On October 30, 1918, German sailors in Kiel, the chief naval base of the German fleet, staged a revolt against their government. Joined by workers, they moved to establish a soviet on Russian lines. Mass protests in Berlin against the government and the war took place on November 8 and 9. The Kaiser abdicated. A German republic was proclaimed. On November 11, the German army in France surrendered to the Allied armies. World War I was over. The German and Austrian armies of occupation in Russia withdrew.

During the period of quiet in Odessa during the German occupation Sioma had decided to return to Petersburg. German forces had not invaded Petersburg or Moscow. The Bolshevik government had moved

---

the Baltic States, Poland, Belarus, and the Ukraine to Germany. Russia thus lost one-third of its population, its grain production, and a considerable part of its industry.

its capital from besieged Petersburg to Moscow. A journey from Odessa required travel through German-occupied regions to the Russian-held territory and on to Petersburg. The only transport would have been by train. A contemporary description of travel by rail gives some idea of the difficulties involved.

> They set fire to literally every train station, beginning from Moscow itself right up to Orsha, stations at which all the platforms and paths were literally covered with vomit and defecation.[12]

It would appear that Sioma made this hazardous journey to obtain documentary evidence of his attendance at the university in Petersburg that would enable him to continue his engineering studies elsewhere. Because there was a complete breakdown of postal services it is probable that he did go to Petersburg. The risks that he undertook went beyond those of the journey, for there was an outbreak of cholera in Petersburg. Between July and September 1918 there were more than twelve thousand registered cases in the city, and more than four thousand deaths. The shortage of food in the city was so severe that at one stage the bread ration was down to one eighth of a pound per day (56 grams) for factory workers. This led to strikes and retribution by Red Guards and Red Army soldiers.

Despite the risks he was able to secure two receipts. They bear consecutive numbers and are dated August 24, 1918. They appear, in part, to duplicate each other. Both are for one hundred rubles. One states that it was for attending lectures in the first and second halves of the 1917–1918 academic year, while the other is for attendance in the second half of the 1917–1918 year. On the same date the institute issued a travel pass that allowed him to travel throughout Russia.

These dates indicate that he would have returned to Odessa in late August or early September 1918. His scrapbook contains another receipt that was issued to him as a second-year student in the Odessa Polytechnic Institute, Civil Engineering Faculty. Dated September 27, 1918, it is for

---

12 Ivan Bunin, *Cursed Days: A Diary of Revolution*, trans. Thomas Gaiton Marullo (Chicago: Ivan R. Dee, 1998), 202.

attendance in the autumn half of the academic year. Another receipt from Odessa Polytechnic is for attendance at the spring half of the 1919 academic year. Later that year, he obtained a certificate from the Odessa campus of the University of Novorossiysk that confirmed that he had left that university to attend the institute in Petersburg in the autumn of 1917.

Sioma's narrative in *Tog* continued:

> A power vacuum was created by the departure of the Germans. A number of different Ukrainian forces, all competing for control of the newly independent Ukraine, occupied Odessa at different times during the following month. The Jewish self-defense force found that it could not rely on any of the Ukrainian forces to maintain order in the city and that task fell on the Jewish unit supported by our student unit. Throughout this period I told all these conflicting interests that our purpose of existence was to watch over the peaceful population of Odessa, and I insisted on our remaining an apolitical group. We carefully refrained from aligning ourselves to any of the competing parties. The final group that moved in on Odessa was the followers of Symon Petlura.[13] A month after the Germans had left Odessa a French fleet carrying the Russian anti-Bolshevik "Volunteer Army" arrived.[14] The aim of this invasion was to provide a port through which supplies could be provided for the White Army forces and the Volunteer Army, both of which were fighting the Red Army in the Ukraine. The Volunteer Army under their successful general, Grishin-Almazov, was landed in Odessa by French war ships and was supported by French forces. On the

---

13   Although Petlura had no military training, from 1917 to 1920 he achieved the position of head of the army and of the fledgling state of Ukraine. On June 11, 1926, the American journal *The Zionist* published a long article by Sioma on Petlura. While sympathizing with the nationalist aspirations of the Ukrainians, Sioma wrote scathingly about Petlura, who turned a blind eye while his army carried out "the more than six hundred pogroms that took place in the Ukraine during Petlura's regime."

14   The Volunteer Army was formed as an anti-Bolshevik force in September 1918 by officers and men of the defeated Russian army. It was most successful in Siberia where, under the command of Colonel Grishin-Almazov, it defeated the Red Army.

evening of their arrival Grishin-Almazov gave the commander of the Petlura troops instructions to clean up Odessa. He allowed the commander until nine o'clock the following morning to do this. Grishin-Almazov refused a request for more time so the following day a pitched battle broke out. The Jewish unit was called in during the fighting to protect the city market, which was being looted by a mob. The Volunteer Army won the battle and the followers of Petlura were forced out of the city.

Grishin-Almazov formed a commission, of which the Jewish fighting unit was part, to keep order in the city. I was their representative on the commission. I was joined by the head of the Jewish student force. Our financial independence of the subsidies given to the other members of the commission by the Volunteers gave us a basis with which to negotiate. We achieved the concession that our members were exempted from military service and that we were not to be involved in actions which were political in nature. This was important because the Volunteers acted against both Bolshevik and Ukrainian separatists at various times. We needed to retain our status as being non-political in this ever-changing scenario. The minutes kept by the commission recorded that the size of our force was over 300. Many thought that it was over 500. In fact there were far fewer than 300 but I did not think it was necessary to convince them to the contrary. Things were quiet under the control of the commission, but toward the end of March 1919 I was receiving reports of arms appearing on the streets and that a group in the city had revived a cell of the Black Hundred,[15] who were recruiting members quite freely. Two members of our unit who did not look Jewish infiltrated the cell. Based on the information that they gave us we decided to strengthen our watch division and to place new units in two of our weaker areas.

---

15 The Black Hundred was an ultra-nationalist group created in 1905 after the failed revolution. Its activities, with the knowledge of the tsar, included fomenting and participating in pogroms throughout Russia.

It was during this period that Odessa was on the verge of anarchy. Thousands of Ukrainians had fled from Odessa to the countryside to escape the Bolsheviks. The city was without heat or electricity and shortages triggered a tenfold increase in prices. The *Odessa News* of March 2, 1919, wrote, "Never before has Odessa passed through such a nightmarish situation. The population is succumbing to starvation and cold."

The French army abandoned Odessa on April 3, 1919. The French government in Paris was shocked by the failure of their army in the Ukraine to establish some reliable form of anti-Bolshevik government. This feeling was reinforced by a strong anti-interventionist movement in France. Orders to evacuate Odessa and all of the Crimea were issued in Paris on April 2, 1919. On April 6, 1919, the Red Army moved in and recovered Odessa.

A diary note by a Russian writer who was stranded in Odessa at the time read:

> May 1, 1919. I went out to look for food. People were saying that everything would be closed and that there will be nothing to buy. Sure enough there is almost nothing in the stores that were open. At night all the homes are dark. There is no electricity. I am writing by the light of a stinking kitchen lamp, using the last of the kerosene.[16]

Sioma was put in the difficult position of having to protect the integrity of his self-defense force and its weapons against pressure from a number of his fellow Jews in the Red Army. They believed that as the Red Army was now in control of the city, a Jewish self-defense force was now no longer necessary and that its arms should be handed over. Sioma refused to do this, believing that the civil war and general unrest might still allow a situation that could result in a pogrom. As a result of this stand, Sioma and several others in his group were arrested and imprisoned.

On April 23, 1933, the Glasgow *Sunday Mail* published an interview with Sioma. Much of the article is in quotation marks. The reporter had written that it was best if Sioma's story was told in his own words.

---

16   Ivan Bunin, *Cursed Days*, 90–91.

On several occasions, Sioma told the story of his arrest by the Red Army. It first appeared in the press during his fund-raising activities for ORT-OZE in South Africa in 1930. It was not told to his audiences in Australia, although photographs of Sioma sitting with the armed men of *Okoyed* were used in Australian newspapers. Curiously, the story is not repeated in his series of articles in *Tog*, but two Scottish newspapers published on April 23, 1933, carried the same story, both in quotation marks, indicating that the report was verbatim. Both accounts read as follows:

> When the Bolsheviks came into power the first thing that they did was to dismantle our self-defence force and place our officials in prison. We were sentenced to death without trial. There were nineteen of us in one cell. The prison was filthy and the food was terrible. Every day the soldiers would come round and read out the names of those whose turn it was to be shot. Men would be dragged out of our cell, conducted to the "death corner" in the yard, and the next minute a few shots would ring out – the men were dead.
>
> The Bolshevik guards did not know who they were shooting. A warder came into our cell and asked for prisoner Nikitin. When there was no reply he shouted out, "Where is Nikitin?" A man jumped forward, it was in fact Nikitin, and asked the warder if he did not remember that Nikitin had been shot a few days ago. Nikitin's name was crossed off the list.

How Sioma escaped from this situation is uncertain. There were several versions of the story that he told to different audiences. It seems most likely that he was released at the end of August 1919 when a new White Army, under the command of General Denikin,[17] attacked Odessa from the sea and on land. In the ensuing battle, two of Sioma's officers were

---

17 Denikin was a Russian general in the war with Germany. He became chief of staff in the provisional government but was arrested for trying to establish a military dictatorship. He escaped and in April 1918 assumed command of the White Army forces in southern Russia. His invasion of Odessa was a step toward taking Moscow

killed by the invading forces, but soon after that the city returned to calm. It seemed as if the White Army had settled for good and that the government would not change again.

Sioma's story continued:

> At that time I left Odessa. I received permission to leave from the government without any difficulty, and I was given a visa from the British consulate to enter Palestine. On November 12, 1919, I was to leave by the ship *Ruslan*,[18] which was carrying homeless people to Palestine. Just before the ship was due to leave I was arrested on board by the White Army investigation unit. But thanks to the intervention of the Jewish community and the city mayor I was released and was able to find another ship that enabled me to leave for Palestine two weeks later.

---

from the south, but he was defeated in a major battle just four hundred kilometers short of the capital.

18   This ship was famous as the first transport available for Jews to leave for Palestine after the mayhem of the Revolution.

Chapter 4

Palestine on Both Sides of the Jordan

Before World War I, Palestine was an ill-defined area within the Ottoman Empire. The biblical Land of Israel included areas on the western side of the Jordan that were home to three Israelite tribes: Reuben, Gad, and Manasseh. After the war, the victorious wartime Allies met in San Remo to determine the division of the old Ottoman Empire. They resolved to establish Syria and Iraq – then known as Mesopotamia – as independent states with borders still to be determined. Palestine, without any attempt to define its boundaries, was to be a mandatory area with a mandatory authority[1] to be appointed by the Allies.

The resolution concerning Palestine included a recognition of the Balfour Declaration.

> The Mandatory will be responsible for putting into effect the declaration originally made on November 8, 1917, by the British Government, and adopted by the other Allied Powers, in favour of the establishment in Palestine of a national home for the Jewish

---

1   A legal commission for the administration of the area.

people, it being clearly understood that nothing shall be done which may prejudice the civil and religious rights of existing non-Jewish communities in Palestine, or the rights and political status enjoyed by Jews in any other country.

On November 2, 1917, Arthur James Balfour,[2] in his role as foreign secretary in the government of Lloyd George, had written to Lord Rothschild,[3]

> His Majesty's Government view with favour the establishment in Palestine of a national home for the Jewish people, and will use their best endeavours to facilitate the achievement of this object, it being clearly understood that nothing shall be done which may prejudice the civil and religious rights of existing non-Jewish communities in Palestine.

The Balfour Declaration had an impact on events in the Middle East from the time of its release, and it still resonates to the present time. There have been many versions of the background surrounding its writing, but because the letter and its repercussions over the following twenty-two years of Sioma's life had such a profound influence on him and his times, it is important to recount the story.

An aspect of its importance is that one of the aims set out in the Declaration of the Central Committee of the newly formed Union of Zionist Revisionists issued in Paris in November 1925 was "the inclusion of Transjordan within the frontiers of Palestine and the area of Jewish settlement." It was a concept that had been spelled out as an aim of Zionism as early as 1919, but long after the League of Nations defined Palestine as the land lying to the east of the Jordan to the sea, it remained an aim of the Revisionist movement that Palestine should be the biblical Land of Israel "on both sides of the Jordan." For the next twenty years after the League of Nations decision on Jordan, the Revisionists maintained

---

2   Balfour, who served as prime minister from 1902 to 1905, was created Earl Balfour in 1922.

3   The second Lord Rothschild, a Zionist supporter.

their stance. Sioma published a newspaper article in 1930 that expressed the view that the Jewish state should encompass the land on both sides of the Jordan,[4] and Jabotinsky included it in a book that he published shortly before his death in 1940.[5]

British interest in the "Holy Land" as the birthplace of Jesus and the site of his execution extends almost as far back as the introduction of Christianity to England. The first English pilgrims made their way to Palestine in the fifth century and the English Crusader expeditions took place in the twelfth century. In both the seventeenth and nineteenth centuries, there were strong evangelical movements in England that believed that the second coming of Jesus would occur only if the Jews were restored to Palestine.

Overlaying this religious interest was the geopolitical importance of Palestine and Syria. Before the Suez Canal was built, the trade route from India and China to Europe was by sea across the Indian Ocean. Rather than taking the long voyage around South Africa, ships sailed up the Arabian Gulf to Tyre and Antioch. There they discharged their cargo, which was sent overland to Mediterranean ports. British concern for the area was heightened during the Napoleonic Wars. After Napoleon invaded Egypt, he had ambitions to capture Jerusalem on his way to dislodge British interests in Mesopotamia, Persia, and India. Napoleon set off through the Sinai Peninsula into Palestine and laid siege to Acre. The prospect of this important seaport falling to Napoleon brought action from Britain. Acre was successfully defended by adding British warships and marines to the Ottoman defenses. It was Napoleon's first defeat on land. He abandoned his plans and withdrew to Egypt.

Thirty years later, another invader threatened this trade route. Mehemet Ali,[6] who had seized control of Egypt when the French withdrew, had plans to conquer the Ottoman Empire. He had to invade Palestine and

---

4   *The Australian Jewish Herald* (Melbourne), April 17, 1930, page 6.

5   Vladimir Jabotinsky, *The Jewish War Front* (London: George Allen and Unwin, 1940).

6   Mehemet (Muhammad) Ali, an Albanian-born commander in the Ottoman army, was sent to attack Napoleon in Egypt but seized power there after Napoleon's withdrawal.

Syria on his way to Constantinople. This posed a threat not only to the British route to India but to the eastern interests of the European powers. An alliance of Russia, Britain, Austria, and Prussia was formed to protect the weak Ottoman Empire. British and Austrian forces were sent to defeat the invader at Acre. France joined the other powers in a treaty that was signed in 1841.

It was during this period that a concept of the Jews being returned to Palestine to bring stability to the area first surfaced. In 1840 Lord Palmerston, the British foreign secretary, suggested to the Ottoman sultan that he should to take advantage of a "strong notion among the Jews in Europe" to return to Palestine. This would be a check on any further invasions of the sultan's territory. *The Times* of London approved this plan that was "to plant the Jewish people in the land of their fathers." The sultan did not follow this advice, but allowed the Jewish population of Palestine to increase. The arrival of the new immigrants, mostly Russian Jews, changed the face of the existing Jewish population that had lived in Jerusalem and other towns in Palestine for two thousand years.

There are no authentic figures of Jewish settlement in this period because of the unreliability of the Turkish census, which in 1890 reported that Jews constituted some 10 percent of the population of Palestine.

During the first years of the twentieth century, Theodor Herzl went to England, seeking the support of the British government for some land where Jews of the world could establish a homeland. On August 14, 1902, the Foreign Office wrote to Herzl that the foreign secretary would be "prepared to entertain favorably proposals for the establishment of a Jewish colony of settlement on conditions which will enable the members to observe their national customs." Herzl read the letter to the Sixth Zionist Congress, which greeted it with applause, but Russian Zionists, some of whom had already settled in Palestine, were opposed to settlement anywhere else. When no suitable site could be found in the British Empire, the suggestion lapsed.

When Turkey sided with Germany during World War I, the prospect of a breakup of the Ottoman Empire in the Middle East aroused a fresh outbreak of imperial ambitions amongst the Allies. France believed that they had rights in Syria and Palestine that went back to the conquest of the area by a French army during the Crusades. Since then, the French insisted, it was they who had protected the lives of Christians who lived there. To support this argument the French quoted their persuasion of the Ottomans in 1851 to accept a treaty that confirmed France and the Roman Catholic Church as the supreme Christian authority in the Holy Land.

Britain was concerned, as always, to protect the interests of its empire in the Far East and now the sea gateway to it, the Suez Canal. Russia, still in the war at the time, wanted control of the seaway from the Black Sea to the Mediterranean. The British prime minister, Asquith, concurred that Russia should have its demands met, provided that "we and France should get a substantial share of the carcass of the Turks."

T. E. Lawrence – known later as Lawrence of Arabia – was in Arabia and Palestine wooing Arab nationalism to support the British army in its war against Turkey. Lawrence's efforts were supported by the British government, which promised, in a letter now known by the name of its author as the McMahon letter, to satisfy Arab national dreams. Specifically, the letter said that Great Britain was prepared to recognize and support the independence of the Arabs in all the regions within those "frontiers wherein Great Britain is free to act without detriment to the interests of her ally, France."

A year later Britain, France, and tsarist Russia completed a secret agreement, known as the Sykes-Picot Agreement, to carve up the defeated Ottoman Empire between them. The French would have Lebanon and Syria, Britain would have Palestine and Mesopotamia, and Constantinople would go to the Russians.

One of the problems with this treaty was the absence of any agreed borders of the countries of Lebanon, Syria, and Palestine. The Sykes-Picot Agreement allowed only scant recognition of the McMahon letter by including the words that the parties were "prepared to recognize and protect an independent Arab State or a Confederation of Arab States." While the agreement made no mention of Jews or Jewish interests, there was a growing interest in Britain in the possible settlement of Jews in Palestine.

The Russian-born Chaim Weizmann, educated in the universities of Switzerland and Germany where he graduated with a doctorate in chemistry, arrived in England in 1904. He settled in Manchester, where he joined the British Zionist movement. Charles Dreyfus was the president of the local branch of the Zionists. Dreyfus was actively involved in politics as a member of the municipal council and a leading figure in the local Conservative Party. Balfour, then the Conservative prime minister, was the local member for Manchester East. Dreyfus introduced Weizmann to Balfour. The following year Dreyfus was the Manchester campaign chairman for Balfour in the general election of 1906. During the campaign, he arranged a much longer meeting between Balfour and Weizmann.

Early in World War I, British munitions production was suffering from a critical lack of naturally occurring acetone. The major source of acetone was from Austria, now an ally of Germany. The chemical, a by-product of wood alcohol, was the solvent that was used to produce cordite, the explosive charge for ammunition. A shortage of acetone, and a consequent inadequate supply of ammunition, was widely blamed for failures of the British army on the Western Front. In addition, an ample reserve of shells was also essential for the retention of British naval supremacy. Weizmann had devised a laboratory process for the bacterial fermentation of acetone. In recognition of his invention in 1916, he was appointed the director of the British Admiralty Laboratory in London. In this position he was known to the future prime minister, Lloyd George, who was the minister for munitions.

Balfour was first lord of the Admiralty and Weizmann's immediate superior. Later that year, Balfour was appointed foreign secretary. Sir Mark Sykes, the man who had negotiated the Sykes-Picot Agreement and was sympathetic to Zionism, was appointed secretary of the war cabinet. Weizmann thus had access to the sympathetic ears of the prime minister, the foreign secretary, and the secretary of the war cabinet, and from there to a number of other influential members of the British government.

Weizmann had the assistance of the Polish-born Nahum Sokolow, who had moved to England before the outbreak of the war. Sokolow, a former secretary-general of the World Zionist Organization, traveled widely seeking support for Zionism. As a duo they were a powerful force both within the Jewish community in Britain and as lobbyists to the government. Sokolow was so highly regarded by the British establishment that he was invited to travel with Sykes to France and Rome seeking the support of Britain's allies to the concept of a British-enabled settlement of Jews in Palestine. They gained the approval of the French and Italian governments and the pope.

The time was now ripe for Weizmann and Sokolow and a committee of English Zionists to put together a memorandum to be submitted to the British cabinet. It proposed the establishment of Palestine as a national home for the Jews, with full autonomy for the Jewish people. Sokolow advised the authors of the Balfour memorandum to confine the message to two simple proposals.

> His Majesty's government accepts the principle that Palestine should be reconstituted as the national home of the Jewish people; and will use its best endeavours to secure the achievements of this object, and will discuss the necessary methods and means with the Zionist organisation.

Balfour responded that he would put the memorandum to the cabinet. There was opposition within the cabinet. Edwin Montagu, who was secretary of state for India and the only Jew in the cabinet, was an ardent anti-Zionist. "I assert," he wrote, "that there is not a Jewish nation." His own family had been English for generations. They were not, he argued, the same nation as Jews in other countries any more than Christian Englishmen were the same nation as Christian Frenchmen. Opposition from the only Jew in the cabinet tended to dampen the enthusiasm of Sykes and Balfour.

While these negotiations were in progress the Palestine issue was clouded by Jabotinsky's efforts to have a Jewish regiment created in the British army. Jabotinsky, who wanted a Jewish fighting force to be part of the British army that conquered Palestine, had come to England to enlist support for this aim. It was opposed by Montagu and other anti-Zionists, including the senior Jewish chaplain in the British armed forces. Would all

Jews already serving in the British forces be required, they asked, to join this new regiment, which would be largely composed of Russians and Poles? Despite this opposition, Jabotinsky was ultimately successful and the regiment was formed.

A decision by the British cabinet on Weizmann's proposal was stalled until the concept had been approved by the American president. Then both Lloyd George and Balfour were absent from cabinet meetings because of illness and travel commitments, so the matter was delayed further. It was not until the cabinet met on October 4 that a version of the declaration prepared by two cabinet members was considered. It differed substantially from Weizmann's efforts. It now used the phrase "a national home for the Jewish race," and to satisfy Montagu it included the words that nothing would be done that would prejudice "the rights and political status enjoyed in any other country by such Jews who are fully contented with their existing nationality and citizenship." The cabinet still waited on direct confirmation from President Wilson of his approval. Support was also required from both the British Zionist movement and representative persons in Anglo-Jewry.

By now Montagu had left England to take up his position as secretary of state for India, so his opposition was not heard at subsequent cabinet meetings. The alternative drafts of the proposed declaration were supposed to have been considered by the War Cabinet in mid-October, but it was not included in the agenda for that meeting because of other pressing matters. By now the proposed letter was common knowledge. *The Times* ran a leader on October 14 called "The Jews and Palestine." "It is indeed no secret that the question of re-establishing the Jews in Palestine has for months been under consideration of the British and Allied Governments…[and] with the British army actually in Palestine…a public announcement has been unaccountably delayed."

It was not until the War Cabinet meeting of October 31, 1917, that the wording of the letter that was to be sent to Rothschild was approved. Legend has it that Weizmann was waiting outside the cabinet room for the decision. Sykes emerged from the cabinet with the wording in his hand and presented it to Weizmann with the words, "Dr. Weizmann, it's a boy."

But the wording of the declaration approved by the cabinet was deliberately vague. The concept of a Jewish state had been reduced to "a national home for the Jewish people." What precisely did that phrase mean? Over the next thirty years, the carefully imprecise wording of the letter became the basis of arguments between the British, Arabs, and Jews.

The final document read:

> His Majesty's Government view with favour the establishment in Palestine of a national home for the Jewish people, and will use their best endeavours to facilitate the achievement of this object, it being clearly understood that nothing shall be done to prejudice the civil and religious rights of existing non-Jewish communities in Palestine, or the rights and political status enjoyed by Jews in any other country.

The imprecision of this wording and the absence of a definition of what was meant by Palestine were to be major causes of dispute between Zionist factions.

On April 24, 1920, the Supreme Council of the victorious Allied Powers acceded to representations from Weizmann to include the Balfour Declaration in their peace treaty with Turkey. In January 1921, the British prime minister, Lloyd George, appointed the forty-seven-year-old Winston Churchill as secretary of state for the colonies. As an army officer, Churchill had seen action in British India, the Sudan, and the Second Boer War. He gained fame as a war correspondent and through the books he wrote about his campaigns. By 1921, Churchill had already spent a long time in government. His first appointment in 1905 was as under-secretary of state for the colonies. During World War I, Churchill was first lord of the Admiralty, but lost his place in the war cabinet, having fallen from grace over the 1915 Gallipoli campaign. While still an MP he served for six months in 1916 as a battalion commander in France, but then returned to a stellar political career.

Churchill took up his new duties as colonial secretary in February 1921. His portfolio included a newly created Middle East Department. Churchill's first decision in his new position was to approve an application from Pinhas Rutenberg for permission to build a hydroelectric power station in Palestine. He approved it the following day.

In March 1920 there had been a series of attacks by Arabs on Jewish settlements in the Galilee. These were followed by an eruption of so-called Arab "riots" in Jerusalem. The use of the word *riot* was a euphemism for a pogrom in which Jews were killed, Jewish women raped, and Jewish property destroyed. In response a meeting of the Histadrut[7] had created the Haganah, a Jewish defense organization. It was, in essence, an unofficial group designed to coordinate the protection of settlements. In May 1921, Arabs initiated more serious attacks on Jewish settlements and on the Jewish quarter of Jerusalem. The newly formed Haganah was outnumbered, and during a week of fighting several settlements were destroyed and forty-seven Jews were killed.

Sir Herbert Samuel, a British Jew, a Zionist, and a former member of the British cabinet, was appointed the British high commissioner of Palestine by Lloyd George. He arrived in Palestine on June 30, 1921, to run the country under the Mandate. But he was in an impossible position of trying to serve three incompatible interests: as high commissioner he was charged with running the country on a peaceful basis, as a Jew he was in favor of the terms of the Mandate, and he had resentful and angry Arabs to placate. He decided that pacifying the Arabs was the most pressing demand, and he did this by announcing a cessation of Jewish immigration.

In an attempt to ease tensions all around he granted an amnesty to all those, both Jews and Arabs, who had been imprisoned under army rule and were held in Acre prison. The released prisoners included Jabotinsky, who had been sentenced to fifteen years' imprisonment at hard labor for carrying his service revolver for protection during the Arab "riots" of 1920, although he had been a commissioned officer in the British army, in the Jewish Legion, during the war.[8] But adding to the outrage already engendered by

---

7   The General Federation of Jewish Labor.

8   Jabotinsky commanded a force that was the first to cross the Jordan and that took part in the capture of Jerusalem. Other members of the Legion included the sculptor Jacob Epstein, three future prime ministers of Israel (David Ben-

Jabotinsky's absurdly severe sentence, the amnesty also included two Arabs who had been convicted of rape during the 1920 pogrom.

Churchill had invited T. E. Lawrence to join his staff in his Middle East Department. They had a high regard for each other. Churchill and Lawrence arrived in Cairo in March 1921 for a conference with British administrators in Palestine, Egypt, and Iraq. They were joined by the local commanders-in-chief of the British army and air force. The Arabs' open hostility to the Jewish presence in Palestine was just one of Churchill's problems. There was the troublesome situation that had arisen between the Arabs and the French in Syria. In 1918, the British army commander in Syria had installed Sherif Faisal, Hussein's third son, to rule in Damascus. This had been done despite his knowledge of the Sykes-Picot Agreement, which gave Syria to France. After the war, Faisal was displaced by French forces. Skirmishes between French and Arab forces ensued in Syria and northern Palestine. At the time it was not clear where the border between the two countries lay.

Early in 1921, Faisal's older brother, Abdullah, occupied the Jordanian city of Maan with two thousand Bedouin soldiers. He was threatening to attack the French army in Syria and recapture Damascus. This was a situation that Britain wished to avoid. The French army would defeat the small Arab force and then might intrude into British Palestine.

Weizmann had written to Churchill that it was the Zionist view that the whole of Transjordan had been part of the biblical Land of Israel and should become part of the Jewish national home. That was the area that now comprises Israel, the West Bank, and Jordan. As the mandatory authority, Britain was given authority "to make such provision for the administration of the territories – lying between the Jordan River and the eastern boundary of Palestine – as may be considered suitable...." This enabled Britain to dispose of Transjordan (the territory that is now Jordan) and reduce Palestine to the tiny area that lies between the Jordan River and the Mediterranean.

Gurion, Itzhak Ben-Zvi, and Levi Eshkol), and several others who later would rise to prominence in the state.

At a meeting in Cairo that included Lawrence and Samuel, resolutions were worked out to Churchill's satisfaction. First, Transjordan was to be separated from Palestine. Transjordan's western border would be the Jordan River and include the whole of the British Mandate to the east. Jewish settlement would not be allowed in what was to be the new Arab kingdom of Transjordan. Thus Jewish settlement would be confined to that part of Palestine that was defined in the west by the sea, in the east by the Jordan River, in the south by Aqaba and in the north by the Upper Galilee on what is now the border with Syria. Palestine as defined by that concept included what is now known as the West Bank (Judea and Samaria) and the Gaza Strip. Transjordan was to be offered to Abdullah as a kingdom for Arabs that would be free of Jewish settlement, provided that he gave up any intention of invading Syria.

Lawrence sounded out Abdullah with this proposition. He appeared to be amenable to the deal, so Churchill formally put the proposal to Abdullah at Government House in Jerusalem over a cup of tea. Churchill confirmed to Abdullah that the Zionist clauses in the Mandate would not apply in Transjordan. The deal was done.

Then Churchill met with Palestinian Arab leaders, who requested that the concept of a national home for the Jews be abolished. "You have asked me to repudiate the Balfour Declaration.... It is not in my power to do so, nor, if it were in my power, would it be my wish," Churchill responded.

Finally, Churchill greeted a Jewish delegation with the words that he was "perfectly convinced that the cause of Zionism is one which carries with it much that is good for the whole world." The following day, Churchill planted a tree at the future site of the Hebrew University of Jerusalem. He said at the ceremony, "My heart is full of sympathy for Zionism. I believe that the establishment of a Jewish National Home in Palestine will be a blessing to the whole world, a blessing to the Jewish race...and to Great Britain...."

No doubt Churchill believed that he had secured a diplomatic triumph. Even Lawrence was pleased that the promises to the Arabs had been fulfilled.[9]

---

9   Lawrence was to write in a footnote in his book *Seven Pillars of Wisdom* (London:

In June 1922 the decisions made by Churchill about Transjordan and the meaning of the words a "National Home" for the Jews in Palestine were spelled out in what was to become known as Churchill's White Paper of 1922. It enshrined the agreements reached with Abdullah. Transjordan was created as a Hashemite kingdom and Jews were excluded from settling there.

The White Paper explained that the terms of the Balfour Declaration "[did] not contemplate that Palestine as a whole should be converted into a Jewish National Home, but that such a Home should be founded in Palestine."

> It is not the imposition of a Jewish nationality...but the further development of the existing Jewish community with the assistance of Jews in other parts of the world in order that it may become a centre for the Jewish people...[and] that it is in Palestine as of right and not on sufferance...internationally guaranteed and that it should be formally recognized to rest upon ancient historic connection.

There was a further sting in the tail of the Paper. Jewish immigration to Palestine must not "exceed whatever may be the economic capacity of the country at the time to absorb new arrivals." This allowed the British high commissioner in Palestine to determine the level of Jewish immigration from time to time based on his interpretation of the "economic capacity" of the country.

In Parliament Churchill was forced to defend his White Paper. The fact that it allowed any immigration of Jews against the Arab opposition was seen as Churchill's increasingly pro-Zionist bias. But eventually the White Paper was passed by a substantial majority. It was presented to the League of Nations and approved as the basis for the Mandate on July 22, 1922. The Council of the League of Nations added that a body to be known as

---

Jonathan Cape, 1935), page 276: "Churchill...in a few weeks made straight all the tangle, finding solutions...without sacrificing any interest of our Empire or any interest of the peoples concerned. So we were quit of the war-time Eastern adventure, with clean hands...."

"the Jewish Agency" be formed "to be recognized as a public body for the purpose of advising and co-operating with the administration of Palestine."

Weizmann wrote to Churchill congratulating him and tendering "our most grateful thanks" for the "unfailing sympathy you have consistently shown towards the legitimate aspirations [of the Jewish people]…and for securing the opportunity of rebuilding its national home in peaceful co-operation with all sections of the inhabitants of Palestine."

Two issues – the split of Transjordan from the biblical Land of Israel, where no Jewish settlement would be allowed, and who should represent world Jewry on the Jewish Agency Executive – divided Jewish opinion. Both matters were discussed by the Zionist executive committee, of which Jabotinsky was a member.

The executive approved the new definition of what constituted Palestine and the prospective limitation of Jewish immigration despite Jabotinsky's objections. The clause added by the League of Nations Mandate that created a "Jewish Agency" – which was to be the recognized Jewish public body that would advise and cooperate with the mandatory authority – created further tensions within the Zionist movement.

Who would serve on the Jewish Agency? Should it be only members of the Zionist movement, or should it include leaders of the Jewish community in America and Britain, the so-called "armchair Zionists," who approved of a national home for other Jews who wished to go to Palestine, but were in a position to provide funds and influence? The Jews of Poland and eastern Europe outnumbered the Jewish population in the rest of the world. Should it represent the Jews of the world on a democratically elected basis or on the basis of wealth and influence?

Jabotinsky proposed that the executive should ask the British government to reaffirm its adherence to the original Balfour pledge and that the Jewish state should consist of biblical Israel, which had existed on both sides of the Jordan. This proposal was not supported. As for the Jewish Agency, Jabotinsky proposed that it should be democratically elected by only the financial members of the Zionist Organization and that there should be no place for non-Zionists on the agency. This proposal was also rejected.

Jabotinsky wrote to a friend, "You know perhaps that Dr. Weizmann and I have parted ways in earnest."

Jabotinsky was also a member of the Actions Committee of the Zionist body. He proposed that the committee should lodge two protests with the British government. The first was based on his recent personal experiences in Palestine, that many of the British personnel in Palestine were anti-Semites, or at best anti-Zionists. The second was that the Zionist movement still stood for Palestine being the Israel of biblical times without Transjordan being ceded to the Arabs. He received no support for his positions from other members of the Actions Committee. Weizmann's views had prevailed.

On January 17, 1923, Jabotinsky resigned from the executive and from the Zionist Organization. His letter of resignation had an air of finality about it.

> In view of the attitude of the executive and the Actions Committee – an attitude incompatible with the interests and the very principles of Zionism – I have decided to resign from the executive and moreover to consider myself no longer bound by the discipline of the Zionist Organization – and therefore no longer a member of it.

It was a decision that would split the Zionist movement and, in time, polarize the political landscape of Israel.

CHAPTER 5

PALESTINE AND THEN TO ENGLAND

Sioma finally left Odessa for Palestine in late November 1919. He carried with him a letter of introduction from the president of the Odessa Zionist Organization and the documents that confirmed his attendance at the engineering faculties of the universities in Petersburg and Odessa.

Within a few weeks he found employment as a draftsman and an assistant land surveyor with Pinhas Rutenberg in Jerusalem. He worked there from December 20, 1919, to June 5, 1920.

Pinhas (Peter) Rutenberg, who was born in the Ukraine in 1879, graduated as an engineer in St. Petersburg. He became active in the Russian social revolutionary movement and participated in the first Russian revolution of 1905. With the failure of the revolution he fled to Italy, where he worked as an engineer. After the tsar's abdication in 1917, Rutenburg returned to Russia and joined the Kerensky government. He was appointed deputy governor of St. Petersburg. After the October 1917 Revolution he was arrested by the Bolsheviks but was released with other political prisoners when the Germans were threatening St. Petersburg. Rutenberg managed to reach Odessa during the French army's occupation of the city. It is possible that Rutenberg met Sioma during that time.

Rutenberg eventually found his way to Palestine, where he conceived the idea of harnessing the waters of the Jordan and Yarkon Rivers in order to create hydroelectric power. He set about surveying and planning this new venture in the Galilee.

Rutenberg and Jabotinsky first met in Italy in 1915. Rutenberg had been converted to the Zionist cause and had independently conceived the idea of establishing a Jewish fighting force to secure Palestine as a Jewish homeland. In 1915 he was living in Italy, where he had heard of Jabotinsky's efforts to form a Jewish Legion in Egypt to fight with the British army against the Ottoman forces, and that Jabotinsky was on his way to London to lobby for his plans. Rutenberg asked Jabotinsky to meet him in Italy. They met in Brindisi, where they agreed that Jabotinsky would pursue his plans in England and Rutenberg would proceed to the United States to try to raise an army of American Jews. While Rutenberg gained no support, Jabotinsky was ultimately successful.

Jabotinsky and Rutenberg renewed their contact in Jerusalem in 1920. Jabotinsky met Sioma for the first time in Rutenberg's planning office. The meeting was the start of a friendship between the charismatic Jabotinsky and Sioma, the bright young man who was a committed Zionist and had already proved his fighting qualities in Odessa. It was a friendship that was to last for the next twenty years. Jabotinsky was eighteen years older than Sioma. In the relationship that developed, Jabotinsky appeared to assume the role of an older brother of a gifted younger sibling. Sioma held a deep admiration for Jabotinsky for his brilliant mind, dynamic personality, and absolute commitment to the Zionist cause.

While Sioma was a committed Zionist and a follower of Jabotinsky, it is apparent from the path that he followed that he was determined to have a career that would make him financially independent. He therefore set out to complete his engineering qualifications. A return to Russia to finish his degree was not possible. He decided that his best course of action was to obtain an English engineering degree, which was highly regarded throughout the world. In May 1920 he obtained a *laissez-passer*, a document issued in lieu of a passport, from the Department of Immigration and

Travel of the British Egyptian Expeditionary Force in Egypt. This allowed him to travel to England. He arrived in London the next month and registered as a draftsman with the London Employment Exchange. He gave his address as 12 Endsleigh Street, London. This street is near both the London University and the British Library.

Sioma kept a scrapbook that documented his activities after his arrival in London. Almost immediately, he became involved with the British Zionist movement. Just weeks after his arrival, he attended the 1920 Annual Conference of the Zionist Organization in London, and several days later he addressed a meeting of the David Wolfsohn Zionist Lodge in Whitechapel. The invitation to the meeting listed him as a speaker, "S. Jacobi, E.Z.F." EZF was the English Zionist Federation.

Within the London Jewish community he was able to earn some income as a teacher of modern Hebrew and Jewish history. From July 1920 he taught modern Hebrew and Jewish history at the West Central Jewish National Institute. At the same time he taught modern Hebrew at the Soho synagogue, a job that lasted for three years.

It is known that at that stage Sioma spoke Russian, Ukrainian, Yiddish, and both modern and biblical Hebrew. Later in his life there are letters that he wrote in fluent French and German. His wife's story was that he learned to speak English by translating a Russian edition of Shakespeare into English.[1] But he had come to England to complete an engineering degree. His first move was to gain entry to the University of London, which had an engineering faculty. In September 1920, he was granted matriculation by East London College, a school of the University of London,[2] under an article of their constitution that allowed entry to the college in special circumstances without having passed the usual examination. He enrolled and was admitted to the engineering faculty of the University of London,

---

1   Taped interview with Edna Jacobi.
2   The East London College was founded as the People's Palace in 1887 to provide Londoners from the East End with education and social activities. It developed into a technical school and was renamed the East London Technical College. In 1902 degrees were awarded to graduates by the University of London. In 1915 the college became a school of the University of London.

where he began his studies on September 27, 1920. His college records show that he was enrolled for five subjects in the intermediate engineering course during the 1920–1921 academic year.

But what must have weighed heavily on his mind was that although he had escaped from Odessa, his family was still there in very difficult circumstances and possibly with their lives in danger.

The plight of Ukrainian Jews during the Russian civil war was well known to Jewish communities throughout the world. In the United States, the *New York Times* carried a full column on September 8, 1919, reporting on a meeting of Ukrainian Jews living in the USA with the headline "Ukrainian Jews Aim to Stop Pogroms." On April 29, 1921, the same paper carried an item that the Federation of Ukrainian Jews in England had called a conference of all Jewish political and philanthropic organizations to decide on measures that could be taken to assist the Ukrainian Jewish pogrom victims.

Sioma's student record at East London College for 1920–1921 was marked "Ill & in Constantinople during 3rd term." Third term would have commenced in mid-April 1921. His entry in the college records for the year 1921–1922 was marked "Re-entered 23 February 1922." He was absent for more than nine months. There are no cuttings in Sioma's scrapbook or other records that indicate that he was in England during this period.

The family legend of Sioma's family escaping from the horrors of the Ukraine during that period was that Sioma went back to Odessa to bring them out to Palestine. Because this is the only long period of his life that is not accounted for by documentary evidence, it is almost certain that he went back to Odessa during the time that he was absent from the college.

In late 1940, the Palestinian weekly news magazine *Ha-olam* (the world)[3] published an obituary of Sioma. Entitled "The Passage of a Life: An Appreciation from Palestine," it was written by Samuel Ussishkin, the son of Menachem Ussishkin (1863–1941).[4] The Ussishkin family came

---

3   *Ha-olam*, which was founded in 1937, ceased publication in 1993.

4   Menachem Ussishkin was a celebrated Zionist leader who attended the First Zionist Congress in 1893 and was part of the Jewish delegation that addressed the Paris Peace Conference in 1919. He settled in Palestine in that year and was elected to

from Ekaterinoslav, a town in the Ukraine northwest of Odessa. It was a heavily industrialized area that was a center of unrest and rioting during the 1905 revolution. There were several pogroms during this period and the Ussishkin family moved to Odessa that year. Samuel was born in Ekaterinoslav in 1894. He was three years older than Sioma. In the obituary, Samuel wrote that he first knew Sioma as a student in Rappoport's high school in Odessa. They were both in the Zionist movement and Samuel's comment about his friend was that as a young man Sioma "was an outstanding figure.... While most of his friends had a fixed outlook – an outlook of Socialist and semi-Socialist ideas, Jacobi was the only one of our group that opposed these ideas and inclined towards a physical and not spiritual struggle."

Samuel went on to outline and praise Sioma's leadership of the self-defense force in Odessa and "to doubt whether any of his contemporaries could have emulated his capacity...of making people forget his age and of being accepted as an equal among old and notable people."

The friendship between the two young men resumed in 1919 when Samuel Ussishkin left Palestine for England. In that year he matriculated at Cambridge University for admission to study law. He earned his BA and LLB from Cambridge in 1922.

Samuel's obituary for Sioma continued with a remarkable story – remarkable because Sioma left no written record of these events and did not relate them to his wife or children, only that he had gone back to Odessa to bring his own family to Palestine.

> One day he [Sioma] told me that he had found something after his own heart, to travel to Bolshevik Russia in order to bring out the family of a wealthy Jew[5] who had also escaped to London.
>
> On arriving in Odessa he was arrested by the Cheka [a state security apparatus formed to suppress counterrevolutionaries]. He told them that he had left the city during its occupation by the

---

head the Jewish National Fund, which was established to acquire agricultural land for Jewish settlement.

5   Nothing is known of the identity of the "wealthy Jew."

Whites, but that he was now prepared to live in Red Russia. He was released because there was nothing against him. He gathered together the family of his employer and after many vicissitudes brought them across the Dniester River out of Russia.

Jacobi received his promised reward and completed his engineering studies. After years of wandering for ORT-OZE he settled in London and as a man economically independent he devoted himself to Zionist work in the Revisionist Party.

Sioma must have brought his own family out from Odessa at the same time. The family story of their journey to Palestine is told as an epic clandestine escape tale. Sioma risked his life by returning to Russia. The legend continued that their journey was largely on foot and that they had to climb over mountain passes to reach safety. The most likely route if they traveled west from Odessa would have been to make for the Romanian port of Constanza on the Black Sea. From there it was possible to find a ship to take them to Istanbul and then to Palestine. Constanza was to figure prominently in 1938 and 1939 as the escape route for Jews fleeing from Nazi persecution by way of the Rhine and making their way to Palestine.

In England Sioma told meetings that the Jewish population of Odessa had been 250,000. In the month of April 1922 the bodies of 7,336 Jews were found in the streets. They had died of disease and famine.

It is not known when the Jacobi family arrived in Palestine. They were known to be living in Tel Aviv in the late 1920s. On Sioma's wedding certificate in 1929 his father, Leib, was described as a merchant. In the wedding photograph taken in Jerusalem, Leib is very smartly dressed in a well-cut suit and a bow tie. All the family in the photograph appear to be in good health and formally dressed for the wedding.

It is possible that Sioma's father was able to bring some wealth with him when they escaped from Odessa. This may have enabled him to set up in business after the family's arrival in Palestine. Certainly their appearance in the photograph indicates that they were already middle class by 1929.

When Sioma returned to London, he reentered East London College on February 23, 1922, in the intermediate engineering course. But on November 19 of that year he completed an application form for a *laissez-passer* to the government of Palestine for permanent residence in that country. He would opt, said one of his answers on the application, for Palestinian nationality. He named Rutenberg and Dr. J. Klausner as references. The latter, who was also from Odessa, was a renowned academic who later became a professor of Hebrew literature at the Hebrew University of Jerusalem. Sioma described himself in the application as twenty-five years old, five feet seven inches (170 cm) tall, and with grey eyes. Why Sioma applied for the travel document is open to conjecture. Did he want to join his family and settle in Palestine? All we know is that he did not go there in 1922. He completed the intermediate engineering course at East London College and in the following academic year, 1922–1923, he was admitted to the full engineering course. He did not take up the offered place. His student record was marked "Not here by 31/10/23."

Sioma had decided to leave East London College. On July 12, 1923, he enrolled in a summer vacation course in civil engineering at Loughborough College. Loughborough is in Leicestershire, in the English Midlands. The college started as a technical school in 1905 but it expanded during the war and developed into a residential tertiary institution in its own grounds. When Sioma enrolled, it offered technical degree courses. The application forms that Sioma completed contain selected information from his early academic career. He included his attendance at the Gymnasium in Odessa from 1907 to 1915, his commencement of an engineering degree course in St. Petersburg from 1917 to 1918, his work as a draftsman and assistant land surveyor in Rutenberg's office in Jerusalem from December 1919 to June 1920, and his being granted matriculation in London. He included neither the various courses that he had undertaken at the university in Odessa nor the intermediate engineering exams that he had passed at the East London College, although in a later document from the Loughborough it was recorded that his completion of first year in London allowed his entry to second year at Loughborough.

On September 8, 1923, he was admitted to the degree course in civil engineering at Loughborough. Although this was a five-year course, Sioma was granted entry into the third rather than the second year. In addition to this concession, the normal fee charged by the college for the course was reduced by half, from £150 to £75 per annum. The registration form gives the principal of the college as the authority for these special considerations. These allowances must have made the Loughborough course very attractive for a young man in a hurry, although it removed him from the center of Jewish activities in London.

It would seem that the story of Sioma being paid for his trip to Odessa is given some credence because of his being able to pay his fees for Loughborough and to live in "digs" in Frederick Street in the town. Employment opportunities in England were scarce at the time. Unemployment was calculated at some two million during most of the 1920s. Part-time jobs were almost unknown. Since Loughborough had no Jewish community, the opportunity of finding jobs similar to the ones that he had enjoyed in London was absent.

On April 9, 1924, there were several local press reports of the results of the Loughborough College Oratory Night. Sioma, who was in his second year at the college, had been speaking English only since his arrival in England four years before. The *Nottingham Evening Post* carried a report of the competition, entitled "Refugee Secures Second Place": "A foreigner got within a hairsbreadth of carrying away the cherished trophy, in the person of a Russian student-refugee from Bolshevik kindness – Mr. S. Jacobi." Another report wrote that his prepared speech on the history of the economic structure of civilization based on the development of engineering skills "held his audience with an enthralling story." This would have won him the competition, the report went on, but the second leg of the contest was an impromptu speech on the subject of "Should Women Preach?" He was not quite as successful there. It brought him down to second place. One report of Sioma's impromptu effort was that "it was rather disappointing due doubtless to the fact that the time allowed for preparation of the speech of just five minutes was all too short a time to prepare a speech in a foreign language."

It was a remarkable performance. He was presented with a certificate by the college that he had been placed second of three finalists in the third annual competition for oratory of its Literary and Debating Society.

Sioma was subsequently in demand as a speaker at Rotary Club lunches in the neighborhood. Newspapers reported his speeches to four clubs in late 1924 and early 1925.

Sioma kept in touch with Jabotinsky after he left Palestine for England. Jabotinsky visited England several times during the early 1920s but it is not known if they were in contact at the time. The first of the surviving letters from Jabotinsky to Sioma was dated February 15, 1924. It was one of the approximately five hundred letters that Jabotinsky wrote to Sioma during the next fifteen years. This first letter is in reply to one from Sioma that has not survived. From Jabotinsky's response it is clear that Sioma's letter had suggested that Jabotinsky should follow up a lead to a group that proposed to establish a Jewish international defense force. Jabotinsky asked for the names of those in the group so that he could get in touch with them. Nothing more on this topic appears in later correspondence.

At the time Sioma's major concern was alleviating the misery of Ukrainian Jews, most of whom were unable to leave the country. The London *Jewish Guardian* of September 5, 1924, under the heading of "Projected Campaign in Provinces," reported that Sioma was now a member of the Council of the London Federation of Ukrainian Jews. He and the secretary of the Federation, the report went on, were about to travel throughout England, Scotland, Ireland, and Wales to establish committees that would raise funds for the council. They had already established nine local committees. Two weeks later, the *Jewish Chronicle* reported that the campaign was "in full swing" and that Sioma had addressed meetings in Cardiff, Liverpool, Birmingham, Blackpool, and Bradford. His speaking tour was carried out during the summer vacation of Loughborough, which lasted from June to October.

Sioma was on a path that led to a career of public speaking to raise funds to help his fellow Jews who were leading impoverished lives in the Ukraine and eastern Europe. It was a task that would occupy the next decade of his life. He used his command of English that he had so recently acquired, and he was able to make public addresses in Russian, Yiddish, both classical and modern Hebrew, French, and German. He had the ability to grip an audience with a logical style that used facts and figures rather than flamboyance. But he recognized that his own experiences in Odessa would add an emotional appeal for his audience. His speeches were fueled by his telling a story of having survived imprisonment and a death sentence by the Bolsheviks. This appealed to the anti-Russian and anti-Communist stance of both the public and the British press of the time, although the story was reported with many differences and embellishments.

He was in touch with Jabotinsky during this period. On February 20, 1925, Jabotinsky wrote from Paris acknowledging an article that Sioma had written on the story of self-defense in Odessa and asked for another article about Rutenberg's plans for a hydroelectric plant in Palestine. Included in that letter is a note of regret that Sioma was intending to return to Russia. There is no other reference or indication from any other source of this intention.

Sioma completed his engineering studies at Loughborough on July 1, 1925. The certificate of his degree from Loughborough College is dated July 25, 1925. He had graduated with a diploma in civil engineering with first-class honors.

Three months later, the principal of the college wrote a glowing reference for Sioma. It included a detailed record that as well as his academic achievements, Sioma had had practical training in the college foundry, its heavy lathe department, and milling shop, in addition to the drawing office. During a surveying camp run by the college he was put in charge of a section of the exercise. The reference concluded that

> Mr. Jacobi has throughout his entire period at the College been in every way an excellent student.... [who] will do himself and the Institution great credit in any position to which he may be appointed.

For the rest of his life he used the title "S. Y. Jacobi CE," and he was unfailingly mentioned in reports as an engineer. But he was destined never to follow the profession.

CHAPTER 6

THE BIRTH OF THE REVISIONIST MOVEMENT

The Balfour Declaration had used the phrase "a home for the Jews" in Palestine. A section of the Zionist movement had always regarded that phrase as insipid. They wanted a Jewish state, not just a home. Their worst fears were confirmed by Churchill's pronouncement in the British government's White Paper of June 1922, which used exactly the same phrasing as the Balfour Declaration. The White Paper further specified that Britain had not intended that the whole of Palestine would become a Jewish national home.

The same phrase was used in the wording of the League of Nations Mandate for Palestine granted to Britain. The Mandate also confirmed the excision of that part of Palestine to the west of the Jordan River as Transjordan, an Arab kingdom in which no Jews would be allowed to settle. The Zionist Organization (ZO) decided to accept both this division of Palestine and the phrase "a home for the Jews." At the time Vladimir Jabotinsky was on the executive of the ZO that had been founded by Theodor Herzl and was now led by Chaim Weizmann. Jabotinsky was so against this decision, which was intended to preserve the Zionist relationship with Britain, that he resigned from all Zionist activity and politics in protest.

Jabotinsky was a journalist, poet, novelist, soldier, and a gripping orator who could address his audiences in any one of seven languages. Chaim Weizmann, the great Zionist leader and the first president of Israel, who was Jabotinsky's opponent on many issues, described him as follows:

> Jabotinsky, the passionate Zionist, was utterly un-Jewish in manner, approach and deportment. He came from Odessa, but the inner life of Jewry had left no trace on him. When I became intimate with him in later years, I observed at closer hand what seemed to be a confirmation of this dual streak; he was rather ugly, but immensely attractive, well spoken, warm-hearted, generous, and always ready to help a comrade in distress; all of these qualities were, however, overlaid with a certain touch of the rather theatrically chivalresque, a certain queer and irrelevant knightliness, which was not at all Jewish.[1]

Horace Samuel, a prominent English barrister, had been a fellow officer with Jabotinsky in the Jewish Battalion in Palestine during World War I. He later defended two of Jabotinsky's followers who were charged with politically motivated murder in Palestine. He wrote of the man that "Jabotinsky…was the most picturesque and melodramatic nationalist that ever performed on the Zionist stage…a magnetic orator, an accomplished litterateur, and an expert journalist."[2]

For nearly two years Jabotinsky had refrained from taking any part in the formal Zionist organization. He devoted himself to writing newspaper articles and developing a publishing house that would produce educational material in modern Hebrew. He revived the Russian-language Zionist

---

1   Chaim Weizmann, *Trial and Error: The Autobiography of Chaim Weizmann* (London: Hamish Hamilton, 1949), 63.

2   Horace B. Samuel, *Unholy Memories of the Holy Land* (London: The Hogarth Press, 1930), 8.

weekly journal *Rasswyet*, which had ceased publication, as a vehicle for his writings and those of his followers.

It was in *Rasswyet*[3] that he published the often misquoted and frequently maligned article with the title of "The Iron Wall." The thesis of this piece was that in recorded human history there has never been an instance where the existing inhabitants of a country have given up their land to new settlers without a fight. He cited North and South America as examples, and added the rider that the manner in which the new settlers acted, even with the best intentions, had no effect on that resistance. His argument went on that the expulsion of Arabs from Palestine was not possible and a view that they would voluntarily consent to Zionism in return for economic benefit was "infantile." It followed that the suggestion of an Arab voluntary agreement to the establishment of a Jewish state in Palestine was wishful thinking. This "colonization," Jabotinsky concluded, could therefore only continue under the protection of British (during the Mandate) or Jewish bayonets – for which he used the euphemism of an "iron wall" – that would deter the local population from interfering with Zionist efforts to settle in Palestine.

In order to raise funds for his publishing and writing activities, Jabotinsky undertook a lecture tour to the Baltic countries. Although he had made his home in Berlin, the postwar inflation that beset Germany and the consequent rise in the cost of living there made him decide to move. There were a number of expatriate Russian Jews now in Paris, where he moved in late 1923. From there he undertook a second fund-raising tour, this time to Austria, Czechoslovakia, and Germany.

The author Arthur Koestler[4] was a young man when he heard Jabotinsky speak in Vienna. Jabotinsky spoke for three hours in faultless German, and Koestler was smitten. He followed Jabotinsky on his speaking tour of Czechoslovakia.

---

3   November 4, 1923, published in Russian.

4   Arthur Koestler (b. Budapest 1905, d. London 1983) was an influential author even in his youth, and had a large following during the 1930s and 1940s. He was a Communist who broke away from the party after Stalin's purge trials.

Jabotinsky's travels in the Baltic countries led to an encounter with a young student group in the Latvian capital, Riga. The group called itself the Histadrut of Zionist Activist Youth in the name of Trumpeldor. They named their movement after their hero, Joseph Trumpeldor,[5] and its name formed the acronym Betar.

Encouraged by his reception in eastern Europe, in March 1924 Jabotinsky and his followers published a series of articles in *Rasswyet* setting out the basis of a new platform for the Zionist movement. The policy stated that the goal of Zionism was the establishment of a Jewish state by mass colonization of Palestine. The Jewish state would be made up of all the land of the original British Mandate on both sides of the Jordan. The articles were widely read. While many readers, including the young Arthur Koestler, were enthusiastic, the leading Jewish newspapers in Berlin, London, and New York supported the mainstream Zionist Organization and condemned Jabotinsky's program on the grounds that it could only harm attempts to reach a settlement with the Arab population.

The members of the youth movement that Jabotinsky had met in Riga had challenged his inaction. They told him that if he really believed in what he was preaching, then he should organize a party that would achieve these ends. Jabotinsky wrote to a friend, "I saw a young generation that is worth believing in. I will try to organise them to the cause." It was a call to action. Betar was founded in Riga in 1923. It would become a significant part of the Revisionist movement as a recruiting ground for those who believed in a strong nationalistic ideology.

Two years later, Jabotinsky decided that he would rejoin Zionist ranks

---

5   Trumpeldor, a volunteer in the Russian army and the first Jew to be made an officer
     in that army, lost an arm fighting in the Russo-Japanese War. He met Jabotinsky in
     1914 in Egypt, where together they conceived the idea of forming a Jewish army
     to fight with Britain to free Palestine from Turkish rule. Out of this meeting came
     the idea of the Zion Mule Corps. It was formed in 1915 as a transport unit to
     bring supplies and ammunition to the British troops and bring out the wounded.
     Trumpeldor was with the corps that served with the British army during the
     attempted invasion at Gallipoli, where he was wounded in action. A survivor of two
     wars, he was killed by Arabs on March 1, 1920, as he led the defense of Kibbutz Tel
     Hai in the Upper Galilee.

and reform the organization from within. He called together a group of disaffected Zionists to a meeting in Paris. Their principal objections to the ZO's policy was that they believed that Britain had promised a Jewish state, not just a "home for the Jews," and that the state should be that portion of Palestine that had been biblical Israel.

In March 1925 Jabotinsky wrote to Sioma, telling him of his intention to form this new party. This letter was followed a few weeks later by another letter from Jabotinsky to Sioma informing him that he was calling a meeting of Zionists sympathetic to his views in Paris on April 26. He asked Sioma to get in touch with two London Zionists who Jabotinsky believed were interested in the concept and encourage them to come to Paris. Twelve men met in Paris on April 25, 1925: six Russian Zionists living in Paris, and five who came from as far afield as Palestine, Riga, Vienna, and Salonika. Meir Grossman came from London.

Jabotinsky called for suggestions of a name for the new group. The youngest person present, a student, made the suggestion of calling it the Revisionist-Zionist group.[6] Jabotinsky accepted the proposed name over "Activist" or "Democratic." The Declaration of the Central Committee of the Union of Zionist Revisionists that was subsequently issued by the conference read as follows:

> The aim of Zionism is the gradual transformation of Palestine (Trans Jordan included) into a Jewish Commonwealth, that is into a self-governing Commonwealth under the auspices of an established Jewish majority. Any other interpretation of Zionism, especially the White Paper of 1922, must be considered invalid.

The meeting also decided that

> The Union of Zionist Revisionists (UZR)[7] is an integral part of the

---

6   If the group could have known the sense in which the word "revisionist" is now used, it would perhaps have adopted a different title. Originally used to label modifications of Marxist-Leninist doctrine or policies, it has come to mean, in the current vernacular, ultra-conservative or extreme right wing.

7   This was the name of the organization that the Revisionists used until it was changed in 1935. In recent times, the name of the Revisionist movement in Hebrew, Zohar,

World Zionist Organization, but it reserves to itself the right of independent propaganda in Jewish and non-Jewish circles.

The office in Paris sought support of known sympathizers on a letterhead bearing the title The League for the Revision of Zionist Policies – Provisional Organizational Bureau. The use of this heading was to explain to the recipients what "Revisionist" meant in the Zionist context. Jabotinsky was back on the battlefield of Zionist politics.

Sioma was not invited to the meeting because he was waiting to hear the results of his final engineering exams, which were not announced until mid-July. A month later, he applied for a Russian refugee's travel permit that would enable him to travel abroad.

On September 11, 1925, Jabotinsky wrote to Sioma, offering congratulations on his success in the examinations. He went on to ask whether Sioma would be willing to "devote a few years to the Zionist cause" with the recently formed Union of Zionist Revisionists. Jabotinsky added that he foresaw that the leaders of the new movement would be in a position to take the reins of the entire Zionist movement at the Fifteenth Zionist Congress, which would take place in 1927. Would Sioma be prepared to move to Paris and work for the party at "a modest income"? Jabotinsky went on to warn Sioma that if he did take up the offer, it would prevent him from taking up a career in engineering and that this might cause difficulties for him if he wished to pursue his professional career in the future.

For Sioma, prospects of a professional career in engineering were not good. In 1925, England was continuing to suffer the aftereffects of World War I. It had lost its market share of its most important export, coal, and its major secondary industry, shipbuilding, was at a standstill. London, the once proud center of the financial world, had lost its place to New York. Unemployment was close to two million. Hunger marches by the unemployed were taking place. It was a situation that would lead to

---

has been translated as the Revisionist Zionist Alliance (RZA). This work will use the original name, Union of Zionist Revisionists (UZR).

the great General Strike the following year. There were few employment opportunities for a recently graduated civil engineer.

Although Jabotinsky suggested that Sioma could expect only a modest income, the offer to join Jabotinsky, a man whom he greatly admired, in a cause that was dear to his heart, was one that he could not reject. Sioma possibly still had means of his own from the money that he received for his expedition to Russia. Sioma arrived in Paris in late September and a week later Jabotinsky wrote from Riga to Paris on October 6, 1925, thanking Sioma for having agreed to take up the position of secretary-general of the Central Revisionist Office.

In November 1925, the Revisionist movement met in Paris to prepare a full platform of the party. This was issued as a declaration. Sioma was a signatory to the document. The declaration issued by the conference was a long one. The essence of its argument was as follows.

There was a growing desire of the Jewish masses to emigrate to Palestine, and the last Zionist Congress had not made a plan to solve the complicated problems facing the Jewish people that would enable them to achieve this aim. The congress had agreed to pass its functions to the Jewish Agency. Because of the composition of the agency, a Jewish plutocracy could now make decisions without reference to over half the Jewish population of the world who now had no voice in the deliberations of this ruling Jewish body.

The Zionist movement should not be cringing before England as if it had given refuge to the Jews out of compassion. Relations with Great Britain should be based on a foundation of mutual loyalty, and if the activity – or inactivity – of the British administration in Palestine proved to be harmful to Jewish interests, the Zionist fight against Britain was justified by its loyalty to Britain. The Palestine Mandate was approved by the League of Nations, an international body. Most importantly the Zionist movement must struggle for the inclusion of Transjordan within the frontiers of Palestine and as an area of Jewish settlement. The control of Jewish immigration to Palestine should be handed over to the Zionist Organization and not be the prerogative of the mandatory authority.

Included in the declaration was a statement that would distance the new movement from the main body of the Zionist movement, which was dominated by the left wing. The Revisionist manifesto stated that the party "firmly takes a position above all classes of society. All classes should be given the opportunity of life in Palestine. Revisionism will resist any attempt at class domination no matter from which side it comes."

"Our immediate aim," they affirmed, was "the conquest of the forthcoming Zionist Congress." A committee of fourteen members, which included Sioma, who was described as a member from Paris, signed the declaration.

The movement did obtain representation on the Actions Committee at the ensuing Zionist Congress. Jabotinsky's speech at the congress was greeted by an enthusiastic ovation, but the congress was "not conquered." In the words of the *New Palestine* newspaper, "the applause was attributed to his fine oratory rather than the logic and power of his political arguments." The rather grand title of Sioma's position as secretary-general of the Central Committee of the Revisionist World Union was undercut by a contemporary description of the organization's head office in Paris. One of Jabotinsky's biographers, J. B. Schechtman, wrote:

> Its "premises" consisted of a corner of Jabotinsky's crowded desk in the study of his five-room apartment in Paris. There was no telephone. To make or receive a call one of us had to run down and then up five flights of stairs to the janitor's lodge. [Because I] was completely ignorant of the art of typing [I] dictated letters and circulars to Jabotinsky, who acted as typist, using…two fingers…. When the rather meager results of a day's work were ready for mailing, there always arose the agonizing question: do we possess enough money for stamps? If this problem was solved satisfactorily – often by digging into Jabotinsky's personal funds – one of us happily ran to the post office, six blocks away…. We never had stamps in stock for another day. To send a telegram was a major, sometimes insoluble problem.

Sioma's duties in Paris involved supporting Jabotinsky's general interests in addition to his functions as secretary-general. One was the short-lived

Hebrew Publishing Company. The language now spoken in Israel, modern Hebrew, was still a new language in the early 1920s. There had been no common language for the mélange of Jews who lived in Palestine in the nineteenth century. Ashkenazi Jews came from Europe with the languages of their own countries of origin, mainly Russian, Polish, German, and Yiddish. They spoke, or had knowledge of, the Hebrew language that was used in the synagogue, for the study of texts and for religious ceremonies in the home, but it was not used in normal conversation. Sephardi Jews who came from Morocco, Yemen, and Persia all spoke the languages of the countries in which they lived, but the Hebrew that they used in prayer had a different pronunciation from that of the Ashkenazi Jews.

If Hebrew was to be developed with a modern vocabulary for common usage, which pronunciation would be used? Although the idea of modern Hebrew as the common language for Palestine was envisaged as early as the late 1880s by a Russian-born settler, Eliezer Ben-Yehuda, there was opposition to Hebrew by both German- and Yiddish-speakers, who wanted their languages to be adopted. The ultraorthodox objected because of their belief that Hebrew should be used only in prayer. In 1913, the Eleventh Zionist Congress decided to adopt Hebrew as the common language. The language had to be extended to include words that had not existed in biblical times. The congress also decided to found the Hebrew University of Jerusalem. The inclusion of the word Hebrew in the title was deliberately chosen to emphasize the new common language. It was not until 1920, against strong opposition from Arabs, that the British mandatory authority recognized Hebrew in addition to Arabic and English as one of the three official languages in Palestine.

A publishing house, Hasefer (the book), had been established in Germany by S. D. Salzman, who was not a Revisionist. Salzman's intention was to publish books in modern Hebrew that could be used in Jewish schools and communities throughout the world. His venture did not prosper. Jabotinsky was a fervent believer in the widespread use of modern Hebrew as a spoken and written language. Therefore, when he resigned from the Zionist executive and decided to resume his profession as an author and journalist, he enthusiastically pursued Salzman's idea. In order to resuscitate the project, Jabotinsky turned the publishing house into a company and issued shares to some of his English friends that raised enough capital to revive Hasefer. The company operated at first in Berlin but it was transferred to Paris in early 1924. Jabotinsky was the editor-in-chief. In 1925, the Hebrew publishing company Hasefer Limited was incorporated in London. Sioma was appointed managing director and holder of the company's power of attorney.

The company published two popular books that were translated into Hebrew, a collection of Conan Doyle's Sherlock Holmes stories and *The Prisoner of Zenda* by Anthony Hope, both in paperback. This was followed by a 288-page almanac for schoolchildren. It contained five chapters by Jabotinsky with topics ranging from the Sephardi pronunciation of Hebrew to the stories of the Zion Mule Corps at Gallipoli and the Jewish Legion in Palestine. There was one chapter on table manners! The company's most important publication was *The Hebrew Geographical Atlas*. Coedited by Jabotinsky, the *Atlas* had an emphasis on Jewish communities throughout the world, giving their location on the maps and their population with economic and cultural strengths.

Sioma endeavored to market the *Atlas* by obtaining recommendations from well-known persons of stature. These included Israel Zangwill,[8] who responded that he did not see the need to publish an atlas in Hebrew when there were already many others available in English. Sir Herbert Samuel[9] replied that while it appeared to be "a very useful publication," he could not provide a formal expression of opinion as it would create a precedent for other similar requests. Einstein sent a card from Berlin declining to help.

Jabotinsky had warned Sioma that he must be prepared to travel in order to market the *Atlas* and suggested that someone else should take over running the Revisionist office in Paris during his absence. His replacement should be paid a salary of 800 French francs per month. It

---

8   Israel Zangwill (1864–1926), English novelist, playwright, and Zionist.

9   Viscount Samuel (1870–1963), British parliamentarian, cabinet member, and the first British high commissioner of Palestine (1920–1925).

is hard to equate such a figure with living standards in France at the time. Postwar inflation was high and during mid-1925, the exchange rate for one British pound sterling was one hundred francs, while twenty-one francs were needed to buy one American dollar. If Sioma's salary was in the vicinity of the one proposed for his temporary replacement, or even if it was twice or three times that sum, it was indeed very modest.

Jabotinsky traveled to the USA in January 1926. He had hoped to set up a strong Revisionist organization in America. Sioma followed Jabotinsky to America in March. The New York *Jewish Daily Bulletin* wrote that the reason for Sioma's visit was as "managing director of the Hebrew publishing company Hasefer of London and Paris." The article did include a reference to Sioma being a member of the Central Committee of the Zionist Revisionists in Paris. Although the announced purpose of his visit was to introduce the *Atlas* to the American public, clearly Sioma's trip was to support Jabotinsky in his mission to attract American Zionists to the Revisionist cause.

From the United States, Sioma contributed an article entitled "Revisionism in America (Letter from New York)" to *Rasswyet*. It recounted his experiences of helping Jabotinsky trying to win the minds and purses of American Jews. In a more than somewhat exaggerated account, Sioma reported the enthusiastic reception that Jabotinsky received when he arrived in New York. This part of his report is in marked contrast to other accounts of the same events. One of Jabotinsky's biographers wrote that he was met on the wharf by just one man who had been trying to set up a Revisionist group in America.[10] Although an audience estimated at two thousand attended a lecture that Jabotinsky gave at the Manhattan Opera House four days after his arrival, the huge auditorium was little more than half full.

Worse was to come. Jabotinsky's arrival coincided with the absence in London of the president of the Zionist Organization of America (ZOA), Louis Lipsky. While Jabotinsky was still in the early phases of his campaign,

---

10   Joseph B. Schechtman, *Fighter and Prophet: The Vladimir Jabotinsky Story; The Last Years* (New York: Thomas Yoseloff, 1961), 46.

Lipsky returned from London and issued a statement that he "regretted that the courtesies extended to Mr. Jabotinsky have in some quarters been construed as an endorsement of his program…[these courtesies]…do not indicate a new direction for the Zionist movement to take."

As a result of this rebuff by the president of the American Zionists, the trip was not far short of a disaster. Jabotinsky wrote later that "I did not succeed in making money – not for myself, not for Hasefer, nor for the Revisionist Central Committee, nor the *Rasswyet*."

Despite five months in America, Jabotinsky's only success was with just one group, the Order of the Sons of Zion. This was a wealthy mutual aid society that had invested heavily in Palestine by establishing the Judea Industrial Corporation, which had a subsidiary insurance company.

In mid-1926 the Revisionist Zionist Alliance (RZA), as it is now referred to in Jabotinsky's correspondence, was in severe financial straits. Jabotinsky wrote several letters to Sioma explaining that he was unable to offer paid positions to two of his staunchest supporters. The financial situation continued to deteriorate. On September 2, Jabotinsky wrote to Sioma that he had not invited him to participate in the administration of the RZA because he would not be able to pay him a salary on which he could maintain himself. Jabotinsky had his own financial problems. Three weeks later he wrote to Sioma thanking him for paying the premium on his life insurance and asking him to send seventy British pounds sterling to the Jewish Settlement Treasury in the name of his wife, Joanna. He promised to repay the debts from the proceeds of a lecture tour of Germany.

In late November 1926 Sioma realized that he must make a break with the RZA as an employer and tendered his resignation from his position. For a young man wishing to create a position for himself in the world it is not a surprising decision. On December 3, 1926, Jabotinsky wrote to Sioma regretting this decision. Sioma was not resigning from membership of the RZA. He would continue as a devoted member of the Revisionist cause for the rest of his life.

Sioma's support for the Revisionist cause included writing several long articles in Russian for *Rasswyet*. The first, published on February 6, 1927, was entitled "Insurance and Markets." It commenced with an analysis of the achievements of the traditional Zionist fund-raising body, Keren Hayesod. This showed a diminution of the funds raised on a worldwide basis from £294,000 in 1923–1924 to £268,000 in 1925–1926. Sioma pointed out that these diminishing sums were inadequate to meet the needs for the development of a national Jewish home. Taking the Judea insurance company as a model, he argued that the Revisionists should establish a Jewish life insurance company that would accumulate funds that could be invested in capital structures in Palestine. This, Sioma stressed, was not a new concept. He cited numbers of infrastructure developments in England and America that had utilized funds from insurance companies for the development of railways, tram lines, water supplies, and subway systems. The AMP Society of Australia was cited as an example of how the premiums paid by its customers were retained and could be utilized for capital development. In respect of markets, Sioma analyzed the trends in production of primary produce grown and exported by the Jewish settlements in Palestine. He predicted that there would also be a market for locally produced goods.

Sioma stayed on in Paris for several months after resigning from the RZA executive. He kept in touch with Loughborough College. In the March 1927 edition of the college magazine *The Limit*, the chatty columns included a section of "what the past students were doing now." It said of Sioma that he was the director of a publishing company "and careers all over the globe." He was, said the editor of the column, enviously and tongue in cheek, "making some money so that he could settle down to an engineering job at two pence a week." The Loughborough alumni records show that in March 1927 Sioma was living at 21 Rue de la Convention, Paris, XVe, and in July he had moved to 9 Bis Rue Vineuse in the same arrondissement.

But soon afterwards Sioma moved back to London. He was looking for a job that would pay a reasonable salary to a young man wishing to make his way in the world. The comments in the Loughborough College magazine of "two pence a week" confirmed that there were very few job opportunities for a recently graduated engineer. So he explored other options. Jabotinsky wrote several letters from Paris to Sioma in London during September and October 1927. The letters referred to negotiations that Sioma was conducting with a British life insurance company, which was not named in the correspondence, to establish an office in Palestine. But these negotiations were not successful.

The first employment that Sioma accepted was a trial as a fundraiser for an organization known as ORT-OZE. He was to go to Egypt to raise funds from the Jewish community there. ORT-OZE and a third party to the group, Emigdirect, all had their own long histories.

The oldest of the three, ORT, was established in the mid-nineteenth century. Jews who lived in the Russian Pale of Settlement had been denied access to mainstream Russian commerce and industry. Although most Jews in the Pale lived in abject poverty, Tsar Alexander II, who reigned from 1855 to 1881, encouraged the growth of trade and industry that would enable the Russian economy to compete with the rest of Europe. This policy enabled a number of Jews to establish themselves in positions of influence in the Russian capital, St. Petersburg. In 1880 a group of them that included Nikolai Bakst, a professor of physiology at St. Petersburg University; Samuel Poliakov, a railway entrepreneur; and Baron Horace de Gunsberg, a financier and banker, petitioned Alexander for permission to start a fund to help the five million impoverished Jews who still lived in the Pale. Alexander was told that the fund was to celebrate the twenty-fifth year of his reign. Flattered by this attention, Alexander allowed the collection of money that would enable Jews to be trained to take their places in the community as skilled tradesmen and agricultural workers. The fund was named the Society for Trades and Agricultural Labor, and the Russian words for that name were used to form the acronym ORT.

After World War I, the Jews of western Europe, Britain, and the United States realized that Jews in eastern Europe and Russia had been unable to acquire the skills that would enable them to survive in the twentieth century. In 1921, ORT was expanded to become a worldwide organization. Its head office was in Berlin and its purpose was to assist eastern European and Russian Jewry to be trained to survive in the new world.

Another factor that had limited the access of Jews to participation in the life of the general population in eastern Europe was their level of health. The shtetls in which they lived were, by Western standards, little better than slums. Many lacked sewage services and running water. In 1912, a group of successful Russian Jews, supported by those living in the West, decided to create an organization that would deliver medical assistance and improved sanitation to the shtetls. The name was also derived from an acronym of the Russian name, the Jewish Health Society, known as OZE. Under the presidency of Albert Einstein, an international body was created at a conference in Berlin in 1923.

As a result of the instability in eastern Europe and Russia during the aftermath of World War I, there was a massive movement of Jews wishing to escape to a more settled existence in the Americas, the West, and Palestine. In 1920 sixty thousand Jews left Poland, twenty-five thousand left Bessarabia,[11] and another five thousand left from Russia and Bulgaria. Most of them – some seventy-five thousand – made for the USA and Canada, eight thousand went to Palestine, and the balance to South America. This emigration continued during the 1920s. On their way the emigrants were held up in various ports waiting for ships to the "new world." The major ports involved were Cologne, Genoa, Danzig, London, and Liverpool. The wait imposed great hardship for the would-be emigrants, who had no income and little savings. Several local voluntary organizations were formed to assist them. Conferences in Brussels and Paris early in 1921 failed to coordinate the activities of these local groups, but in October of that year a further conference in Prague created a United Committee for Jewish Migration that came to be known as Emigdirect.

In 1926, the executives of ORT and OZE formed a United Committee. The head office of ORT-OZE was established in Berlin under the chairmanship of Albert Einstein. A British office, chaired by Lord Rothschild, was established in London. The chief rabbi of the British Empire was a vice president, and the executive included Colonel Levey, DSO, MBE, and Neville Lasky, KC.

---

11   The country was bounded by Ukraine on the west, by Romania to the east, and by the Danube and the Black Sea to the south.

The British establishment had its office in the fashionable London area of Upper Gloucester Place, which was, and still is, the London West End center of Jewish activities. There was a considerable contrast between the offices of Sioma's new employer and the Revisionist "head office" in Paris.

Sioma's engagement by ORT-OZE and Emigdirect started in early 1927. The French-language Cairo newspaper *L'Aurore* of February 26, 1927, carried an item that read: "We announce the imminent arrival in Egypt of Solomon Jacobi, an envoy for three great organizations." There was a heading in the first of two full columns of the paper that set out the purpose of his visit. The heading would be Sioma's watchword throughout his fund-raising efforts for the next seven years: "If you think you are tired of giving, you do not know what it is to be tired." On his way to Egypt, Sioma went to Palestine to visit his family, who were living in Tel Aviv. Jabotinsky addressed a letter, dated March 5, 1927, to Sioma in Tel Aviv which thanked him for looking after his sister, Tamar, while he was there. On March 19, another Cairo newspaper, *La Liberté*, reported some extracts of the speech by "S. Y. Jacobi C.E." The next reference to his work there was in another Cairo newspaper, *La Bourse Egyptienne,* on May 12, 1927. It reported that Sioma had spoken to a number of groups in Cairo and Alexandria, including B'nai B'rith lodges, and that he was due to leave Egypt at the end of the month.

In terms of his employment by ORT-OZE, this was a most successful trip. In June 1927, Jabotinsky congratulated Sioma on the success of his endeavors in Egypt. He was reported to have raised £10,000, an astonishing sum for that time. It was perhaps the equivalent of £250,000 at today's values. The brotherly correspondence from Jabotinsky referred to Sioma's problems in seeking other employment in England and encouraged him not to be put off by some of the "difficulties" that he was encountering with ORT-OZE. The situation would improve, advised Jabotinsky, and Sioma should not withdraw from his engagement there.

At the time Sioma was pursuing a job with the Norwegian explosives manufacturer Nobel. The company, which had a large factory in Scotland, was looking for an engineer to supervise work with their explosives on construction projects in Britain. Jabotinsky had written to Sioma counseling him not to accept the position. He also suggested that Sioma should not resign from the head office of the Revisionist movement in Paris until he had seen the results of its reorganization, where there was the possibility of a well-paid job. The job with Nobel did not eventuate, nor did employment with the Revisionists.

However, Sioma had come to satisfactory arrangements for permanent employment with ORT-OZE and Emigdirect. His assignment was to travel to the major centers of Jewish communities to raise funds for all three organizations for the next five years. Although the specific arrangements are not known, it would seem that Sioma's traveling expenses were paid in full and he was remunerated at least in part on the basis of his success in fund-raising.

Although Sioma would remain a staunch Revisionist for the rest of his life, he was clearly not prepared to live a hand-to-mouth existence while he worked for the organization, as many other Revisionists,[12] including Jabotinsky, were prepared to do. He had an ambition to achieve a successful professional or business career in his own right.

---

12 A number of signatories to the original Revisionist manifesto signed in Paris in 1925, the brothers Tiomkin, Grossman, Trivus, and the Hoffman brothers, worked consistently for the movement over the years.

CHAPTER 7

ORT-OZE AND EMIGDIRECT – THE 1928 JOURNEY

Sioma left London for his three sponsoring organizations on January 17, 1928, on travels that took him to Egypt, India, the Dutch East Indies (now Indonesia), Australia, New Zealand, and the United States. Although this presented opportunities to express his belief in the Revisionist movement, he agreed with his employers not to cloud his fund-raising efforts for their humanitarian causes with Zionist issues.

Sioma's travel diary records that he went first to Paris on his way to his employer's Berlin office and then backtracked to Paris. He traveled down to Marseilles, where he picked up a ship to Bombay. His journey around the world took nearly eighteen months, and he did not return to Berlin until June 6, 1929.

He carried letters of introduction to establish his credentials. One, from OZE in Berlin, dated January 23, 1928, described him as a member of their world executive committee. In Britain, OZE was known as the Jewish Health Organisation of Great Britain. The letter of introduction from the British organization was dated December 15, 1927. It described him as their "emissary" for a fund-raising tour of the world and "a member of the Central Committee of OZE."

He remarked that on the passage down the Suez Canal, he could see the trains on their way to Palestine and that there were twenty-seven Christian missionaries on the ship on their way to India. On February 10, 1928, he arrived in Bombay, where he spent two weeks. He visited a Jewish school and noted that the women wore Indian dress while the men wore European suits. From Bombay he went by train to Agra, then Delhi, and on to Benares, where he watched the population bathing in the river at different times for men and women. From there he went to Calcutta and on to Rangoon before traveling to southern India. The map on which he drew lines to record his journeys on this trip is criss-crossed over the subcontinent.

Amongst Sioma's papers is an unfinished article, "The Jews of India," which he wrote three years after this visit. He made contact with three separate Jewish communities during his journey. The largest, which consisted of some three thousand Sephardi Jews in Bombay, had been established by the Sassoon family in 1830 when they emigrated from Baghdad. Although a few Ashkenazi Jews had also settled in Bombay, the two communities did not mix. But it was the Jewish communities of Southern India that fascinated Sioma. Known as the Bene Israel, they looked very much like the Indian population. Their skin was dark brown. The men wore dhotis and not trousers, and the women wore saris, not dresses. It was not known when their forebears had arrived in India, but they still celebrated an approximation of the major festivals. They knew only a few words of Hebrew. Sioma added that the Sephardim did not recognize the Bene Israel as Jews and referred to them as "the colored," while the Bene Israel referred to the Sephardim as "the colorless."

From India, Sioma took a ship to Penang and Singapore, where there was an active Jewish community of seven hundred. This was a very successful visit. The diary entry of his ten-day stay concluded with a note that he had cabled to Berlin £1,348 that he had raised in the town; there was still more to collect and "the balance [would] follow."

Sioma's diary includes his observations on the occupations of the Jews in the East. There were "cotton Jews" in Egypt and Bombay, "jute Jews" in Calcutta, and "rubber Jews" in Penang and Singapore.

His major destination for the trip was Australia. He had to get there by way of the Dutch East Indies (now Indonesia) and touched on the ports of Batavia, Samarang, and Surabaya. There was a small Jewish community in Surabaya who were descendants of Jewish Dutch merchants who had settled in the Indies during the Dutch colonial period. He noted that he collected 831 florins from the group. From Surabaya he took a small ship of only three thousand tons with one cabin for eight to ten passengers. The trip to the next port of call took five days in these cramped conditions.

He made landfall in Australia on the tiny northwest coast town of Derby, in his description "a very small god forsaken place…very hot and full of insects, mosquitoes, etc." He was traveling on a coastal steamer that traded from the East Indies around the west coast of Australia. The ship, a cattle boat, sailed from Derby to Broome and to Port Headland. Sioma remarked on the tides at each place which left the ship high and dry until the tide turned.

He made interesting notes on the Aboriginals he saw – "a fairly quiet people, not wild…have no idols, believe in good and evil spirits." He was made aware of some aboriginal customs by a missionary on the boat: their hunting-gathering way of life, initiation ceremonies, marriage practices, the taboos within their family relationships, and mourning practices. He recorded a particularly grisly tale from the area. A white man was speared for taking the wife of an Aboriginal. Four police officers went to investigate and killed "some thirty natives." A cleric who lived in the town where the police were stationed demanded an inquiry and a trial of the police officers responsible. They were acquitted by the local court. Although Sioma made no direct comment on this incident, his record implies shock and disgust at the murders of Aboriginals and the acquittal of the police officers.

The ship reached Fremantle, the port of the West Australian capital, Perth, on April 26. The journey from Surabaya had taken two weeks. He spent only a day in Perth. His diary records that his reception by the Jewish community was cool because he was competing with local appeals for funds. He decided to return to Perth in October.

So he took another ship to his major Australian destination, Melbourne.

He arrived there on May 1, 1928. The journey so far had taken nearly four months.

The Melbourne Jewish community was facing its own problems of raising enough funds to settle the European Jewish immigrants who had been arriving in Melbourne since 1925. They landed with little money, no English, and nowhere to live. An informal group of Polish Jews who were already settled in Melbourne had organized a committee to meet ships and help those who arrived to find accommodation and work. In 1926, this committee was formalized as the Victorian Jewish Welcome Society (VJWS). The society recorded that from August 1926 to March 1927, it assisted 354 immigrants. However, a penciled undated note beside this record read "700 new arrivals since March 10th 1926." Not all of them had been assisted by the society, but the figure of seven hundred would represent an addition of 10 percent to the existing Melbourne Jewish community. An analysis of the arrivals recorded by the VJWS showed that most of them came from Poland, some from Palestine, and a few from Russia and Germany. The small committee of the VJWS could not cope with the problem of finding housing and work for this number.

In March 1927 the VJWS passed the problem on to the wider Jewish community. The ruling body of the Victorian Jewish community was the Melbourne Jewish Advisory Board. The board reacted in a traditional manner: it created a subcommittee to examine the problem. The subcommittee was given the somewhat grandiose title of the Victorian Jewish Immigration Questions Committee. The president of the committee was a prominent Melbourne solicitor, Albert Jones, LLD. Dr. Jones, as he was known, was also president of the oldest and largest Melbourne synagogue, the Melbourne Hebrew Congregation, whose synagogue was in the heart of the Melbourne central business district in those days.

In 1913, the Melbourne Jewish community had faced a similar problem with the arrival of a considerable number of Russian Jews. These immigrants had been settled most successfully on irrigated agricultural land that had been bought by the Melbourne community near the central Victorian town of Shepparton, where they grew stone fruit for the local canning industry. The immigration committee decided that it would try to repeat this project in another rural area and set about raising the considerable sum of £50,000 for a new settlement. Some new arrivals were found work and accommodation in Shepparton, but the Welcome Society was left with the task of supporting a seemingly neverending stream of new arrivals. By early 1928 it was reduced to handing out meal coupons and offering just a few pounds in cash to the unemployed.

It is little wonder that the Melbourne Jewish community did not wish to face competition for their fund-raising. The fortnightly Melbourne Jewish newspaper, the *Australian Jewish Herald* (AJH), had reported as far back as March 29 that the Victorian Jewish Immigration Questions Committee had cabled the office of Emigdirect in Berlin requesting cancellation of Sioma's trip. It had heard that three-quarters of the funds that Sioma might raise in Melbourne would go to overseas relief and only one quarter would remain to go toward their problems. Emigdirect responded from Berlin that the emissary, Sioma Jacobi, was already on his way.

But despite their misgivings, the CV that Sioma presented to his Melbourne hosts impressed the immigration committee. It outlined his Russian background, his organization of the self-defense force in Odessa, and that he was a qualified engineer who had worked with Pinhas Rutenberg on the generation of electric power in Palestine. The letters of introduction and support were signed by Lord Rothschild, the chief rabbi of the British Empire, Albert Einstein, and the board of the joint organization of ORT-OZE and Emigdirect in Berlin. Sioma's background and his endorsement by this array of prestigious Jews impressed the local community.

The AJH announced Sioma's arrival with the headline "Reconstructing European Jewry: Distinguished Visitor Arrives." The article that followed this introduction was illustrated by photographs of Lord Rothschild, Albert Einstein, and Sioma. Included in a bordered box within the article was a copy of the letter from the chief rabbi of the British Empire recommending Sioma to "my brethren in Australia." These photographs and two others of the Odessa self-defense force, which included Sioma sitting in his position as leader, were to become his calling cards for his visits to other Jewish communities throughout the world. They were included without exception by all local Jewish press in his ports of call throughout Australia. Usually they were accompanied by an article written by Sioma that outlined his message.

The only reference to Sioma's Zionism was one line: "He is a prominent Zionist and a member of the Central Committee of the Revisionists."

The immigration committee arranged a public meeting in a large hall at the Montefiore Home on St. Kilda Road, Melbourne, on May 10, 1928. On May 17, the AJH reported the meeting on its front page. Sioma's full address was set out on later pages. The meeting, said the *Herald*, was for Sioma "a veritable triumph. When he had finished his address those who had come to the meeting with a whole satchel full of arguments against his mission found themselves without anything to say."

Sioma's considerable charisma, presence, speaking ability, and, most importantly, his message had persuaded those who had opposed his coming to Melbourne that they should support his mission. The AJH reporter wrote that "It was a remarkable effort, remarkable for the intensity of feeling that accompanied it, and at the same time for the sane logical argument in which the case was presented. There was no attempt at rhetoric…no endeavor at creating an atmosphere of hysteria…simply cold hard facts."

The text of his speech, as reported by the AJH, set out the past horrors that eastern European Jews had endured and the plight of those who had survived. It read, in part:

> Will the distress of our people ever cease, their social and economic life be re-established? 896 pogroms; more than 100,000 killed; 86,000 mutilated; 200,000 orphans; thousands of ruined homes; famine that has wiped out whole communities; a terrible succession of epidemics; that is the history of East European Jews during the last few years; 30 per cent of the total Jewish population – more than two million souls – without economic basis, without means of support, physically shattered; morally broken; this is their present position.
>
> In Russia the Government of the day has appropriated to

itself all the commerce, and [to] the co-operative institutions…
only workmen and peasants have the right to exist in the economic
structure of the society and there are therefore, today, 900,000
"déclassé" [fitting into neither category] unemployed Jews.

Sioma went on to outline the work being undertaken by the organizations
that he represented: OZE, ORT, and Emigdirect, which was working with
both the British Jewish Colonization Association (ICA) and the Hebrew
Immigrant Aid Society (HIAS). The latter was an American organization
created in 1881 to assist immigrants to the United States, but it was now
assisting Jewish immigrants throughout the world.

Sioma showed a number of lantern slides (photographs projected
onto a screen by an electric lamp) to illustrate his speech. The AJH
reporter wrote that he had never seen an audience so profoundly stirred.
The trustees of the Levinson Estate contributed £500 to the fund on the
spot.

The meeting elected a subcommittee to assist "in placing his message
before the Victorian community." The chairman of the subcommittee was
Dr. Albert Jones.

This enthusiastic reception disheartened the Englishman, Mark
Ettinger, who was in Australia at the same time as the organizer-secretary
of the nascent Australian Zionist Federation. Not only was Sioma
stealing the headlines, but Ettinger was worried that Sioma's Revisionist
connections would undermine his efforts.[1]

Two of the Melbourne morning newspapers reported the meeting in
the Montefiore Hall. The *Sun* used the headline "2,000,000 Jews Starving."
The *Argus* headline read "Jews in Eastern Europe: Story of Post War
Plight."

Albert Jones arranged an evening reception in his home for Sioma to
meet the leaders of the local Jewish community. Albert's older daughter,
Edna, recalled in an interview when she was eighty-six years old that it
was there that she first met Sioma. During the evening, he asked her if she

---

1   Eliyahu Honig, *Zionism in Australia, 1920–1939: The Formative Years* (Sydney:
     Mandelbaum Trust, 1997), 54.

would help in his office with mail and general office work. She went in each weekday and "after nine days I was engaged to be married to him," she said.

Sioma's diary notes of the meetings with Edna and their decision to marry could not be briefer or less sentimental. They read:

> 23 May. Dr. Jones. E.
> 30 May. Dr. Jones. Tea.
> 9 June. Fateful.

Sioma set up an office in the Melbourne CBD. He received a letter from General Sir John Monash dated June 5, 1928. It read, in part: "No one can hear from you a statement of the urgent need…without being profoundly impressed, as I have been, with the duty and responsibility of all Australians, and particularly members of Australian Jewry, to do what they possibly can, by financial support and sympathy, to aid you in your splendid efforts."

Monash, the son of German Jewish immigrants, was the very successful and greatly respected commander-in-chief of the Australian army in France during World War I. In a rare honor, he was knighted on the field of battle by the king. He was worshipped by those who served under him. At the time, he was the most highly regarded citizen in Australia and the best-known Jew in the country. Sioma used the letter in the other state capitals of Australia when he arranged for publicity in the local Jewish press.

The Council of Jewish Women organized two functions, one an "at home" in reception rooms in the suburb of St. Kilda, at which Sioma spoke, and a dance at Monash House in Carlton to raise funds.

On June 3, Sioma gave a lecture at the Carlton Hall on a recently published book, *The Seventh Dominion,* by Josiah Clement Wedgwood. The author, who was the great-great grandson of the potter Josiah Wedgwood, joined the army with the rank of captain and served in South Africa during the Boer War. He served in the army during World War I, was awarded the DSO at Gallipoli, and was promoted to the rank of colonel. He entered the British Parliament as a Liberal in 1906 but switched to Labour in 1919 and was appointed to the front bench when Labour came to power in 1924. Churchill offered him a peerage in 1942, which he accepted, but he died the following year. Throughout his life, Wedgwood was a radical. He staged filibusters in support of women's suffrage and against a Mental Deficiency Bill that he thought was unjust. In 1920 he criticized the British government's role in Palestine and throughout the 1920s and 1930s was a staunch Zionist. *The Seventh Dominion* was one of several books that he wrote. Published in London in 1928, it proposed that it was in England's interests to turn the whole of Palestine, including Transjordan, into a Jewish dominion that would then form part of the British Empire. It was a concept that the Revisionists greeted with great enthusiasm.

The American *Time* magazine reported on March 4, 1929, that a Seventh Dominion League had been founded in London by three parliamentarians: Wedgwood, Lt. Commander Joseph Kenworthy, and Lord Harrington. In May, a Seventh Dominion League was established in Jerusalem with Jabotinsky as chairman.

In his speech in Melbourne, Sioma spoke warmly of Wedgwood's hypothesis that with "a pipeline and a railway finishing at Haifa with Mount Carmel on one flank, and the Suez Canal on the other, the British Fleet could look after the Near East in comfort and safety." But, Sioma went on, in his view this could not be achieved without massive immigration of Jews to Palestine. In 1926, seventy-two thousand Jews had immigrated to Palestine, but in 1927, with a downturn in the economy, there had been a net loss of some twenty-five hundred Jews. Given the area's Arab population and their rate of natural increase, Palestine needed the immigration of some forty thousand Jews per year if there was to be a Jewish majority in the country by 1978.

The Jewish Telegraph Agency reported on July 22 that Sioma's mission to Melbourne had raised over £2,000 and that now he had moved on to Sydney and Brisbane. A subcommittee in Melbourne had been formed to continue the campaign.

Sioma exchanged letters with Jabotinsky throughout the course of this journey. A long letter had been waiting for Sioma's arrival in Perth. It reported on Jabotinsky's trip to London, where he made contact with members of Parliament and other influential people. Two further letters arrived while he was in Melbourne. One dealt with Jabotinsky's decision to immigrate with his family to Palestine, where he would take up a position with the American insurance company Judea, despite his being told of the poor state of the company in Palestine by comparison with its success in America.[2] The letter also dealt at length with the internal politics of the Revisionist movement, and Jabotinsky expressed doubts that the present approach of the Party to gain power within the World Zionist Federation was likely to succeed.

In early July, Sioma went to Sydney, where he worked for six weeks. The pattern of Sioma's campaign in Sydney followed closely on the one that he had established in Melbourne. The local Jewish press, the *Hebrew Standard* and the *Australian Jewish Chronicle*, reported large attendance at meetings of the general community in the Maccabean Hall, and at functions organized by the Council of Jewish Women. One paper commented that "Mr. Jacobi is probably the most popular and painstaking emissary that has ever visited the Australian Jewish community." The same Jewish press reported that over £2,260 were raised in New South Wales.

Before leaving Sydney, Sioma was invited to address a meeting that was called by the chairman of the Sydney Jewish employment bureau to consider the problem faced by the local community of settling Jews who had immigrated to New South Wales. Influenced by his Melbourne visit, he recommended a land-settlement scheme in view of the present employment situation and the few opportunities for trade.

Sioma returned briefly to Melbourne and then was off again. His journeys appear to be somewhat convoluted. From Melbourne he traveled to Adelaide for a stay of ten days before returning to Sydney, where he celebrated the Jewish High Holy Days, and then went on to Brisbane. He worked in Brisbane for three weeks and then traveled across the continent

---

2　　Jabotinsky proceeded with his engagement with the Judea as a vice president and managing director in Palestine at a salary of $6,000 per year. Although Jabotinsky was attracted by the prospect of a steady income and being able to return to Palestine, the mandatory authority refused to renew his permit to stay in the country after a year.

to Perth. It was a month before he returned to Melbourne. By this time he had been in Australia for over six months.

The total Jewish population of Australia at that time would have been in the vicinity of twenty-two thousand people. Only two census counts were conducted in Australia in the interwar years. The first, in 1921, showed a Jewish population of 21,615, and the second, in 1933, showed 23,553. More than 80 percent of Australian Jews lived in Sydney and Melbourne. There do not appear to be any precise records of the money raised by Sioma in Adelaide or Brisbane. In Perth the figure of £645 was published. Assuming some funds were raised in Adelaide and Brisbane, the total sum would have been in the vicinity of £5,000. Converting that sum to 2010 currency, it would have amounted to over $300,000. A successful exercise.

On November 12, Sioma went back to Sydney to catch a ship that would take him to New Zealand, where he arrived on November 20. Between then and December 28, when he sailed for the United States, his fund-raising took him to Auckland, Rotorua, Waitomo, Wellington, Dunedin, Christchurch, and then back to Wellington to board a ship for the Pacific crossing to the United States. Although the *Jewish Times* of New Zealand devoted more than half of its December 14, 1928, issue to Sioma's visit, including several articles that he wrote for the paper, it gave no indication of the amount that was raised.

Sioma's successful visit to Australia carried an afterglow in a letter published in the London *Jewish Chronicle*. The paper had reported a resolution passed at a recent meeting of the London Relief Federation that deplored the poor response of the Australian Jewish communities to the Federation's appeal for funds. In response, Newman Rosenthal, the editor of the Melbourne *Jewish Herald*, wrote to the Chronicle pointing out that Sioma's visit to Australia had raised "some £6,000" for ORT-OZE Emigdirect. This was despite the Federation's attempt to discredit this appeal even before Sioma's arrival. Rosenthal finished his defense of Sioma's mission with this enthusiastic endorsement: "No emissary that has come to Australia on behalf of a European Organization has made quite as deep and lasting impression upon this community as has Mr. Jacobi."

On January 18, 1929, Sioma arrived in San Francisco, where he stayed for a month. From there he went to Los Angeles, where he stayed for two weeks. He did not record in his diary the results of his fund-raising in either city, but in Los Angeles he was in touch with members of the film industry.

Sioma made a record of an interview that he had with Cecil B. DeMille.[3] The discussion was about DeMille's 1927 film *The King of Kings,* which portrayed the last years of the life of Jesus and came in for a deal of criticism from Jews wherever it was shown. DeMille defended his film to Sioma, saying that it showed that political intrigues, not the Jewish people, were responsible for the execution of Jesus. Furthermore, it showed that Jesus was a Jew who founded the Christian religion. DeMille went on that his mother was Jewish, a niece of the well-known London Samuel family, and he was disappointed at the reception of the film from some Jewish quarters.

From Los Angeles, Sioma set off for New York City by way of the Grand Canyon, Chicago, and Niagara Falls. He reached New York on March 9, 1929. From there he continued the efforts that he'd begun in Los Angeles by correspondence with several film producers to sell the rights of Jabotinsky's latest novel, *Samson the Nazarite.* He had no success with his letters and eventually he engaged the services of a Pathe screenwriter. Their lengthy correspondence continued through the months of April and May 1929 to no avail. Because of the costs of producing another biblical epic there was a great reluctance to become involved with films set other than in current locations with contemporary dress. Furthermore, the film producers felt, why pay for Jabotinsky's book when they could get the story in the Bible for nothing?

Sioma's efforts on behalf of ORT-OZE in this American journey seem to have been unsuccessful. There is a letter in Sioma's files on OZE letterhead dated April 23, 1929. Written and signed by Albert Einstein, it was addressed to Professor Michelson at the University of Chicago. The

---

3   There are several alterations to the typewritten record prepared by Sioma. They were made by Barrett C. Kiesling, who signed the amended document "OK. Personal Representative of Cecil Demille."

letter introduced Sioma, "a member of the Central Committee of the Union 'OZE'…. He has already done much for preserving the health of Jews…. I should be glad if you would find it possible to help Mr. Jacobi in his task to establish a Committee in your country for supporting the cause of 'OZE.'" Despite this introduction, there is just one cutting in Sioma's scrapbook that relates to this American journey. It was in the *B'nai B'rith Messenger*, a Jewish monthly, dated May 21, 1929. The *Messenger* gave a brief biographical outline and that he was fund-raising on behalf of OZE. "Single handed Mr. Jacobi has raised more than $50,000 for the cause he represents. He is now in New York." As far as one can tell, most of this money would have been raised during his journeys before he reached the USA. There is no other record of any funds that he may have raised in America.

While Sioma was in New York, he handled a transaction on behalf of five others to buy the shares in the Judea Industrial Corporation. He had bought shares in the company himself in 1926. He not only sold the shares at a profit of approximately $1,000, but he also received a commission of $675 from Judea for the transaction.[4]

Sioma did not leave New York until May 25, when he set off for Berlin to report back on the results of his trip. The careful diary notes that Sioma kept of his travels for ORT-OZE and Emigdirect listed each journey from one city to another, noting the miles traveled between each one. This trip, which lasted from January 1928 to June 1929, was headed "Trip I." He would undertake another three long journeys to raise funds for those organizations.

---

4   Jabotinsky wrote to other members of the Revisionist group on February 7, 1930, advising them of a letter he had just written to the Judea group in New York. It suggested that he should try to sell shares in Judea Life in South Africa and Australia. The idea was a revival of "S. J.'s suggestion made in 1926 after his London attempt to sell shares in Judea Industrial."

CHAPTER 8

MARRIAGE

Sioma met Edna Jones, a beautiful young woman of twenty-six, in Melbourne shortly after his arrival. Four years before, Edna had married a Brisbane Jew, Roy Mirls. All that Edna's family knew of Mirls was that he had served in the Australian Imperial Forces in France. From enlistment as a private, he had reached the rank of lieutenant. Edna met the handsome young ex-army officer at a tennis party in Melbourne. Neither she nor her family knew that he had been hospitalized with shell-shock several times during his military service and had been wounded in action twice in France. Finally, in 1918, Mirls was admitted to a neurological hospital in England with a severe case of war neurosis. He was in such poor health that he was invalided back to Australia in August 1918 before the war ended. In 1925, he was still severely afflicted by his war service, but this only became evident to Edna once they were married. The marriage lasted only a short time.

Edna had not obtained a divorce from Mirls when she met Sioma. Also, she had been involved in a serious car accident only two months before. Thrown against the windscreen of the car that was being driven by her brother, she suffered serious cuts to her forehead and above her upper lip. In the days before plastic surgery, the injuries were sewn up by her GP uncle. She was left with bad scars at the time, although they faded completely in later years. When she met Sioma, she was convinced that the scars and her unresolved marriage would put a stop to the possibility of any romance, "but when I met your father it didn't make any difference," she recalled in a recorded interview with her daughters.

Their engagement was complicated by Edna's unresolved first marriage and by Sioma's work for ORT-OZE and Emigdirect. He was committed to raise funds in the rest of Australia, New Zealand, and the USA before he returned to the head office in Berlin. After that, he was to attend the Zionist Congress in Zurich. He would not have time to return to Australia for a wedding and then go back to Europe. The only method of travel from Australia to Europe or the Middle East was by ship. It took a month to make the journey from Europe to Australia and three weeks to travel from Australia to the Middle East. It was decided that Edna, who had no commitments, should be the one to travel and that they would meet and be married in Palestine, where Sioma's parents and other members of his family lived. Sioma appeared to have no permanent residence of his own at the time. He moved between London, Paris, and Berlin as his commitments demanded.

They set the date for the wedding that would allow time for Sioma to travel to Palestine after his return to Berlin. Edna would have to make her way by ship on her own to meet Sioma somewhere along the way. It was arranged that they would meet when the ship berthed at Port Said after it had made its way through the Suez Canal. From there the couple would travel by train to Palestine.

Sioma left Berlin on May 25, 1929, and Edna left Melbourne three days later. Edna had never been overseas before. She was heading off by herself to marry a man she had known for only a few weeks. As the ship traveled up the Red Sea toward the Suez Canal, she received a cable from Sioma from the famous Shepherd Hotel in Cairo. He asked her to get off the ship at the port of Suez, the Egyptian town at the southern end of the canal, rather than at Port Said at the northern end. He would be waiting for her on the wharf. There was nothing unusual about this. A number of Edna's fellow passengers were disembarking at Suez to travel overland to Cairo, where they would go sightseeing and spend the night. The following day, they would catch a train to Port Said to reboard the ship, which had by then made its way there through the Canal.

When Edna disembarked at Suez early in the morning on June 29, Sioma was not there to meet her. She tried to phone the hotel in Cairo where he was staying but could not get through. The other passengers who had disembarked for their Egyptian tour offered to take the forlorn little blonde Australian, sitting on the wharf surrounded by her luggage, with them. But Edna knew that if she went with them, Sioma would have no way of finding her. So she stayed on by herself with her pile of suitcases in a totally strange land. She had no foreign languages and very few locals spoke English. It is easy to imagine her state of mind. Had she been stood up? How would she get to Palestine? She had never met Sioma's parents and didn't know where they lived. How could she get back to Australia? She had no return ticket and not enough money to pay for one.

The ship left the wharf for its passage up the Suez Canal. There she sat with her luggage on a largely deserted wharf. A young, white, unaccompanied woman was the subject of close scrutiny by the Egyptian men who passed by. It was three hours before Sioma turned up, sitting high on the back of a car with its top down and waving an umbrella to attract her attention. The ship had arrived in Suez at 8:00 a.m. Sioma had been told that it was due in at 11:00 a.m. There was a tearful reunion on the wharf.

The couple went to Cairo where they went on the usual tourist round: a camel ride, a visit to see the Sphinx, and then to the museum to view the recently discovered golden sarcophagus of Tutankhamen with its accompanying funerary objects. Then they left by train for Palestine to meet Sioma's family.

Edna stayed with Sioma's family in Tel Aviv for two weeks. They could not marry until Edna's Australian divorce decree came through. The papers did not arrive until July 9. Then they had to arrange for a Jewish divorce[1] in Palestine. After all the legal and religious requirements had been observed, Sioma's mother insisted on a formal engagement with a rabbi officiating.

---

1   In Hebrew, a *get*.

It was traditional Jewish practice in Russia that the contractual nature of a formal engagement was more important than the wedding. Both the engagement and the wedding, with Vladimir Jabotinsky as best man, took place in the Jerusalem home of Rabbi Abraham Isaac Kook two days later on July 11, 1929. Kook was the first Ashkenazi chief rabbi of Palestine.[2] The witnesses who signed the marriage certificate were Jabotinsky and his wife's brother, the lawyer Eliyahu Galperin.[3] Sioma's father gave his occupation on the certificate as "merchant," and stated that he and his wife Sara were residents of Tel Aviv.

The wedding photograph was taken in a studio. The arrangement of the group is not as it would have been in Anglo custom. All the women are seated in the front row. Edna is seated next to her mother-in-law, who is on her left. Sioma's sister, Manya, is seated on her right and an unidentified woman is on Sioma's mother's left. Sioma stands in the center of a row of men at the back. The closest that he gets to Edna is placing one hand on the back of the chair in which she is sitting. Jabotinsky, as best man, stands on Sioma's left. On his right are one of his brothers and his father. Two unidentified men are to the left of Jabotinsky. Presumably one of them is Eliyahu Galperin. In the photograph only one of the eleven in the group, the bridegroom, is smiling, even though it is a very subtle smile. It is one of the few surviving photographs of Sioma in which he is smiling. In all the other extant photographs of him he seems, purposely, to adopt a serious demeanor.

After the wedding there was a family celebration in a kosher restaurant in Jerusalem. Then the wedding party drove to Rachel's tomb in Bethlehem. There Edna's new mother-in-law bought a ribbon which she tied around Edna's waist to ensure that she "would have many children."

---

2   Rabbi Abraham Isaac Kook (1865–1935) was born in what is now Latvia. He went to Palestine in 1904 to work as a rabbi in Tel Aviv. During World War I, he was stranded in England and was appointed rabbi in the Spitalfields Synagogue in London. He returned to Palestine after the war to become the Ashkenazi rabbi in Jerusalem. He was appointed chief rabbi in 1921.

3   In a letter to Sioma on May 23, 1929, Jabotinsky expressed concern for his brother-in-law's health. He was finding it difficult to settle in Palestine.

Edna commented wryly sixty years later that it hadn't done much good as she bore just two daughters.

From Jerusalem the couple returned to Port Said to take a ship to France. They landed on the Riviera and spent a week there on their honeymoon before traveling through France to Switzerland in time to arrive in Zurich in late July 1929 for the Sixteenth Zionist Congress.

The conference was the scene of high drama. On the first day, the Revisionist group was physically attacked by members of the left-wing faction. Amid an uproar, the session was closed. The cause of friction at this conference was the election of new members to the Jewish Agency. It was proposed at the conference that the number of delegates on the Executive of the Jewish Agency should be increased and that US delegates would be given forty-four seats. Weizmann's supporters saw that the capital needed to advance the economy of Palestine would be provided by rich American Jews if they were encouraged by offering them places on the Jewish Agency Executive.

Many Jews who lived comfortably in America, England, western Europe, and Australia rejected the concept of Palestine becoming a Jewish state. They were first and foremost citizens of the lands in which they lived. As far as they were concerned, Judaism was a religion, not a race or a nation. They regarded themselves as American, English, or Australian citizens of the "Mosaic persuasion." They supported Zionism as a philanthropic gesture for "others" who wished to live in Palestine. Their views were anathema to the Revisionists and their supporters. Although the Jewish population in America was much the same size as it was in Poland, the Americans were given twice the number of seats on the agency as those allotted to Jews from eastern European countries. The great bulk of Revisionist supporters were from eastern Europe.

Edna recounted that she was largely oblivious to this high drama. Although it was customary for wives who accompanied their husbands to Zionist Congresses to sit next to their spouses, she said that she understood very little of what was taking place. The proceedings were conducted in languages that were foreign to her: Yiddish, Russian, and German. As she spoke only English, her recall related to the people that she met. Jabotinsky presented her with a book of poems by Bialik that had been translated into English. She sat with Mrs. Weizmann on one occasion and met the wives of other leading Zionists.

This conference, and the decisions made regarding the composition of the Jewish Agency, had a lasting effect on the Zionist movement. It created a split between Weizmann and Jabotinsky that was never healed.

After the conference, Jabotinsky made a decision to transfer the head office of the Revisionist movement from Paris to London, where it would be under the control of Meir Grossman, who had been a Jabotinsky supporter since the campaign to create the Jewish Legion in 1915. Grossman lived in Copenhagen at the time but moved to London at Jabotinsky's request the following year to edit a daily Yiddish newspaper. Jabotinsky liked Grossman's organizational abilities. Although by 1929 Grossman had views that diverged from Jabotinsky's plans, Jabotinsky believed that Grossman would abide by the decisions of the Revisionist executive.

At the end of the congress, Sioma and Edna made their way to Berlin, where they met with the leaders of ORT, OZE, and Emigdirect. From there, Sioma took Edna on a tour of eastern Europe. Sioma's interest was to see for himself where the results of his fund-raising would be spent. For Edna, coming from her sheltered life in Melbourne, it was a confronting educational tour to see the conditions under which Jews were living in that area at the time.

They went first to Kovno, the capital of Lithuania, where Jews had lived since the fifteenth century. At the time of their visit, the Jewish population was estimated at thirty thousand, constituting some 25 percent of the population. Edna recalled that she was horrified at the desperate poverty that she saw for the first time in her life. They went into a number of homes that had only earthen floors, and years later she recounted that her overwhelming memory was the smell of untreated sewage. She was so distressed at seeing so many poor people and the lack of hygiene that she could bring herself to eat only boiled eggs. She was also appalled by the contrast when she and Sioma were treated to a magnificent meal at a formal dinner provided by the leaders of the community for the "distinguished guests." Outside the city, they visited the suburb of Slobodka, which had once boasted a celebrated yeshiva. The school had been moved to Hebron in Palestine in 1923, so Edna was shown the empty building. She was very impressed by the first yeshiva she had ever seen. But again she was distressed by the poverty. The wooden houses with earth floors had front doors that were so small that even Edna, who was five feet four inches tall, had to duck her head to enter. The synagogue was in a state of disrepair, with large holes in the roof.

From Kovno, the couple visited the nearby town of Keidany and then on to the town of Ponevezh. Again, Edna saw primitive wooden homes in a town that was home to some sixty-eight hundred Jews. Their "great synagogue" was, by her standards, a small stone building.

From there they traveled to Riga, the capital of Latvia. The Jewish population of Riga at the time was some forty thousand and there were up to forty synagogues in the city. The couple were taken to a summer camp for children in the forest outside the city that was run by OZE. Edna was horrified to learn that one child at the camp had lived on bread and water for the whole of his life until he was taken to the camp for six weeks. Before they traveled south, they stopped for a day in Dvinsk, the second largest city in Latvia. From there they went to the Lithuanian city of Vilnius, which was then part of Poland.

Moving on to Warsaw, they saw the vibrant Jewish quarter of the city as well as the poverty of the crowded poorer areas. They visited the OZE summer camps run for underprivileged children. None of this was new to Sioma. He was giving his new wife an understanding of why he was so committed to his work.

Then it was back to Berlin for Sioma to visit the head offices of ORT-OZE and then Paris to spend some time in the Revisionist office there. After ten days, they went on to London, where they stayed for two weeks to liaise with the British branch of ORT-OZE before taking a ship to New York.

Although Berlin was the head office of the three organizations, the London office was very influential within the British Jewish community and with non-Jewish sympathizers. Lord Rothschild was chairman of the British group, and the committee included the chief rabbi of Britain and Neville Lasky, KC.

The *American Jewish Year Book* of 1929 reported that the American Jewish community had created their own ORT Reconstruction Fund. It had determined to raise $1 million. In addition, American Jewish trade unions had determined to raise another $1 million over five years. ORT America was also acting as the agent for collecting tools and machinery to send to Russia. This was in addition to another fund for the same purpose. It aimed to raise $10 million, of which John D. Rockefeller had contributed $500,000. Some of the money raised had already been sent by the American Society for Jewish Farm Settlement in Russia. It was hoped that it would work in conjunction with the Soviet government.

In addition to these ORT organizations, American Jews had their own organization to help immigrants. This was the Hebrew Sheltering and Immigrant Aid Society (HIAS), which had been functioning since the late nineteenth century. HIAS was already working in conjunction with Emigdirect.

In 1929, a referendum was held of all Jewish Americans who had contributed to overseas aid for Jews in Europe since the outbreak of war in 1914. They were asked whether this aid should be continued. The vote was in favor of maintaining aid. At the time, there were many American Jewish fund-raising groups doing this work. A meeting of community leaders determined to reorganize a committee known as the American Jewish Joint Distribution Committee. All the monies raised for overseas aid would be funneled into this central fund and the committee would be delegated to handle the work of reconstructive relief in central Europe. This Committee (known worldwide just as the Joint) is still functioning to assist the resettlement of Jewish immigrants and their continuing social welfare throughout the world.

Thus the only organization that Sioma represented that the Americans were not already assisting on a grand scale was OZE. But by the time Sioma was ready to return to America, it was reported in *The American Jewish Year Book* of 1928–29 that a group of American doctors and sanitarians[4] had established an organization to sponsor the work of OZE.

---

4   Defined in the OED as "one who studies sanitation or who favors sanitary reform."

Sioma and Edna set off with a letter of introduction from OZE Berlin dated September 2, 1929, on the next leg of his fund-raising journey. It authorized him to act as OZE's representative in the USA and Canada. The couple went by ship to New York. They had been on the move for the three months after their marriage in Jerusalem on July 11, 1929, until their arrival in New York on October 6.

Sioma finally met with the American National Committee of OZE later that month. The committee gave itself the full title of the Society for Preserving the Health of the Jews in Eastern Europe. The meeting was reported in the *Jewish Daily Bulletin* of October 31, 1929. The Wall Street crash of 1929 had occurred just days before. "Black Thursday," October 24, 1929, heralded the major crash of "Black Tuesday," October 29. The Committee of OZE decided that it would not compete with the Joint appeal that was currently underway. Therefore, it would not organize or allow any public campaigns for OZE, nor would it allow solicitation from individual contributors. The only exception allowed Sioma was that he could approach "established foundations."

There was thus a double blow to Sioma's planned campaign in America. The first was the local OZE decision. The second was the Wall Street crash, which made many potential contributors, even from foundations, extremely cautious. The *Daily Bulletin* concluded its report of the meeting with the laconic footnote that "S. Y. Jacobi, member of the Central Committee of the OZE, who recently arrived in the United States, reported on his tour in Poland, Lithuania and Latvia during the summer." No doubt Sioma had planned his usually successful oration on the plight of his fellow Jews, but this was all that was reported in the Jewish press.

Sioma's diary records only that after New York, the couple traveled to Washington and then visited several American cities. These included Niagara Falls, Detroit, Salt Lake City, Denver, Colorado Springs, and San Francisco. They left for Australia in early March 1930.

There do not appear to be any references to "business" undertaken by Sioma during this extended journey in America. If he was effectively barred from fund-raising for OZE, was he spreading the word for the small

American Revisionist Party? There is nothing in the surviving literature or correspondence to indicate that he did so.

Edna was pregnant with their first child when they sailed from the West Coast for Melbourne. She would be with her family for the birth. They arrived in Melbourne in late March 1930 and stayed in a house that Edna's father had rented for them in St. Kilda.

During his first visit to Melbourne, Sioma had struck up a particularly strong friendship with Newman Rosenthal (1898–1984), the editor of the *Australian Jewish Herald* at the time. Rosenthal, who was born in Ballarat, was the same age as Sioma and a graduate of Melbourne University. After World War II, he founded and directed the university's audiovisual department, and was a prolific author on film and on local Jewish history. Rosenthal and Sioma were of like critical minds concerning the politics and strategies of the Zionist body headed by Weizmann at the time of Sioma's visits.

When Sioma was in Melbourne on his 1928 fund-raising trip he made no reference, apart from a lecture on the book *The Seventh Dominion*, to his views on the Zionist movement. Sioma clearly felt no constraints about expressing his Revisionist views when he was in Melbourne on a purely family visit two years later. Sioma wrote two long articles for the AJH while he was in Melbourne in 1930.

The first article, which was published on April 17, 1930, was introduced with a boxed editorial note by Rosenthal stating, "We take pleasure in presenting the first of a series of articles written for the *AJH* by Mr. S. Y. Jacobi…a leading member of the Central Committee of the World Union of Zionist Revisionists." Sioma explained his position in the opening paragraphs of the first article, which was provocatively entitled "The Zionist Leadership Has Failed."

> The views of the Zionist Revisionists, to whom I belong, are in many instances diametrically opposed to those of the official leadership of the Zionist movement and my criticism would [have] hamper[ed] the efforts of the Australian Zionists to build up an organization here. I obeyed. Now, two years later, the worst of our – revisionists' – predictions have been fulfilled, the Palestine

> Administration continued to be anti-Zionist, the economic crisis
> has not been overcome, and above all a pogrom took place in
> Palestine and 134 Jewish men, women and children were killed.

This explanation must be seen against the background of contemporary developments in the Zionist movement and the situation in Palestine. In his articles, Sioma detailed the major differences between the Zionist movement led by Weizmann and the Revisionists led by Jabotinsky. These centered on two issues.

First, the main Zionist body had abandoned a concept of a Jewish state in Palestine, being prepared to settle for a "homeland for Jews" in the country expressed in the Balfour Declaration. Second, the Jewish Agency, the body designated under the Mandate to negotiate with the British mandatory authority, now included wealthy and influential American Jews, some of whom were openly anti-Zionist and saw their participation as a philanthropic gesture to help other Jews settle in Palestine. They had been included at the expense of those who would have been elected by the Zionist movement at large.

The pogrom to which Sioma referred was the most recent of the Arab "riots." This was the term used by the mandatory authority to describe the indiscriminate murder of Jews by Arabs in Palestine. From August 23 to 29, 1929, pogroms were carried out against Jews in Jerusalem and then spread to other towns and to kibbutzim. The number of Jews killed throughout the country totaled 134. Eighty-seven Arabs were killed, mostly by British troops and police trying to halt the bloodshed. Weizmann had accused the Palestine Administration of having known what was brewing before the outbreak of violence but doing nothing to prevent it.

Sioma's article set forth the viewpoint of the Revisionists. In reviewing the history of the Balfour Declaration, he cited the various authorities who supported the essential notion that the declaration's aim was to establish a Jewish state in Palestine rather than, in the words in the declaration, "a national home." This interpretation, wrote Sioma, was endorsed at the peace conference at the end of World War I, where it was supported by the leader of the Arab delegation to the conference, Prince Faisal.

But, continued Sioma, the British administration of the Mandate continued to maintain that the words did not promise a Jewish state – and for geopolitical reasons, the British were now pursuing a policy of conciliating the Arabs. The Arabs had been offered a legislative assembly with no Jewish representation. This was despite the £11 million in donations collected from the worldwide Jewish community and the £45 million in private investment for Palestine from Jewish sources, both of which benefited the whole country. These sums did not include £6.7 million paid to Arabs for land that had been bought by the Jewish National Fund.

Sioma went on to accuse Weizmann of no longer speaking of the creation of a Jewish state in Palestine. This demonstrated, Sioma argued, that the traditional Zionist movement no longer believed in "the great idea of Zionism – the creation of a Jewish state." He argued that the British administration in Palestine favored Arabs over Jews. The restrictions placed on Jewish immigration meant that the eight thousand Jews admitted each year was less than Arab natural increase.

To add injury to insult, the Zionist executive had written to the Revisionist executive that the direction of political work has been passed to the executive of the Jewish Agency. The Revisionists regarded this as unacceptable because the composition of the Jewish Agency included known anti-Zionists who regarded their position as a philanthropic one to help others who wanted to go to Palestine.

Sioma closed his article with the assertion that if the mandatory authority intended handing over the running of the country to an Arab majority, this would prohibit further Jewish immigration and then there could never be a Jewish majority in Palestine. The country would end up as another ghetto for the Jews who had gone there.

Sioma's second article in the AJH appeared on May 1, 1930. It was primarily an expansion of one of the issues raised at the end of his first one: the inclusion of Jews who were non-Zionists as members of the Jewish Agency. The heading of the article was "What of the Jewish Agency? A Jewish National Home or a New Jewish Ghetto?"

He continued to attack the inclusion of declared anti-Zionist Americans in the Jewish Agency. They might bring money, he argued, but money alone could not rebuild Palestine. The Zionist dream was being undercut by the body that was supposed to be bringing it to fruition. One of the leaders of the Americans had declared that while they approached their work for the agency as purely philanthropic, they would not agree to provide funds unless they could share in the agency's decision-making process.

Sioma went on to include German Jews among those who "disagreed with the national conception of Zionism…[and] the words 'Jewish National Home' in the Balfour Declaration [for them] constitute[d] an undesirable term…. We reject the conception of a Jewish people…[and] that Palestine should be a National Home for other Jews, other than for those living here."

To illustrate the influence that this thinking had on the newly constituted Jewish Agency, he included two photographs of the halls in which the conferences had been held. One showed an enlarged image of Herzl over the podium that had dominated the meeting of the Sixteenth Zionist Congress. The second photograph, taken in the same venue, was of the first meeting of the newly elected and expanded Jewish Agency. Herzl's image had been covered over.

Sioma suggested that in order to change these views, it was necessary to broaden the base of those who elected the members of the Jewish Agency to include all those who contributed to Zionist funds, shareholders in the Jewish Palestinian banks, and all those participating in work for Palestine.

In the same issue, the AJH published an article entitled "We Must Have a Jewish Majority," with the subhead "Powerful Address by Mr. S. Y. Jacobi at Carlton Hall." The meeting, which was held under the auspices of the Jewish National Fund, was chaired by the doyen of the Zionist Organization in Melbourne, Samuel Wynn. Sioma attacked the current international Zionist leadership and the Jewish Agency under several headings, but the central thrust of his speech was that without a Jewish majority in Palestine there was no hope of establishing a Jewish state. The AJH reported that several speakers disagreed "vehemently" with Sioma and objected to his campaign against the Zionist leadership. He replied that he had given them the facts and if they did not agree with his solutions, then they should offer their own proposals because the present course of action could not lead to a Jewish state. His "spirited reply" was that the present approach had been a failure and would continue to fail unless their methods were changed. Rabbi Brodie, who chaired the meeting, thanked Sioma and declared himself "profoundly stirred by his able and eloquent appeal."

There was another reason for the couple's trip to Melbourne. Although Sioma had graduated as a civil engineer, he had never put his qualifications into practice. Still hoping to practice his profession, he was prepared to move to Australia and had put out feelers for a job as an engineer with the Melbourne City Council. The job did not materialize. Sioma was destined never to practice as an engineer.

While he was in Melbourne awaiting the arrival of his and Edna's first child, he received a cable from ORT-OZE asking him to undertake a fund-raising trip to the Far East on their behalf. He could not afford to turn down the offer. He left Melbourne on May 1 to travel to Sydney, where he boarded a ship that took him via Manila to Hong Kong. From there, he visited Chinese cities where there was a nucleus of wealthy Jews. He did not return to Melbourne until August 7. The couple's daughter, Naomi, arrived on June 8 during his absence.

CHAPTER 9

MELBOURNE, CHINA, MELBOURNE, SOUTH AFRICA

There was a small but wealthy Jewish community in China. The modern Jewish presence in China started in the middle of the nineteenth century.[1] Britain had fought the Opium Wars in order to force China to allow British commercial interests to import opium into their country. After the British victory in 1843, China, apart from ceding Hong Kong to Britain, also granted the British trading rights in the major port cities of China, including Canton and Shanghai, and most favored nation status for Chinese trade.

Once China had been opened to foreign trade, Jewish settlement followed. Among the most notable arrivals were the Kadoories, the Sassoons, and the Hardoons – Sephardi Jewish families who originally came from Baghdad. They had followed the British colonial trail to India for the cotton trade, and then moved on with Britain to the new markets in

---

1   The history of Jewish settlement in China goes back to the first century CE. The remnants of several first-millennium migrations of Jews to China were unknown in the West until the sixteenth century. These Jews, who had no contact with the outside world, were absorbed into Chinese culture by the nineteenth century.

China. These families were largely responsible for the wealth and growth of Jewish communities in Shanghai, Canton, and Hong Kong. Shanghai, which was settled by Jews in the 1840s, had the largest Jewish community. Its major synagogue, which could seat seven hundred people and housed thirty Torah scrolls, was built in 1887. The population was increased by an influx of Russian Jews during the 1920s. At the time of Sioma's visit to Shanghai, the Jewish population of the city was estimated at seventeen hundred. In Hong Kong there were only about 150 Jews, but it was a wealthy community.

It was the usual practice for ORT-OZE to advise the Jewish communities in advance of Sioma's arrival. This would allow the arrangement of press interviews and the planning of meetings. Sioma arrived in Shanghai on June 5, 1930, by way of Manila, Hong Kong, and Canton. In each city he spoke to members of the Jewish community, seeking funds for ORT-OZE. If the community was large enough, a public meeting would be arranged. In Shanghai, three English-language newspapers interviewed Sioma on his arrival and gave him extensive coverage. One headline read "World Wide Appeal for the Suffering Jews of Eastern Europe."

The Shanghai Jewish newspaper, *Israel's Messenger*, was published monthly. It came out after Sioma had left the city. It reported that he was welcomed in a "palatial private home" where he spoke to a select group from the Jewish community. He subsequently spoke at two synagogues in the city. The press report of these functions mentioned that there had already been a "liberal response from the community in Hong Kong." Two articles by Sioma were published in the *Messenger*. Each included the text that had become his standard press release, "Tired of Giving?" and "Reconstructing Jewish Life in Eastern Europe," with photographs of Lord Rothschild, Einstein, Sioma, and the Odessa self-defense force.

The only ships available for Sioma's return journey to Melbourne took him via Saigon, Singapore, Batavia, Samarang, Surabaya, and Macassa. If there were any Jews in these stops, he contacted them in order to raise funds. From there, his journey took him down the east coast of Australia, and he made his way back to Melbourne by way of Brisbane and Sydney. He arrived to see his firstborn child, Naomi, on August 7, 1930. She was two months old. Sioma had been away from Melbourne for three months.

While he was away, the *Australian Jewish Herald* in Melbourne published three long articles that he had written before leaving. They appeared in three different issues of the paper on June 12, June 24, and July 24, 1930. They were entitled "The Way Towards a Jewish Majority in Palestine" and subtitled "Revision of the Zionist Economic Policy."

The articles were closely argued, using demographic and economic figures to support several theses. Sioma's analysis of the position in Palestine included the population and its projected trends, a study of the land area available for settlement, existing protective tariffs and customs agreements, and the negative outcomes if the present regime were not amended. Overall it was a realistic but depressing image of Jewish settlement in Palestine at that time. Sioma detailed how the considerable sums of money that had been raised for Jewish settlement in Palestine had been spent and how they should be better used in the future. The funds that he examined included those of the Zionist Organization; Hadassah, the Women's Zionist Organization – founded in America in 1912 to fund health improvements in Palestine; and the Jewish National Fund, which was founded in 1901 to acquire land in Palestine for Jewish settlement.

The intent of Sioma's demographic studies was to show that from 1919 to 1927, the number of Jews in Palestine had increased by 90,200, while the non-Jewish population increased by 109,300. Unlike many writers of the time, Sioma avoided using the word *Arabs* throughout his three articles, preferring instead the term *non-Jews*. Of the Jewish increase, only 74,100 was by immigration and the rest, 16,100, was by natural increase. The increase in the non-Jewish population was almost all by natural increase.

Sioma made two points from these figures. His first point was that with the present rate of Jewish immigration there was no prospect of achieving a Jewish majority in the country. If the existing rate of Jewish immigration continued, then the rate of natural increase of the Arab population would always exceed the combined figures of Jewish immigration and natural increase. With the uncertain economic conditions arising from the already apparent world financial crisis, from 1927 to 1929 the net increase in the Jewish population in Palestine was only 6,670.

His second point was that with the non-Jewish rate of natural increase, they would number one million in twenty-five years. The present Jewish population was 150,000. To match the projected population of non-Jews would require an increase in the Jewish population, by immigration and natural increase, of 850,000, an average of thirty-five thousand a year for twenty-five years. In the past nine years, the annual average of both natural increase and immigration had been only ten thousand.

In terms of the land requirements of such a large Jewish population, assuming that one-third were to be settled on the land, this would require an investment of some £30 million just to provide each family with twenty-five acres. The present rate of donations and investment was not nearly enough to reach this target.

Sioma's second article attacked the mindset of those who supported Jewish settlement in Palestine. Sioma wrote that they saw the country only in terms of groups of pioneers "sowing and reaping in the fields of Judea." The economic reality of Palestine was that because of a lack of investment in industry, there was, and continued to be, a huge trade deficit. In the five years for which figures were available, imports were four and a half times greater than exports. In the ten years to 1927, the Zionist executive in Palestine had invested only 2 percent of its funds on the establishment of secondary industry. The mandatory authority, he suggested, should be persuaded to impose protective tariffs on goods manufactured in Palestine and to impose high import tariffs on raw materials that were, or could be, produced in the country.

The last of the three articles stressed again the paucity of Zionist funds from all sources that went toward the development of secondary industry – £88,000 out of 4.8 million. But he then went on to illustrate that in education and health, Zionist funds were being used for the benefit of the whole population of Palestine, while the mandatory authority had reduced its spending in these areas. He cited figures of the total Palestinian budget. In 1921–1922, the proportion of the budget spent on health was 7.6 percent. It had fallen to 3.9 percent in 1927–1928, and the Zionist Organization had stepped in to make up the difference.

A similar set of figures applied to education. Why, asked Sioma, should the Zionist movement be asked to subsidize health and education for the population when this was the government's responsibility? In the seven years before 1927, the mandate authority showed a surplus of £1.5 million which, according to a British parliamentary report, was "mainly due to items derived from the influx of Jewish capital into the country." The surplus was achieved after paying off the "debt" incurred by the British government from the military administration of the country.

After his return to Melbourne, Sioma set about trying to create a Revisionist organization there. The *Australian Jewish Chronicle*, a short-lived pro-Zionist Sydney paper, in its issue of September 11, 1930, reported a meeting held at the Toorak Road Synagogue in Melbourne on September 3. Dr. Albert Jones, Sioma's father-in-law, was elected chairman and called on Sioma to address the meeting. Sioma was reported as saying that the main reason for the meeting was to establish a Revisionist branch in Australia. A subcommittee to examine the position was formed at the end of the meeting. Rabbi Brodie, the rabbi of the Toorak Road Synagogue where the meeting was held, was the president of the Australian Zionist Federation. He told the subcommittee that he was sure that the Australian Zionist Federation would welcome the affiliation of a branch of the Revisionists, but stressed that the Revisionists should not seek their membership from existing Zionists. They should enroll those who were not presently committed to the Zionist cause. The newspaper report finished with the comment that Mr. Jacobi appeared to be extremely disappointed at the lack of enthusiasm displayed.

That comment elicited a response from Sioma. In a letter to the *Jewish Chronicle* in its next issue on September 25, 1930, he denied that he was disappointed at the meeting. He had invited only twelve people to attend. Obviously Rabbi Brodie, as the president of the Australian Zionist Federation, could not join a Revisionist committee, but of the remaining eleven who attended, seven agreed to serve on a provisional committee of Revisionists. Sioma was pleased with this outcome. His letter continued that the provisional committee had since met. It had elected Newman Rosenthal as chairman and Dr. Albert Jones and Dr. David Rosenberg (a prominent general practitioner who later changed his name to Roseby) as vice chairmen. They were a distinguished trio of Melbourne Jewry.

The Zionist movement was not in a strong position in Australia at the time. Its appearance on paper – with General Sir John Monash as its patron, Rabbi Israel Brodie as its president, and the youthful Alec Masel as secretary[2] – was a strong one. However, this belied its true position. The Third Australian Zionist Conference was held in Melbourne in July 1930. The conference was described by its recently appointed organizer-secretary in a report to the Zionist offices in Jerusalem:

> In Sydney, Falk[3] is a destructive force.... The Union of Sydney Zionists is nothing more than a JNF [Jewish National Fund] committee making a noise. Their last meeting ended in uproar and they could not elect a president, intrigues and fights.... The Honorary Secretary...Honig is a really nice chap...[but] from others nothing can be expected.... Brodie is indolent...the others are just harmless.

Sioma left Melbourne in late September 1930 to continue fund-raising for ORT-OZE in South Africa. After he left, the Revisionist Provisional Committee issued a circular letter on a letterhead that read "Union of Zionist Revisionists, Victorian Branch," with an office at 34 Nicholas Street, East Brunswick. A two-page letter in eight-point type, it summarized the arguments set out by Sioma in the articles that had been published in the AJH.

But events in Palestine and the onset of the Great Depression contributed to the demise of the fledgling Revisionist movement in Australia. In Sioma's scrapbook is a newspaper clipping dated November 26, 1930. It is a report of the effect of the Great Depression on the Australian Jewish communities, and it relates how the rabbis of the East Melbourne synagogue, Adelaide, and Brisbane had all been dismissed

---

2   Masel, a prominent solicitor, later became a leader of both the Melbourne and the Australian Jewish communities, particularly in the immediate post–World War II period.

3   Rabbi L. A. Falk was an ardent Zionist. He had been a chaplain in the Jewish Brigade during World War I. He had served with Jabotinsky and was one of his great admirers.

because the communities were unable to pay their salaries. Other rabbis in Australia were having their salaries cut, and ORT-OZE-Emigdirect had cancelled all fund-raising activities.

An Arab riot, known as the Wailing Wall incident, occurred in Jerusalem on August 16, 1929, when more than sixty Jews – men, women and children – were killed in the space of five hours. The violence spread throughout Palestine, notably in Motza, Hebron, Safed, and Jaffa. The Haganah was able to mount a defense and further attacks in Jerusalem were repulsed. Some attacks on Jews in Tel Aviv and Haifa were also thwarted by Jewish defenses, but there were sixty-seven Jewish deaths in Hebron and eighteen in Safed. In total, 134 Jews were killed and some three hundred were wounded. Eighty-seven Arabs were killed, "mostly shot by British troops and police seeking to halt the violence," to use the words of Martin Gilbert.[4]

In response to the outbreak of violence, the British government set up yet another inquiry, the Shaw Commission. The inquiry led to the issue by the government, on October 1, 1930, of the Passfield White Paper, so named because it was issued by the secretary of state for the colonies, Lord Passfield.[5] It was seen by Jews as being anti-Zionist and pro-Arab. Passfield found that Jewish immigration had directly contributed to the present level of unemployment in Palestine during the Great Depression and concluded that existing agricultural development had already used all the arable land in Palestine. Therefore, Jewish immigration must be severely restricted and British approval would be required for the sale of any more land to Jews.

The White Paper effectively repudiated the Balfour Declaration when it suggested that the sale of land to Jews should be prohibited and Jewish immigration should be reduced to a trickle. International outcry against the Passfield proposals was such that the prime minister, Ramsay MacDonald, withdrew the main provisions of the paper that restricted Jewish immigration and land purchase.

---

4   *Israel: A History* (London: Black Swan, 1998), 60.
5   Before his elevation to the peerage, Passfield was Sidney Webb, the noted Fabian socialist and associate of George Bernard Shaw.

Jabotinsky, who had given evidence to the Shaw Commission, was subsequently barred from visiting Palestine. The grounds for this decision was a "seditious" address that Jabotinsky had made to a crowd of six thousand in Tel Aviv the previous December. Jabotinsky was fighting a losing battle against the power of several self-confessed anti-Semites in the Palestine administration and the British Colonial Office.[6]

There were Jewish meetings throughout Britain, America, Europe, and Australia to consider reactions to the White Paper and MacDonald's watering down of its suggestions.

In Australia it led to a closing of the Zionist ranks. It appears that those who had supported the establishment of a Revisionist movement in Melbourne now went back to supporting the traditional Zionist party. A protest meeting against the Passfield Paper was held at the Carlton Hall on August 26, 1930. On the platform, those who called for solidarity in the face of this new threat to Zionist aims were the committee of the Revisionist Party: Rosenthal, Rosenberg, and Jones. They spoke on the same platform as the staunch supporters of the main Zionist movement, Rabbi Brodie and Samuel Wynn. This was the death knell of the Revisionist movement in Australia at the time. There is only one subsequent public mention of a Revisionist Party in Australia. In an article in the AJH on March 31, 1932, the author, Newton Super, described himself as honorary secretary of the Union of Zionist Revisionists, Melbourne branch. Sioma was not present. He was on his way back from his trip to the Far East.

Sioma had to leave Melbourne to continue his fund-raising activities in South Africa. It had been decided that their new baby, Naomi, was too young to travel. So Edna stayed with her family in Melbourne for six months before she and the baby set off to join him. Sioma left in late September 1930 for South Africa by way of Adelaide and Perth across the Indian Ocean. After a voyage of three weeks, he arrived in Durban on October 15, 1930.

---

6   William B. Ziff, *The Rape of Palestine* (New York: Longmans, 1938), vol. 2, chapter 3, "Bureaucracy Looks at Jews," 192–233.

CHAPTER 10

SOUTH AFRICA

In February 1930, Vladimir Jabotinsky and his wife Joanna traveled to South Africa, where they stayed for two months. During that time he met with the leading political figures in the country including the prime minister, General Hertzog, several members of the cabinet, and General Smuts, who had served as the prime minister of South Africa from 1919 to 1924. Jabotinsky had known him in London during World War I, when Smuts was included in Lloyd George's war cabinet.

The South African Jewish population was staunchly pro-Zionist. Jabotinsky spoke to large crowds. Three thousand came to the City Hall in Johannesburg to hear the "much criticized Revisionist leader," but the tour was not a success in terms of funds raised for the movement. Jabotinsky left South Africa before Sioma arrived there from Australia.

Although Jabotinsky was unaware of the implications at the time, he had converted a South African Jew, Michael Haskel, to his cause. A successful businessman with interests in mining, Haskel would later become the major financial backer of the Revisionist movement.

The letters of introduction that Sioma carried from ORT-OZE had been carefully prepared for this visit rather than the more general ones that he used for his earlier fund-raising tours. The letter provided by the head office in Berlin was signed by Albert Einstein. The letter from the London office was addressed to the president of the South African Jewish Board of Deputies. It was personally signed by Lord Rothschild just as "Rothschild," and it introduced Sioma as a member of the Central Committee of the OZE, stating, "He is in a position to give you a full account…of the activities for which we are appealing."

Sioma was successful in attracting an influential group to head a local committee. The honorary president was Sir George Albu, a German-born mining magnate who had been knighted in 1912. The two vice presidents were the chief rabbi of South Africa, Dr. J. L. Landau, and Justice Leopold Greenberg. Another South African Jewish knight, Sir Harry Grauman, was vice chairman. Sioma was widely publicized as conducting the "South African Campaign for the Reconstruction of East European Jewry." The committee published a twelve-page booklet that was liberally illustrated with photographs of the work that was being undertaken in eastern Europe by the three organizations. The opening message in the publication, from Sioma, was the familiar "Tired of Giving?" The rest of the pages, although not attributed to an author, were most probably written by Sioma if they are judged by his established method of getting his message across. The article quoted facts and figures with comparative percentages to support the arguments.

The composition of the Jewish population of South Africa was quite different from other communities that Sioma had canvassed, in particular Australia. The original Australian Jewish community was composed largely of British Jews. The Australian gold rush of 1851 brought German Jews for the next two decades. Beginning in the late nineteenth century and lasting well into the first quarter of the twentieth there was a steady flow of immigrants from Russia, Poland, and Palestine. What followed in Australia was a pattern that had been seen in the United States, particularly in New York, France, and Germany during the nineteenth century, where the Western and Eastern Jewish cultures were dissimilar. In each of these countries, this resulted in two quite distinct groups of Jews that did not mix. By comparison, there was a common culture among the Lithuanian Jews in South Africa.

Jewish congregations were formed in several South African cities in the mid-nineteenth century. During the nineteenth century Lithuania had been known as a leading center of Jewish thought and culture. The capital, Vilnius, was called the Jerusalem of Lithuania. Lithuanian Jews fleeing Russian tsarist persecution started arriving in South Africa in the late nineteenth century. They were followed in a chain migration pattern by other Lithuanians seeking the commercial opportunities created by gold and diamond mining in South Africa. These were much more appealing than the cramped economic possibilities of the Baltic States. By the 1930s it was estimated that some 80 percent of the South African Jewish population had come from Baltic countries.

The Jewish population in South Africa in the 1930s was approximately ninety-five thousand – 4.75 percent of the white population. In Australia the Jews were only 0.5 percent of the white population. Although South African Jews had mostly settled in the major cities of Johannesburg, Cape Town, and Durban, they were widely spread throughout the British Dominion of the Union of South Africa. Sioma visited and spoke wherever he could find an audience. His scrapbook has excerpts from newspapers in Bloemfontein, Volksrust, George, Kimberley, Bulawayo, and a number of other cities and towns. A South African newspaper reported that by the end of his tour he had visited and spoken at thirty-eight centers.

The many South African Jewish newspaper reports of Sioma's fund-raising reflected a more welcoming and sympathetic tone than the press reports in other countries. In its November 1930 issue, the *Ivri*, a new Jewish newspaper in Johannesburg, published a long interview with Sioma. In this report he was quoted as speaking of the present situation of Jews in both Russia and Poland. According to official data published by the Soviet government in June of that year, 1930, Jews comprised 28 percent of the unemployed in the Ukraine, where they were only 5.5 percent of the Ukrainian population. In White Russia (Belarus), the comparative figures were Jews comprised 42 percent of the unemployed and 8 percent of the population. Sioma quoted a report from the American Joint Distribution Committee that estimated some 70 percent of all Jewish children in Russia suffered from some form of tuberculosis. Sioma went on to enlarge on the appalling condition of Jews in Russia. This was largely attributable to the government's economic policy, but the Soviet government was now trying to alleviate the problems it had created. It was granting land for settlement and timber for building, and allowing duty-free entry for agricultural machinery and tools for industry that were supplied by Jewish charitable organizations from abroad.

Sioma continued his interview by pointing out that although the situation in Russia was dire, the position of Jews in Poland was much worse. In Poland, the government was pursuing a deliberately anti-Semitic policy. Jews were taxed much more severely than ordinary Polish citizens. While Jews comprised 11 percent of the population, they paid 40 percent of all tax revenue. Non-Jewish Poles could borrow money for business at the going bank rate, while the borrowing rate for Jews was between 25 and 30 percent. In 1929, 891 Warsaw Jews had committed suicide. More than a quarter of the Polish Jewish population required free matzos and charitable gifts in order to celebrate Passover. Jews were being deliberately frozen out of middle-class occupations by Jewish-specific taxation and the cost of borrowing funds. Government and semi-government employment was not open to Jews.

The *South African Jewish World* reported in its issue of December 19, 1930, on a mass meeting that had been held in the Standard Theatre in Johannesburg the previous Sunday. The reporter recorded Sioma's blunt message. The expulsion of 150,000 Jews from Spain and the horrors of the Spanish and Portuguese Inquisitions during the fifteenth century were recorded as one of the major tragedies of Jewish history. But in eastern Europe, more than three times that number of Jews had died as a result of pogroms and starvation during the last decade. "Never before has humanity allowed such inhumane persecution where two million civilized people were denied elementary human rights and treated like outcasts," Sioma said.

The *Ivri* in its issue of January 1, 1931, reported the same public meeting. The report opened by quoting two resolutions that were "carried with applause." The first was that this meeting, "having heard Mr. S. Y. Jacobi's address...expresses its great satisfaction with the activities of ORT-OZE-Emigdirect." The second resolution was that "this meeting pledges itself…to respond generously to the appeal now being made by Mr. S. Y. Jacobi."

A twelve-page pamphlet with photographs of the South African leaders of the campaign, together with a list of the prominent men and women who were already supporting the appeal, was included with pledge forms. The pamphlet was prepared for the Johannesburg community. An identical one, but with appropriate sponsors on the front page, was prepared for the Cape Town community. It appears that Sioma was the author of the text of the pamphlets. The opening pages included his photograph and his well-known question, "Tired of Giving?" The text, accompanied by several photographs, outlined the conditions of Jews in Russia, Poland, and Lithuania and the relief work being undertaken in those countries by the organizations that he represented. Among the photographs was one of a group of some forty men, women, and children taken on a ship. The caption read "Jewish Emigrants on their way to Australia."

The *Zionist Record*, a weekly newspaper founded in 1908, gave Sioma many opportunities to publish his own writing. At first, the paper published articles directed at the readers who would support "OZE in Lithuania" and later published Sioma's articles on Revisionism.

The *South African Jewish Chronicle* published a long article about the Thirteenth South African Zionist Conference, which was held in Cape Town in mid-January 1931. The Revisionists were represented at the conference for the first time. The reporter wrote in glowing terms about Sioma's contribution to the proceedings:

> Jacobi, the leader of the delegation, was probably the most interesting personage at the Conference.… He made a speech on the (Passfield) White Paper which shows deep thinking and clear vision. His quiet manner, his earnestness and convincing demeanour carried his audience with him. He is of a type too seldom met in this country.

At the conference, the main topic of discussion was the Passfield Paper. Sioma put forth the view that although the main concerns had been the restrictions of Jewish immigration and land purchase, he was certain that these restrictions were so unjust that they would be modified by public pressure. His major concern was the composition of the legislative council proposed by the paper, as it would have a majority of non-Jews. He added two further points: first, that Jews should revive the fight for Transjordan to be reclaimed as part of Palestine and it should be open to Jewish settlement, and second, that Jews in Palestine should be allowed to defend themselves by recognized Jewish self-defense forces.

Sioma continued to speak about the Revisionist philosophy on every possible occasion. Addressing the Women's Zionist League in Johannesburg, he put forward the Revisionist view that the aim of Zionism had to be a Jewish majority in Palestine and that the composition of the Jewish Agency, half of whose membership were non-Zionists, did not share this view of the ultimate aim of Zionism.

By April 1931, Edna felt that the baby was old enough for the long journey by ship to South Africa. The trip to Durban took three weeks. The united family visited Cape Town before settling in Johannesburg, where they lived until October.

In the meantime, Sioma had speaking engagements throughout South Africa. One newspaper column listed his itinerary during the month of April 1931 as addressing six meetings in the geographically widespread South African Jewish communities.

Jabotinsky's files include an excited letter that he wrote on August 20, 1931, to Mark Schwartz, the manager of the Judea Insurance Company in Tel Aviv. It set out a cable that he had received from Sioma that told of discussions that Sioma had conducted with the Jewish president of the South African Life Assurance Company. The concept was that the South African company would take over the business of the Judea Insurance Company in Palestine but that the Judea would continue to operate under its own name. The plans that were discussed included the possibility that Judea, under its new ownership, would set up branches in both England and South Africa. The plan was dependent on a report on the Judea's business, including balance sheets, income statements, and actuarial reports. Sioma's cable included his decision to go to Tel Aviv in September to negotiate the matter from there.

Jabotinsky's letter to Schwartz contains insights into the high regard that he had for Sioma:

> He can attract people of the stamp required…he has a knack of extracting money – he has made thousands of pounds for ORT-OZE all the world over – be absolutely frank with him about the weak points (of the Judea)…he must know everything. He is a man of great discretion, and a first rate chap all round.

But nothing more of this plan is recorded. Presumably, Judea's figures did not win the approval of either Sioma or the South African company.

In June, Sioma had spoken on several occasions about Jewish self-defense in Odessa. He titled his talks "In the Days of the Pogroms." His speech was published in full by the South African *Zionist Record* on June 12, 1931. He continued speaking of his experiences of self-defense in Odessa and his fund-raising efforts until September 1931. His appearance at the Community Hall on September 23 in Bloemfontein was announced as his last in South Africa.

The Jacobis left South Africa at the end of September 1931 on a Dutch ship that traded up the east coast of Africa. This was the most direct route to Palestine. On the way they called at Dar es Salaam, Port Arthur, Mombassa, Aden, and then through the Suez Canal, where they disembarked in Port Said. From there they took a train to Palestine. In Tel Aviv they showed off their baby, Naomi, to her other grandparents, Sioma's parents. They stayed in Tel Aviv for a month before making their way to London. By then, Edna was pregnant again.

After they left South Africa a local paper, the *Zionist Record* of October 9, 1931, reported that contributions to ORT-OZE and Emigdirect by Sioma's efforts were "close upon £11,000." Sioma's own figures showed that he had raised £10,558 less his expenses of £964. The net figure would be in excess of half a million Australian or US dollars in present values – an extraordinary result for the middle of the Great Depression.

Sioma cabled these results to the Head Office of ORT-OZE in Berlin. They responded by cable congratulating him for his "great success," but he left Johannesburg before it arrived. Eventually, he received an effusive letter from the Berlin office written in Russian and dated October 7, 1931:

> We wish to express our feelings of great satisfaction with the results achieved. In the circumstances [of the Great Depression] this is indeed a great success…that exceeded our expectations.… Words cannot adequately express how grateful we are. On a number of occasions…you have helped us to overcome seemingly insurmountable difficulties and relieving the most critical state of affairs. We sincerely hope that after your holiday in Palestine you will continue your work in our organizations.

Chapter 11

To London – The Revisionist Split

Sioma and his family arrived in London in December 1931. They rented a house in Golders Green before they bought in the same suburb at 48 Hodford Road. Golders Green was, and still is, very much a Jewish area. The house that they bought was only three doors away from the Golders Green Synagogue. The proximity to the synagogue was coincidental. Sioma went to synagogue when the occasion demanded. During his fund-raising trips, he was often asked to speak from the pulpit, but at home in London he attended synagogue only on the important holy days, and observed major Jewish rituals, including those of mourning when his father died.

In 1932 Sioma was looking for sources of income in addition to ORT-OZE. It would seem that opportunities for civil engineers were nonexistent in that period. In January he was engaged to encourage British companies and other organizations to participate in an international fair in Tel Aviv. This was a period when cities in the Western world held international fairs to show off their primary and secondary production.

Tel Aviv had held its first fair in 1924. The second, held in 1932, was named the Levant Fair.[1]

Sioma sought a reference from Loughborough College to assist him with his efforts to promote the fair. The principal of the college provided the reference: "Mr. Jacobi had a very distinguished career with us, and in a remarkably short space of time – three years – he obtained the College Diploma in Civil Engineering, with First Class Honours."

Sioma continued his fund-raising for ORT-OZE in Britain. The British group had taken a new name, the Joint British Committee (JBC) for the Reconstruction of East European Jewry. Although this was rather a mouthful, it explained in English what the fund was for rather than having to decipher ORT-OZE to audiences and potential subscribers. In a publicity document printed in March 1932, Sioma was named as a member of the Central Committee of the JBC.

His activities for JBC took him to the major provincial English cities and to Scotland. Sioma carried with him a letter of introduction which was signed by the president, Lord Rothschild, and the treasurer, Lieutenant Colonel J. H. Levey, DSO, OBE.

Sioma was in Scotland for JBC when Carmel, his and Edna's second child, was born in London on January 24, 1932. Jabotinsky wrote from Paris to the parents of the new baby, "We have drunk Polish vodka in honour of *our*[2] new grand-daughter. Don't you dare to grumble she's not a boy."

There are a number of references in the London *Jewish Chronicle* to Sioma's activities for JBC throughout 1932 and into the early months of 1933. Jabotinsky wrote to Sioma in April congratulating him on his fund-raising successes.

The JBC Reconstruction Campaign attracted wealthy and influential British Jews. In March 1932, a fund-raising dinner was held at London's Savoy Hotel. It was chaired by Lord Rothschild and the guest of honor

---

1   Two more fairs were held in Tel Aviv in 1934 and 1936. A large new exhibition building was erected for the 1934 event. Arab civil unrest caused the abandonment of subsequent Levant Fairs.

2   Underlined by Jabotinsky in his letter.

was Professor Albert Einstein, who had flown over from Berlin for the occasion. Sioma was included as a member of the executive of the campaign in the event's program.

At the dinner, the vote of thanks to Einstein was moved by George Bernard Shaw. Shaw's speech, which was recorded live, is still available to be heard. This is a partial transcript:

> Napoleon and other great men of his type, they were makers of empire, but there is an order of men who go beyond that. They are not makers of empires, but they are makers of universes. And what they have made in those universes, their hands are unstained by the blood of any human beings on earth. They are very rare. I go back 2,500 years and how many can I count in that period? I can count them on the fingers of my two hands. Pythagoras, Ptolemy, Aristotle, Copernicus, Kepler, Galileo, Newton, and Einstein. And I still have two fingers left vacant.

A newspaper report of a lunch given by Lord Marley[3] in the House of Lords on July 4, 1933, to support JBC mentioned Sioma one of the speakers. It was announced that the fund-raising activities now included help for German Jews. Michael Haskel was included in the guest list.

A publicity pamphlet for the JBC set out the work and achievements of ORT-OZE. ORT had trained fifty-five thousand artisans, provided raw material and machinery for twelve thousand artisans, established cooperative workshops and factories that supported fifteen thousand workers, and given material and technical assistance to 126 cooperative farms. OZE maintained seventy maternity and infant welfare centres, ran 121 summer holiday camps for children and recuperation units for adults, and fed over thirty-five thousand children in Poland.

---

3   Lord Marley was chief Labour Whip in the House of Lords at the time. He graduated as a British naval officer, won a DSC during World War I, and subsequently entered politics as a Labour member. Although he was not Jewish, he took a great interest in Jewish matters. A non-Zionist, he published and spoke about the evils of the Nazis in Germany from 1933 onward and actively sought Birobidzan in the Soviet empire as a place of refuge for Jews fleeing Nazism.

JBC maintained a high profile among the wealthy sector of the Jewish community in Great Britain. An advertisement for the eighteenth annual ORT ball in 1933 announced that it would be held in the fashionable Dorchester Hotel in Park Lane.

Although he was listed as the honorary secretary of JBC in several of their publications, it appears that Sioma's engagement with the organization was still his major source of income. At the same time, he was exploring other commercial possibilities and continued an active interest in Revisionist matters. He remained in close contact with Jabotinsky by mail. There are copies of a number of letters in the Jabotinsky archive that Jabotinsky wrote to Sioma while Sioma was in Australia and South Africa in 1932. Unfortunately, Sioma's responses have not survived.

To confirm his status in England, Sioma became a naturalized British citizen in September 1933. Edna was naturalized at the same time. As an Australian, she had been a British subject all her life, but this was lost when she married Sioma, who had no nationality at the time.[4] They had traveled on what was known as a Nansen passport, which the League of Nations issued after World War I to people who had lost their nationality.

The other business interest developed by Sioma during this period was acting as London representative and adviser for the South African mining magnate Michael Haskel. In a letter that Weizmann wrote to a London colleague on February 8, 1934, Weizmann referred to Sioma as "the Haskel Director in London."[5]

Michael Haskel was born in Vilna, Lithuania, in 1880, to a large family of four boys and four girls. Lithuania was then part of the Russian empire and Haskel's political activities as a student brought him to the attention of the tsarist police. When his father was warned of this development, the

---

4   Australians were British subjects until the Australian Citizenship Act became law in 1969.

5   The concerns expressed in Weizmann's letter were that Haskel was negotiating to acquire 49 percent of the shares in the *Palestine Post*. This would lead, wrote Weizmann, to "complete and intransigent control" of the paper by the Revisionists. Furthermore, Sioma was making "a determined effort to influence the policy of the Jewish Telegraphic Agency."

eighteen-year-old Michael was sent to live with members of the Haskel family in Hamburg, where he was employed in the family business for the next nine years. After a severe illness in 1907, he was advised to live in a warmer climate, so he followed the trail of many other Lithuanian Jews and emigrated to South Africa. In a complete change of direction he took up farming in the Cape District and introduced irrigation into his farming practices. But gold mining in the colony was a contagious fever, and three years after his arrival there, he bought his first interest in a gold mine. During World War I, he went to England and served as a commissioned officer in British army intelligence as a Russian interpreter. After the war, he returned to South Africa and expanded his interests in gold mining. In 1925, he added the new field of asbestos mining to his business concerns. By the early 1930s he was a wealthy man.[6]

As a youth, Haskel had been involved in Zionist activities with his father's encouragement, and he continued this interest in South Africa. In his will he included a paragraph about his "political faith." "I was a Zionist from the first years of my conscious life and have always understood Zionism as a complete and final solution of the Jewish tragedy through the rebirth of Palestine as the Jewish State."

It is probable, but not recorded, that Haskel met Sioma during the latter's fund-raising tour of South Africa for ORT-OZE in 1931, but Haskel was not mentioned in any of the reports of the thirty-eight meetings that Sioma addressed in the country. In July 1931, Haskel attended the international Zionist Congress in Basel and came out as a supporter of the Revisionist movement.[7] Unmarried and with no family in South Africa to support, Haskel "adopted" the Revisionist movement,

---

6   When Haskel died in 1942, his estate was valued at £30,000, which in 2010 values
     was approximately £4 million. His executor's statement was that in the mid-1930s,
     the value of his estate was "very much more." In a will drawn up in 1934, he
     bequeathed £5,000 to Sioma. In a revised will in 1938, he revoked a large number of
     bequests in the previous will and reduced Sioma's legacy to £2,500. Because Sioma
     predeceased Haskel, Sioma's widow, Edna, received nothing.
7   In 1931, Haskel published a paper in Johannesburg entitled "Ideals and Compromise:
     The Present Situation in the Zionist Movement."

becoming its principal financial backer. In 1933 he was appointed South Africa's honorary commissioner in Palestine. When Haskel arrived in Jerusalem, a correspondent of the *Palestine Post* described him as "slight and dapper, unassuming, slightly stooped, quick in movement and speech, with a demeanour betokening intense vitality, power of concentration and resolution…of the type that at once commands attention." During the 1930s, Haskel divided his time between South Africa, England, and Palestine.

The Revisionist movement had transferred its administrative world headquarters from Paris to London in August 1929. One of Jabotinsky's stalwarts, Meir Grossman, who had lived in London since 1917, was one of the signatories to the original 1925 Revisionist declaration. Grossman was another Russian-born committed Zionist. A journalist by profession, he had emigrated from Russia to Berlin. He moved to Copenhagen to be with the Zionist Organization when it relocated its headquarters there after the outbreak of World War I. In Copenhagen Grossman set up a Yiddish language paper, *Di Tribune,* which became the first organ of Jabotinsky's activism. When Grossman moved to London in 1917, he made contact with Jabotinsky, who was already there lobbying to establish the Jewish Legion, which would form part of the British army to fight the Turks in Palestine. Grossman became an integral part of Jabotinsky's circle and was supported in London by a group of fellow Zionists who had contact with Jabotinsky.

Jabotinsky admired Grossman's organizational skills. Jabotinsky, who was frequently absent from Paris, was aware that administration was not one of his strengths. Therefore, in 1929, Jabotinsky asked Grossman to take over the administration of the movement from London, while the movement's political center remained in Paris, where Jabotinsky lived and ruled. This division of power within the Revisionist movement would eventually lead to its fracture.

The first evidence of the schism occurred soon afterwards. There was a difference of opinion between Jabotinsky and Grossman on how to react to a political situation that arose over the British reaction to an inquiry into the outbreak of Arab violence in Palestine. It occurred during the year of the transfer of administrative power to Grossman in London.

Chapter 9 above described how the Arab "riot" known as the "Wailing Wall incident," which occurred in Jerusalem on August 16, 1929, had reflected on Zionist opinion in Melbourne's Jewish community.

The British government issued the White Paper following the Shaw Commission of Inquiry into the riots. It proposed greatly reduced immigration of Jews to Palestine and the restriction of the sale of land by Arabs to Jews. As a result of Jewish outcry throughout the world over these proposals and the Paper's overall anti-Semitic tone, the British prime minister, Ramsay MacDonald, wrote to Weizmann on February 13, 1931. His letter said that Britain had no intention of withdrawing from the terms of the League of Nations-approved Mandate, which included the Balfour Declaration. While this seemed to appease some Zionists, many others saw it as inadequate, and it exacerbated the controversy within Zionist ranks over future relations with Britain as the mandatory authority. The mainstream Zionist movement, although only somewhat mollified by MacDonald's letter, held the view that the movement had nowhere else to turn, and that neither the mandatory authority nor the British government should be antagonized in a manner that would jeopardize what remained of British goodwill.

Jabotinsky would not accept this view and delivered a public speech in Paris that called for the unqualified cancellation of the White Paper. The Revisionist executive committee in London under the chairmanship of Grossman took a stand that was in direct conflict with Jabotinsky's views. It agreed with the general Zionist view of not antagonizing Britain.

Following this difference of opinion, Grossman and his executive set about destabilizing Jabotinsky's position. It made decisions without consulting him. He learned about their pronouncements in the Jewish press. Grossman, it was found, was negotiating behind Jabotinsky's back with the Weizmann-led Zionists. This lead to a showdown between Grossman and Jabotinsky over the leadership of the party. In March 1931, Grossman wrote to Jabotinsky that he "wanted a trial of strength...I want to fight it out, to face the issue."

A meeting of the Executive Committee of the World Union of Zionist

Revisionists to try to resolve the struggle took place in the French port of Boulogne on April 5 and 6, 1931. Boulogne was selected as neutral territory between the two centers of the power struggle: Paris, where Jabotinsky and his close followers lived, and London. No minutes of the meeting survive, nor were the names of those attending recorded. Sioma was not there. He was still in South Africa. An anonymous verbal report recorded by Jabotinsky's biographer described an acrimonious beginning to the meeting, but ultimately an agreement was reached. The Revisionists would put forth a motion at the forthcoming Seventeenth Zionist Congress, which was to be held in Basel later that year, that the aim of Zionism was a Jewish majority in Palestine. The Boulogne Agreement, as it came to be known, was that if this motion was lost, then the Revisionist movement would secede from the main Zionist organization.

At the previous Zionist Congress – the sixteenth, which was held in Zurich in 1929 – the Revisionists had twenty-one delegates representing some eighteen thousand votes. Since then, Jabotinsky had spent a lot of time electioneering in eastern Europe. He went to the Seventeenth Congress, which was held in Basel in 1931, with nearly fifty-six thousand votes, which allowed a delegation of fifty-two, representing some 24 percent of the votes at the congress.

At the congress, Jabotinsky demanded a clear statement from the meeting that the aim of Zionism was a Jewish majority in a Jewish state in Palestine. Jabotinsky asked the meeting, "What is a Jewish National Home?" Answering his own question, he went on:

> It is a national State, a State with a predominant Jewish majority, where the will of the Jewish people will determine the forms of collective life. Palestine is an area whose essential geographical characteristic is that the Jordan River flows not along its frontier but through the middle of it. The purpose of Zionism is to create a living space for millions of Jews on both sides of the Jordan.[8]

---

8   Schechtman, *Fighter and Prophet*, 112.

Subsequently Weizmann gave an interview to the Jewish Telegraphic Agency in which he said, "I have no understanding of, and no sympathy for a Jewish majority in Palestine." This statement caused a commotion amongst the delegates at the congress. A motion was presented at its next session that the statement by Weizmann was unsatisfactory. This was effectively a vote of no confidence in Weizmann. The motion was passed by the congress and Weizmann resigned the presidency.

Sensing victory, Jabotinsky proposed his motion that the ultimate aim of Zionism was a Jewish majority in Palestine. But it was supported only by the Revisionist delegates and a handful of other votes, and was defeated by 121 votes to 57. A furor erupted during which Jabotinsky stood on his chair and tore up his Zionist delegate's card. He did not return to further meetings of the congress and was not elected in Weizmann's place. The new president was Nahum Sokolow, a Polish-born journalist and author who had been a member of the Zionist executive committee since 1907 and had worked closely with Weizmann in negotiations for the Balfour Declaration. Sokolow, who was to remain president until 1935, when Weizmann resumed the position, was a trenchant critic of the Revisionist movement, particularly of its epicenter in Poland.

Relations between Jabotinsky's supporters and the Grossman faction within the Revisionist movement soured even further after the congress. Jabotinsky endeavored, unsuccessfully, to convince the Revisionist executive to adhere to their "Boulogne Agreement" and to withdraw from the main Zionist movement. He failed to achieve this aim, and in a huff he unwisely took a leave of absence from his role as chairman of the Executive Committee of the World Union of Zionist Revisionists. Notwithstanding these tumultuous developments, Jabotinsky still found time to keep Sioma in touch with the affairs of the Revisionist movement. Sioma had not been involved in this struggle for power as he was overseas in Australia and South Africa. Jabotinsky wrote to Sioma in Johannesburg from Paris, describing the break and explaining that he needed a rest and time to think out a means of repairing the rift.

In the meantime, the head office of the movement remained in London under the control of Grossman. It was a situation that could not last. Grossman and his supporters wanted neither a split from the main Zionist party nor to antagonize the British, and they saw Grossman replacing Jabotinsky as the leader of the Revisionists. Two months after taking his leave of absence, Jabotinsky resumed his role as chairman and sought a compromise between his position and Grossman's. He called another meeting of the Revisionist executive on the neutral territory of the French coast, this time at Calais. At this meeting, Jabotinsky agreed that the question of establishing the Revisionists as a separate Zionist organization would not be raised at the forthcoming Revisionist World Conference, and peace was temporarily restored.

But despite this "Calais Agreement," Grossman continued to try to undermine Jabotinsky's position as leader and to press his own claim for the position. In order to defeat Grossman's moves, Jabotinsky ordered a plebiscite amongst Revisionist members to decide who should lead the party.

There is a gap in the surviving correspondence from Jabotinsky to Sioma from July 1932 to January 1933. When it resumed it was about the internal politics of the movement. But on April 5, 1933, Jabotinsky wrote from Warsaw that he gave Sioma his full power of attorney to supervise the plebiscite that was due to be conducted in England on April 16. On the same day he wrote again, suggesting that the opposing faction of the RZU in Britain might refuse to conduct the poll. He asked Sioma to organize the poll if this should occur and authorized him to appoint assistants to conduct the poll.

When the results of the poll were counted, Jabotinsky had won 94 percent of the vote. Badly defeated by the plebiscite, Grossman and his group decided to leave the Revisionist camp and to remain in the main Zionist movement. The big split in Revisionist ranks had occurred. Grossman's adherents formed a new party, the Jewish State Party, which would operate within the Weizmann Zionist movement. The departure of Grossman and his colleagues left the London office without leadership.

In 1933, in addition to his business interests and a relationship that was developing with Haskel and his work for ORT-OZE, Sioma became more actively involved with the Revisionist movement. Jabotinsky had been addressing letters to Sioma in London regularly since early 1932. The letters related to the internal politics of both the Zionist Organization and the Union of Zionist Revisionists (UZR). It appears that by the end of 1932, Sioma had taken up a position with the UZR that he managed to fit in with his other activities.

The tenor of Jabotinsky's letters to Sioma changed during 1933. In addition to the politics of the UZR, there are references to its finances and administrative functions that Jabotinsky expected Sioma to perform, as Sioma had been appointed a member of its executive committee. On June 16, 1933, Jabotinsky appointed Sioma the Revisionist bureau chief in London. As one of Jabotinsky's biographers put it, "Sioma became Jabotinsky's closest confidant and right hand man."

On that same night, June 16, 1933, Haim Arlosoroff was shot while walking with his wife on the beach in Tel Aviv. He died shortly afterwards in the hospital.

Dr. Arlosoroff, Russian-born and German-educated, was the leader of Mapai, the Zionist socialist party that had been formed in 1930. David Ben-Gurion was the main activist in Mapai. Arlosoroff was a highly regarded member of the World Zionist Executive, where he had been appointed to chair the committee that handled political affairs. He had maintained contacts in Germany from the years that he lived there, and had just returned from a trip to Germany where he had gone to negotiate what became known as the Transfer Agreement. At the time, there was a Jewish embargo on trade with Nazi Germany that the Revisionists strongly supported.

The proposed Transfer Agreement was an offer that if the embargo was abandoned, Jews would be allowed to emigrate from Germany to Palestine on condition that they took their capital with them in the form of German exports. The exports would then be sold in Palestine and other world markets. The proposal would achieve two aims for Germany: it would export both Jews and German goods at the same time. The Revisionists did not support the proposed agreement. They wanted the embargo to be enforced. The Transfer Agreement, which was concluded in 1933, was to remain a bone of contention between the Zionist parties.

Arlosoroff was an avowed opponent of the Revisionist movement both on political grounds and on their moves to split from the Zionist Organization. In relation to the latter he was party to a blunt statement by the Zionist executive condemning the possible moves by the Revisionists to secede.

In Palestine there was open dissension between the Revisionist movement and the Labor movement generally. Disagreements had led to violence. The Jewish left-wing parties, both in eastern Europe and in Palestine, regarded the Revisionists as being so far to the right that they were fascists.

From the mid-1920s Jabotinsky had been widely known within the Zionist movement as "an enemy of labor." In 1925, when *Rasswyet* was transferred to Paris, Jabotinsky published several articles that were critical of the attitude of the left-wing parties toward the basic problems of Zionism. It was his view that their undue attention to activist political programs resulted in the diversion of Zionism from everyday constructive work in Palestine. In contrast to their emphasis on the class struggle and the rights of workers, he argued strongly that economic progress in Palestine would be advanced by the introduction of a Jewish middle class and self-employed artisans. These articles earned him the bitter animosity of the Labor leadership.

In response to the criticism, he wrote an article in May 1927 entitled "We the Bourgeois" that only served to increase the opposition. His championing of bourgeois ideals turned his critics from describing him as a mere "enemy of labor" to calling him a proponent of "Jewish fascism."

In addition to this perfidy, Jabotinsky's view of a class struggle in Palestine was that it would give rise to a battle where Jewish workers would consider themselves enemies of Jewish capitalists. He looked on that prospect with abhorrence. It was his view that building a Jewish state in Palestine needed not only the workers, but also capital that could be provided only by a middle class. A flow of private capital that employed Jewish labor was a necessity. He wrote, "Expressed in terms of social economy, it means letting people trade and build and compete as they like, triumph or fail, accumulate millions or lose their last penny, provided no one is allowed to go hungry and homeless, and no one need submit to slavery for want of food and home." To use twenty-first-century terminology, Jabotinsky advocated a free-market economy in a social welfare state, but this was well before its time.

Finally, Jabotinsky further enraged his political opponents by his attitude to strikes. He proposed that strikes should be prohibited and that workers be required to engage in compulsory arbitration as the only way of settling industrial conflict. This was the attitude to labor disputes that Mussolini espoused at the time. Those views alone were sufficient to brand Jabotinsky a fellow traveler of the fascists.

Mainstream Zionists believed that the Revisionist youth movement, Betar, was a militarist and fascist-style training ground for Revisionist youth. Even the brown shirts worn by Betar members were alleged to be the same as those worn by Nazi storm troopers. The Revisionist response was that the Betar uniform had been created in 1923 to reflect the color of the land in Palestine, long before Hitler's rise to power and the later introduction of the SA uniform. An undated photograph on the Betar website, taken sometime during the late 1920s or early 1930s,[9] shows Jabotinsky seated in a group of eighteen Betar members. The Betarim wear military-style uniforms with leather belts and leather shoulder straps in the style of the British army. They all wear hats that are similar to those worn by US soldiers in World War I and those still worn by Boy Scouts.

In Palestine there was mutual hatred between the Jewish left and the Revisionist right. Betar members who immigrated to Palestine were denied employment by the left-controlled Histadrut. The left wing branded them as anti-unionist and strikebreakers, and there was physical violence between the two groups.

On June 15, the day before Arlosoroff's murder, the Revisionist newspaper in Palestine, *Hazit ha-Am*, edited by Abba Ahimeir, ran an intemperate attack on Arlosoroff entitled "The Stalin-Ben-Gurion-Hitler Axis."

---

9   Jabotinsky and two others in the photograph are in civilian clothes: suits, collars and ties. Their dress is consistent with these dates.

> We have read…an interview with Mr. Arlosoroff…. Among other meaningless words and stupidities in which this red mountebank excels, we find that the Jewish problem in Germany can be solved only by means of a compromise with Hitler and his regime. These men…have now decided to sell for money the honor of the Jewish People…to Hitler and the Nazis…. Jewry will welcome the triple "Stalin-Ben-Gurion-Hitler" axis with repulsion and detestation. The Jewish people has always known how to deal with those who have sold the honor of their nation and its Torah, and it will know today how to react to this shameful deed.

Because of this article and Arlosoroff's open political opposition to the Revisionists, the Revisionists were immediately suspected of having committed a politically motivated murder despite Arlosoroff's statement from his hospital bed that he did not know his assassins and was sure that they were not Jews. On June 19, the Palestine police searched Ahimeir's premises and arrested him together with his lodger, Abraham Stavsky, a member of Betar who had recently arrived from Poland. Another Revisionist, Zevi Rosenblatt, was also arrested. Ahimeir was charged with having plotted a politically motivated murder, and Stavsky and Rosenblatt were charged with having committed the crime.

Abba Ahimeir was born in Belarus in 1898. He studied philosophy in Vienna and Liege and wrote his doctoral thesis on the decline of the West. He went to Palestine in 1924 and became active in harassing the British authorities. He was jailed by the British on a number of occasions. One writer described his personality as combining a mixture of intellectual curiosity and fanaticism, of rationalism and nationalistic mysticism.

In 1932 Ahimeir headed a group of some twenty-five delegates, known as the Club of Revisionist-Maximalists, at the Revisionist World Conference in Vienna. They demanded that the democratic structure of the Revisionist movement be abandoned and that the movement be organized on dictatorial lines as a paramilitary unit. The conference rejected their demand. Ahimeir pressed Jabotinsky to take on a dictatorial role within the movement. Jabotinsky refused. Earlier in 1933, Ahimeir and nineteen of his associates had been arrested by the British police. Five of them were charged with belonging to an illegal terrorist organization. Ahimeir was arrested again after the murder of Arlosoroff. A month after his acquittal, he was arrested again on the charge of belonging to a terrorist organization and sentenced to twenty-one months' imprisonment at hard labor.

Stavsky and Rosenblatt were indicted for Arlosoroff's murder.

CHAPTER 12

MICHAEL HASKEL AND THE STAVSKY AFFAIR

The question of who was responsible for the murder of Haim Arlosoroff has never been answered, and more than seventy years later, it is still an issue between Zionist left and right factions. One of the many unexplained facts of the killing was that Arlosoroff's wife did not accompany her wounded husband to the hospital after he was shot. She went to the hospital some time later and then only when the driver of the private car that had taken the wounded man to the hospital had returned to look for her.

Although two young Arabs confessed to the crime, the British police force, the Palestine Police, brought no charges against the two and refused to allow them to be called during the trial.

At the trial, Rosenblatt was found not guilty because there was evidence that he could not have been at the scene of the crime at the time. The nineteen-year-old Abraham Stavsky was found guilty and condemned to death. The death sentence was overturned on appeal and he was released. The case came to be known as the Stavsky Affair. The left wing, led by Ben-Gurion, used the trial as the basis of an anti-Revisionist crusade on the basis that Arlosoroff's murder was a politically motivated Revisionist "kill."

Sixty years later, the Israeli government, led by Menachem Begin, set up a formal investigative committee, chaired by a retired judge of the High Court of Justice, to put the matter to rest. The committee reached the unanimous conclusion that neither Rosenblatt nor Stavsky were guilty, but that there was not enough evidence to determine who had committed the murder.

Sioma's involvement in the case started when legal counsel was sought in Palestine to act for the defense. It was found that the three leading Jewish barristers in Palestine had all been retained to represent Arlosoroff's widow. This was a further conundrum in the matter as Mrs. Arlosoroff had not been charged with any crime. If she were to be called during the trial, it would be only as a witness.

In his new appointment as the Revisionist London bureau chief, Sioma now had the responsibility of engaging a suitable English lawyer to defend the accused. In addition, he was called upon to secure services of independent expert witnesses and to seek financial support to fund the defense.

Sioma had to work from home as he had no access to the old Revisionist offices. The London-based former members of his party had stripped the old offices of files and of office equipment that had any value. The only things they left for Sioma were unpaid debts for expenses that they incurred before the split.

Sioma's first letter to Jabotinsky after he had taken up his new position referred to "Mr. H." Later letters referred to "our friend." This was Michael Haskel, who was the only wealthy backer of the Revisionists. Otherwise, the movement had to rely on Jabotinsky's personal appeals to the mass of his mostly impoverished followers for small donations from each. Sioma wrote that during the course of his conversation with Haskel he had passed on a message from Jabotinsky asking for financial help. Haskel had replied that there was no need to ask and that Jabotinsky would not be unhappy with his support.

In July 1933, Haskel was taken seriously ill in London. He was admitted to the hospital for surgery and made a slow recovery over several months. Sioma was a constant visitor to the sick man but he felt that it was not appropriate to ask for funds at the time. It was not until October that Sioma wrote to Jabotinsky that he had felt that he could raise the question of money. Haskel had agreed to contribute thirty pounds per month to establish a London office for the Revisionist movement. This was enough to cover rental and other expenses, including secretarial assistance, but not enough to pay Sioma a reasonable salary.

In Sioma's files are two tickets to the Eighteenth Zionist Congress, which was held in Prague from August 21 to September 3, 1933. Jabotinsky had booked a room for him in Prague at the same hotel where he and his wife would be staying. The conference was a rude awakening for Sioma and the Revisionist contingent. It was overlaid by the Arlosoroff murder and Labor's accusation of Revisionist guilt. The Labor Party, with their allies, had a commanding majority at the conference. When the Revisionist spokesman went to the platform, the Labor Party and its supporters walked out. When Jabotinsky was preparing to speak on the topic of a boycott of German goods, he was ruled out of order.

An independent American rabbi later wrote that "it was not a Zionist Congress.… The Labor people converted the Congress into a war on Jabotinsky, on the Revisionists…and on the General Zionists."[1] It was a nightmare for the Revisionists.

From January 1934 Sioma's letters were typed on the letterhead of the Revisionist's new office at 47 Finchley Road, London, N.W. 8. Finchley Road runs past Regent's Park and is the route to Golders Green from London's West End.

After Sioma took over the London office, he and Jabotinsky had an extensive exchange of correspondence during the six-year period from June 1933 until Sioma's death in 1939. At times, they wrote letters on a daily basis. It was the sort of communication between officers in an organization that we now conduct by email or by text messaging. But at that time, such exchanges were labor intensive and time consuming. Letters were either typed, using carbon paper to create a copy, or handwritten.

---

1 Shmuel Katz, *Lone Wolf: A Biography of Vladimir (Ze'ev) Jabotinsky* (New York: Barricade Books, 1996), 1383.

They were then folded and placed into envelopes, and had to be taken by hand to a post office or a post box. The Revisionist movement rarely had sufficient funds to employ an experienced typist or other staff to perform these tasks. At times, it lacked even the means to buy stamps.

The first surviving letter from Sioma to Jabotinsky, dated June 16, 1933, was written from his home at 48 Hodford Road. Much of the correspondence at the time relates to the Arlosoroff murder. The first mention of the case was in Sioma's letter of June 22. He wrote of his concern that not only would the Zionist "Labour Party" try to take advantage of the accusation against the three Revisionists, but that Meir Grossman would take advantage of the "excitement" to strengthen his position within the Zionist movement against his old party.

It was not until July 10 that Sioma received specific instructions regarding the appointment of an English barrister to appear for the defense. Jabotinsky cabled from Warsaw that the Revisionist Party in Palestine "insists [on] Horace Samuel for the defence promising participation expenses please elucidate acceptability possibility."

Horace Samuel was a highly regarded English barrister with a sound knowledge of the practice of law in Palestine. He had served in the Jewish Legion with Jabotinsky during World War I and had then conducted a legal practice in Palestine for several years before returning to England. Samuel wrote prolifically about Palestine under the Mandate, among other topics. His books on Palestine include *Beneath the Whitewash: A Critical Analysis of the Report of the Commission on the Palestine Disturbances of August 1929* and *Unholy Memories of the Holy Land*. A partially completed manuscript of the Stavsky trial, for which he could find no publisher, is in the Jabotinsky Institute in Tel Aviv.

Sioma responded immediately to Jabotinsky's cable. He had seen Samuel that day, but Samuel was not certain that he still had the right to appear in Palestinian courts or whether he would be available during September when the trial was expected to start. He undertook to let Sioma know within a few weeks whether he could take the case. During their conversation, Samuel had told Sioma that he regarded the cases against the accused that were known to him to be so "sketchy" that he doubted whether anyone could be indicted on the evidence. But Samuel added a rider. He knew from his practice at the bar in Palestinian courts of cases that had been brought on political grounds that had resulted in guilty verdicts despite the tendering of inadequate evidence by the prosecution.[2]

On July 24, Sioma cabled Jabotinsky in Warsaw that the barrister had not yet been able to establish his right to appear and whether he would be free of his other commitments. It was not until September 18 that Sioma was able to inform Jabotinsky that Samuel would probably be able to go to Palestine, but that his fee would be £1,000 for the trip plus £200 per month for the length of his stay. This was a substantial sum of money that the Revisionists did not have. The letter also contained Samuel's comments on the weakness of the prosecution's case that had been submitted for the committal hearing. Although a cable had been received from Palestine urging that the barrister's presence was urgently required there, his response had been that he would only travel to Palestine if there was a committal for trial.

On October 5, Sioma wrote to Jabotinsky that he had seen Samuel, who had been consulting English experts on medical jurisprudence, and outlined to Sioma how he would conduct the defense. The next day, Sioma wrote to Jabotinsky again. He had seen Samuel on three occasions in the last few days, most recently with a Dr. Danziger, who had been at the hospital when Arlosoroff was admitted. Danziger had been able to give evidence of the track of the bullet that had led to Arlosoroff's death.

A day later, Sioma wrote that he had spent the evening before and that day with Danziger and had brought Samuel into the discussion. He had also brought Colonel Patterson into the conference. Colonel J. H. Patterson, DSO, had been the commander of both the Zion Mule Corps at Gallipoli and the Jewish Legion, which was a part of the British army during its campaign in Palestine. Patterson was a committed supporter

---

2   There were no jury trials in Palestine under the Mandate. Two Palestinian judges, sometimes with a British judge, sat in district courts. Capital cases were heard in the assize court by two British and two Palestinian judges, and the Supreme Court was presided over by a British judge (Horace B. Samuel, *Unholy Memories of the Holy Land* [London: The Hogarth Press, 1930], 175).

of the Zionist cause and a friend of Jabotinsky's from the Legion days. Sioma wrote to Jabotinsky that Patterson intended to leave England but would offer free advice before he left. Sioma wrote that because of the movement's financial straits he had felt "uncomfortable" about not being able to offer Patterson a fee.

Five days later, Sioma reported that Samuel had been working very hard on the case and that he had spent all of three days reading the reports in the *Palestine Post*. On October 10, 1933, Sioma wrote a three-page letter to Jabotinsky that was mainly concerned with the impoverished state of the movement. He was unable to either establish an office for himself or to provide office accommodation and a secretary for Patterson.

In between these involvements Sioma attended a conference "for the Relief of German Jewry" that was held in the West End of London on October 29. Admission was "by ticket only, not transferable" and Sioma's ticket was labeled as a Delegate. In red ink, Sioma crossed out "Delegate" and wrote "Expert." Sioma made no reference to the meeting in his correspondence.[3]

In a letter in December 1933, Sioma advised Jabotinsky that he had interviewed two men who had been head of the British CID in Palestine. One of them, Major Broadhurst, told Sioma that he was keen to help because he was absolutely certain that the three men charged were innocent. Despite this certainty, he was aware from his sources in Palestine that the British administration in Palestine was desperately keen to obtain a conviction. Broadhurst offered to go to Palestine to help if his fare and out-of-pocket expenses were covered. The other man, referred to by Sioma just as "Leach," offered a written "opinion" of the case that suggested the innocence of the accused.

Yet again, Sioma told Jabotinsky about the financial difficulties that he faced. Not only was there no money for these two men, but he was unable to send Samuel his monthly fee of £200 that had been due on the first of the month. Sioma's first letter for the New Year, January 4, 1934, was short

---

3   No active plan to rescue German Jews was undertaken in Britain until after the Nuremburg Laws were passed in September 1935.

and on the same topic. Samuel was now due for another £200 by January 23, and Sioma had "no idea where the money [was] to come from."

In his letter to Jabotinsky two weeks later there is a tantalizing reference to copies of correspondence received from both Horace Samuel and Winston Churchill that Sioma had sent on to Jabotinsky. As no copies were attached to the file we do not know what was in them. There are a number of references to Sioma's discussions with Churchill in his letters to Jabotinsky during the trials. There is no record of these meetings in either Churchill's biography or in Gilbert's book on Churchill's relationship with Zionism and with Jews.[4]

In another letter to Jabotinsky, Sioma reported that he was frantically busy looking after Haskel's business affairs in London, "and on the other hand Churchill takes up a lot of my time."

In a later letter in January 1934, Sioma wrote:

> I enclose a letter just received from Horace [Samuel]. I have communicated with Churchill and asked him to send me the information that Horace requires. I shall forward Churchill's Report and your letter in the usual way, in two sealed envelopes, so as to make certain that it will not be interfered with. You will see from Horace's letter that he wants money.

We do not know what was in either document.

Sioma flew to Paris for discussions with Jabotinsky on several occasions. During a visit that he made in October 1933, Sioma raised the issue of the financial plight of the movement in England and pressed Jabotinsky to come to London to raise some badly needed funds. Jabotinsky was renowned as an orator throughout the Jewish community in Europe and in Palestine, and for his ability to touch both the heart and the purse strings of his audiences. But his letter is an insight into the man behind the public person.

---

4   Martin Gilbert, *Winston S. Churchill*, vol. 5, *The Prophet of Truth, 1922–1939* (London: Heinemann, 1976), and companion vol. 5, part 3, *Documents: The Coming of War, 1936–1939* (London: Heinemann, 1982), and *Churchill and the Jews: A Lifelong Friendship* (London: Simon and Schuster, 2007).

Dear Solomon L'vovich,

Forgive me that I did not reply immediately to the question you posed for me. It is a very painful one, doubly painful: speeches, they are very difficult for me, and especially in London, my entire political intuition rebels against them. Although I feel well, my health will not cope with a new series of speeches; so I have established a rule for myself – this year up until the summer – neither here nor anywhere else, no speeches. If it is necessary to say something at a small function or in a private conversation, that is not a speech, and does not cause the stress of a formal lecture. I am already committed to several formal lectures. In Warsaw it will be necessary to sell myself as a circus to raise funds rather than just being a tourist; and in Antwerp, I have promised to arrive there in time for the elections.

But the most important thing is that I have had an extensive experience with public speaking in England. I simply do not want to make speeches in Whitechapel. It is not worthwhile to use me for recruiting a hundred additional members. But in the case of the West End – it is necessary for you to investigate who will come. I am confident that some of our people will come but most will just be ordinary members of the Jewish community. In London I have never yet drawn a Jewish crowd similar to the ones that come in Poland, Romania, and even in Berlin and Paris on grand occasions. There the cream of Jewish society attends. If you can be sure that it will now be otherwise, it will be necessary for you to establish this to my satisfaction. Therefore I request, in the strongest terms, that you put off this question entirely. For a luncheon or simply for a meeting with whomever you want, I will arrive in response to your first summons. A trip or even three trips will not tire me. But a public presentation in the West End has to be arranged at a time when you are confident of the interest of those circles. Their absence would diminish the effect of the occasion. Be patient, my dear fellow, let's not hurry.

Hugs to you all.[5] Yours, V. E.

---

5   This was for Sioma's family, his wife Edna and their two children, Naomi and

There is another insight into how this renowned orator felt about speechmaking. In a response to a series of questions that had been put to him in 1929, Jabotinsky wrote:

> I prepare speeches in detail, even to the jokes, pauses and nuances. Only then do I succeed. I prevail only in the Russian language. Only through it can I express everything until the last thought, but this does not mean that it is easier for me to speak or lecture in Russian. Perhaps, on the contrary, because of the abundance of words which I have at my command in Russian, I have difficulty in choosing the correct words. In French and Italian I sometimes find myself in difficulties, but not in other languages.
>
> I do not like to change from language to language while speaking. This tires me in a speech. I find it much easier to speak in public than to converse.[6]

In a long letter of January 15, 1934, Sioma recounted details of a meeting of the Actions Committee of the World Zionist Organization, of which he was a member. Although Sioma set out a number of issues that had been reported at the meeting, the most significant was that the Mandate government had appeared to have hardened its stance toward Jews. The high commissioner had announced a further limitation of Jewish immigration to Palestine in a conversation with leaders of the Arab community, rather than informing the Jews first. Several members of the Actions Committee, including Weizmann, defended the British administration. Weizmann's view was that the British government and the British people should be told that Jews believed that their promises would be kept, and that it was his opinion that the Jews in Palestine who fought the police and threw stones at British embassies would destroy any goodwill that still existed in Britain.[7]

Carmel. Jabotinsky was a frequent visitor to the Jacobi home when he was in London.

6   Published in the South African *Jewish Herald* on the tenth anniversary of Jabotinsky's death, July 21, 1950 (page 15).

7   This probably refers to a large demonstration in Tel Aviv on December 9, 1933,

Sioma added a P.S. to the letter. He enclosed a copy of a cable that he had just received from Palestine that read: "Two arrested Arabs confessed to murder Arlosoroff and attempted rape." It was commonly assumed that these two Arabs had accosted the couple on the beach and either raped or attempted to rape Mrs. Arlosoroff. Her husband had attempted to intervene and was shot. Although this created great excitement at the time, when the trial finally commenced in May 1934, the police prosecutor rejected the confession of one of the Arabs and, extraordinarily, was allowed by the judge to refuse to have him called to the stand. When Stavsky was convicted, the chief rabbi in Palestine issued a statement that was signed by 108 other rabbis that they swore "before God that…Stavsky is completely innocent.…"

There are two postscripts to this story. The first is that when Stavsky and Rosenblatt were to be called up to the Torah in a synagogue to celebrate their acquittal, a contingent of Histadrut members invaded the synagogue and broke up the service. The second postscript is that Avraham Stavsky was killed by gunfire at the ship *Altalena* from the shore on June 21, 1948. Stavsky had successfully run the British blockade bringing illegal immigrants to Palestine on thirteen previous occasions. But on board the *Altalena* there were not only nine hundred immigrants, but also five thousand rifles and 270 machine guns and a number of volunteers all destined for the Irgun (the Revisionist armed wing). Although the Irgun had officially been incorporated into the Israel Defense Forces (IDF) three weeks earlier, those on the ship now defied demands from Ben-Gurion that the arms be handed over to the IDF. From its first landfall on the coast, the *Altalena* sailed on to Tel Aviv. There, on Ben-Gurion's orders, the IDF fired upon the ship with machine guns from the shore. The ship was set on fire, and Stavsky was killed by machine-gun bullets as he swam ashore.

---

protesting against the hunting of "illegal" tourists. In an effort to stop Jews from arriving in Palestine on tourist visas and then "disappearing," the police hunted down suspected "illegal" arrivals. The British opposition to the issue of tourist visas made entry for Zionist supporters as tourists extremely difficult.

CHAPTER 13

THE JORDANIA EXPERIMENT

During their visit to America in 1926, both Sioma and Jabotinsky had been impressed by the achievement of the American company Judea Industrial Corporation. This firm had a subsidiary life insurance company, Judea, which invested its reserves in Palestine. Both Sioma and Jabotinsky were enthusiastic about the Judea Corporation, particularly its life insurance company. Sioma was so impressed with the Judea Corporation as a whole that he asked Jabotinsky to buy shares in the company on his behalf. His order was for one hundred shares at $37.50 per share for shares that had a par value of twenty-five dollars. In addition to that purchase, he reserved the right to buy an additional nineteen hundred shares at the same price. It would seem that these shares were reserved for other Revisionists if they wished to take them up. There is no further reference to this share investment in correspondence or Sioma's records.

In 1927, a number of Jabotinsky's letters to Sioma referred to discussions that Sioma was holding with an unnamed British insurance company in the hope that it would enable the Revisionists to establish their own insurance arm. It appears that these negotiations were unsuccessful.

But Jabotinsky was not to be put off the insurance concept. To gain some experience in the field for himself, he accepted an offer from the

Judea Life Insurance Company in mid-1928 to become a vice president of the company and managing director of the Palestine operation. He accepted the offer despite warnings that the Palestine operations of the Judea were not squeaky clean. Then Jabotinsky found that there were problems involved in him obtaining a visa to work in Palestine. His activities and conviction in Palestine in earlier years were counted against him. He had encountered similar problems earlier in the year when he had been refused entry to England. Then he had needed the influence of his powerful friends in the British government and English society in England in order to receive a visa. Now, the Immigration Department of the Palestine government told him that permission for his entry to Palestine would be granted only if he undertook not to engage in any political activity. He had to use his influential friends to have this proviso overturned.

Jabotinsky finally arrived in Jerusalem in October 1928, but his stay did not last long. He left to attend conferences in Europe two months later and was there for several months before going back to Palestine. He left for Europe again in July 1929 to attend the Sixteenth Zionist Congress in Zurich. Afterwards he went on a speaking tour of South Africa. While he was there he was informed from London that he was barred from returning to Palestine because of a "seditious speech" that he had made in Jerusalem in the previous December. This ended, among other consequences, his involvement with the Judea Life Insurance Company.

Adding to Sioma's favorable impression of the Judea Corporation and its insurance arm, during his trips to Australia he had admired the activities of the Australian life assurance company the Australian Mutual Provident Society (AMP). The AMP used its funds to invest widely in Australian agricultural and industrial enterprises, and provided mortgage loans for domestic and commercial properties. On his return to England from his journeys around the world for ORT-OZE, Sioma resumed the search he had started in 1927 for a suitable insurance vehicle in England.

In mid-1932, Sioma achieved success. A life insurance company, Jordania Society Limited, was registered in July with a capital of one hundred pounds. In Sioma's archives is a share certificate for eight hundred one-shilling shares in the company paid to sixpence each. This involved him with an investment of just over sixteen pounds. It took another six months to finalize arrangements for Jordania to commence business. On January 25, 1933, the financial page of the *Times* in London carried a subhead that read, "A Jewish Assurance Enterprise." The column outlined a scheme whereby a newly incorporated company, Jordania Society Limited, had been established to undertake life insurance in the United Kingdom on the basis that policies would be underwritten by the Royal Exchange Assurance until premiums reached an annual figure of £17,500. Thereafter, a new life insurance company would be incorporated by Jordania to take over the funds and the risks from the Royal Exchange. Part of the funds would be invested in "safe" investments in Palestine. Sioma was named managing director of Jordania, which was to be an investment venture of the Revisionists. In Sioma's CV, dated 1933, he included "Appointed Managing Director of the Jordania Society Limited from 1ˢᵗ December 1932, with a salary of £800 per annum and Director's Fees of £50." This was a very handsome salary for the time. The chairman of the company was the distinguished Lieutenant Colonel J. H. Levey, who was also chairman of the executive of ORT-OZE in England.

But Jordania faced an established competitor for Jewish life insurance business in the British market. Preparations for Jordania's launch would have been common knowledge in the City of London. Two days before the Jordania announcement in the *Times* there was a double column advertisement in the *Jewish Chronicle* inserted by the Jewish National Fund (JNF) Assurance Department. The advertisement was directed at the Jewish community to remind them that for the past year the JNF had an arrangement with the Prudential Assurance Company that would benefit settlement in Palestine. Three days later, the *Times* published a note that it had received a letter from the Zionist Federation asking the paper to inform its readers of its activities.

Notwithstanding his late entry into this market and competition for the same customers, Sioma went about publicizing Jordania throughout England and Scotland in the manner that he had developed so successfully for ORT-OZE. He organized meetings in the provinces in the centers of

Jewish communities in England and Scotland as well as in London. He spoke in Newcastle, Manchester, and Glasgow. A full-page advertisement in the *Jewish Chronicle* on June 9, 1933, announced that Jordania, in addition to life insurance, was now offering all manner of general insurance products: fire, burglary, motor vehicle, and house insurance. The advertisement carried recommendations from Lord Allenby, Lord Lytton, and several other non-Jewish peers of the realm.

Then Jordania found itself in competition for the same market from yet another Jewish enterprise. This one was to support Jewish religious institutions throughout the world. The vehicle was another British life assurance company, the Eagle Star.

Sioma inserted a number of advertisements for Jordania in the *Jewish Chronicle* in October, November, and December 1933. From the middle of 1933, Sioma was managing the affairs of the Revisionist Party in London and had little time to devote to the Jordania. Between December 1933 and February 1935, there does not seem to have been any publicity for Jordania in the London Jewish press. On February 8, 1935, the *Jewish Chronicle* published a large advertisement for the company. Sioma was still named as managing director. The advertisement was opposite a single small paragraph "interview" with Sioma. Both the interview and the advertisement appeared in the last section of the paper, on page 37. Later that month, Sioma was forced to invest more capital in the company. On February 27, 1935, he was issued with four hundred shares of one pound each and ten shares paid only to one shilling each. This seems to have been Jordania's swan song. In a letter that Jabotinsky wrote to Sioma from the United States on March 23, 1935, he "regretted the bad state" of Jordania. Sioma's letter to which Jabotinsky was responding has not survived. Nor, it would seem, did the insurance company.

CHAPTER 14

LONDON, 1933 AND 1934

There are no indications that Sioma ever received an adequate salary from the Revisionist movement. This would also be true of all of its workers, including Jabotinsky. The movement lacked both capital and material assets, and consequently was chronically short of funds. Membership fees were low and the generation of additional funds relied heavily on Jabotinsky's public appeals.

In 1933, Sioma had three sources of income that enabled him to provide services to the Revisionists, and these sources afforded him and his family a comfortable lifestyle. In all the correspondence there is no reference to the Revisionists paying for Sioma's expenses or reimbursing him for them. He often flew to Paris to meet with Jabotinsky and his executive, and he traveled overseas for the UZR on a number of occasions. There is no indication in the surviving correspondence of how these expenses were met.

Sioma seems to have had a source of income from ORT-OZE, although it is not known how much, or on what basis this was paid. Whether he was paid a retainer or a percentage of his fund-raising is not recorded. We have seen that after his return to England he continued raising funds for them throughout the UK.

His second source of income was as managing director of the Jordania insurance company.

Finally, a letter that Sioma wrote to Jabotinsky on June 22, 1933, contains a reference to a company that Haskel was floating on the London Stock Exchange. It was not named in the letter but it is known from later correspondence that it was Kenya Consolidated Goldfields Limited, a company that had been incorporated in Kenya in February 1933. Sioma was referred to as Haskel's London agent by others, a position in which he would have been paid, but it is uncertain whether he was also appointed a director of the gold mining company.

These three sources of income enabled him to afford to send his wife, Edna, and their two children on a trip to Australia to visit her family in 1934.

Although Sioma remained a committed Revisionist throughout his life, there are indications that he did not enjoy the cut and thrust of the politics that were played within the Zionist movement. It was mentioned in the previous chapter that Sioma had attended a meeting of the Actions Committee (AC) of the World Zionist Organization. He expressed his reaction to the internal politics that bedeviled the Zionist movement in a letter that he sent to Dr. Jacob Hoffman.[1] The letter gives an insight into Sioma's character and his reaction to the mainstream Zionist movement. The meeting had been called by issuing a circular letter rather than calling a regular meeting of the committee.

Sioma's letter read:

> The chairman opened the meeting and then called on Brodetsky[2] to deliver his report. Before he commenced, I got up and demanded the floor. I asked Locker[3] point blank, whether a regular meeting of the AC is going to be called. He replied by

---

1   Hoffman was a longtime supporter of Jabotinsky and the Revisionist movement. A Latvian, he was part of the group that had established Betar in 1922. At the time of Sioma's letter, Hoffman was a member of the Executive Committee of the World Union of Zionist Revisionists.

2   Professor Selig Brodetsky, a member of the London Zionist executive.

3   Berl Locker, another member of the London Zionist executive.

stating that all information concerning this meeting was circulated among members of the AC, but financial and other considerations prevented them from calling a formal meeting. Again, I demanded a definite statement of when the AC is to meet. Locker answered that he could not add anything to his previous reply. I said that it seemed to be an indication that the original statement issued by the executive that the AC will be called in March or April is not going to be complied with.

Having finished the question of the AC, I read out the telegram regarding the recent events in Haifa,[4] and I demanded that the executive submit to the meeting all the information they have with regard to these events, and that the meeting deal with the question. Both Brodetsky and Locker objected saying they had no information whatsoever, and that the meeting was called for another purpose and that this was a manoeuvre on my part to create a panicky atmosphere. As far as they were concerned, they must treat the information as a pure rumour. I sharply protested, saying that in submitting the telegram I was not acting as an individual, but as a representative of my party…but Locker and Brodetsky demanded that the question shall not be gone into and accordingly, the chairman ruled me out of order. I protested and demanded that my protest be entered in the minutes.

I felt like leaving the meeting, slamming the door behind me, but then decided that they would be only too happy to see me go, and consequently remained.

Weizmann spoke to the meeting in his usual strain, of one goat, one brick, one house, ten houses, one hundred houses – that is how the country is being built. We must tell the British government and the British people that we believe that they will keep their word; that we have a community of interests both spiritual and material. He

---

4　Histadrut employees in the city had attacked workers on two building sites being constructed by Revisionist contractors, and had then attacked other Revisionist sites.

dwelt on the madness of those who wished to destroy sympathetic understanding between us, and almost the only great power that is friendly to us. "By fighting police and by throwing stones into British embassies, they will destroy whatever favourable public opinion there exists in this country; but if we proceed quietly at the present tempo we may create in the next years, a Jewish community of half a million souls."

I felt so disgusted that I had no intention to speak at all. But when Brodetsky asked me whether I wished to say anything I obviously accepted the challenge. I told them frankly that Brodetsky's report was void of any information or any plan, that it was hard to understand why they had called this meeting; that instead of criticizing the boys who threw stones into the windows of the British embassies, they should put themselves in these boys' place, with Palestine their only hope, being denied to them by the British administration. I asked them to put themselves in the place a Revisionist who attends such a meeting as this: a Revisionist, who knows what he wants and who believes he knows the way of forcing the gates of Palestine, to be opened for the Jewish people. When such a Revisionist comes to this meeting and listens to a report like the one submitted by Brodetsky, a report which demonstrates the executive's utter helplessness and shows the position as void of any hope, how can they expect such a Revisionist to change his views one iota. I asked them what they had done…to stop the government's new methods of catching illegal immigrants and what they had done to protest against the legalization of the Arab demonstration on January the 16th, and so on…half a dozen questions.

I must say that on the whole they treated me with respect. Although I spoke for ten minutes only, they devoted more than half their replies to me. Brodetsky…went into a long excited speech about the damage which the Revisionist demonstration in Palestine had done to the goodwill towards the Jewish people in this country.

Finally in reply to my question of why in such critical times the Executive did not consult with other leading members of other Jewish groups living in London, Brodetsky said that there were no important leaders in London other than the Revisionists, but that their ideology and methods were so different that consulting with them would be of no use.

Ten days later Sioma wrote a long letter to Jabotinsky in a similar vein.

The Jewish National Fund people are getting on my nerves, and I have to divide my energy between working up the Jordania and fighting them in their campaign against the Jordania in order to protect their own insurance interests.

Horowitz is a very unpleasant fellow. I personally would not have any dealings with him. This is not only because he is a member of the National JNF Fund Committee and that he visited various members of the Advisory Boards (that I had set up) in the provinces trying to induce them to resign from the Jordania, but he is an unpleasant fellow.

I enclose a copy of the letter I received from Horace Samuel, and of my reply, and a copy of the letter which Churchill received from Samuel and his reply. I also enclose Churchill's report and his covering letter to it.

There is now quite a crisis in the Jewish Telegraph Agency (JTA) office. The manager tried to stop my statement about the meeting of the members of the Actions Committee after I had given it to be published, as he had made arrangements with Locker and Brodetsky that nothing should be published about that meeting except their statement. So I told him to go to blazes, and my statement was published. However, the crisis is on.

In an ill-conceived plan, Jabotinsky had sought to enlist support from the British government to recognize the moral and humanitarian right, according to the terms of the Mandate, for the Jews of eastern Europe to immigrate to Palestine. The plan was to collect a large number of signatures to several petitions. One was addressed to the king of England, another to the British Parliament and to the prime ministers of the states in which the petitioners lived. By 1934 the Revisionists had attracted some six hundred thousand signatures to the petitions from around the world, but largely from their supporters in Poland and eastern Europe. It was ignored by the British government. Under British law a petition to the crown or Parliament is recognized if it is signed only by British subjects. It further divided the Revisionists from the World Union of General Zionists, who felt that the petition would create an impression that world Jewry was anti-British, and that this would be counterproductive to Jewish interests in Palestine.

Sioma had been shown the wording of the petition when he was in Paris. When he saw the final wording of the petition, he complained in a letter to Jabotinsky that his opinions were not accepted.

> I see that the text of the Petition to the King is worded exactly in the way I found it when I was in Paris, notwithstanding the fact that you agreed with some of my remarks particularly the one objecting to our saying that "Our people are successfully building the Jewish national home." Why have you decided not to change the words?

In the same letter, he grumbled about his workload.

> It is humanly impossible for me to take upon myself any more work at the present moment. I shall be unable to do justice to the Petition movement. Haskel takes up lots of my time for things of his own connected with Palestine. I have to do it – I cannot help myself – work for him, draft his letters, and discuss at great length matters that affect his investigations in Palestine. On the other hand Churchill takes up a lot of my time. Add this to the fight I have to conduct for the Jordanian [*sic*: Jordania] and my continuous battle in the JTA, and you will see there is very little time left.

A JTA Bulletin on February 23, 1934, was devoted to the Revisionist "Petition Movement." It referred to a statement issued that day by "Mr. S. Y. Jacobi, Chairman of the Executive of the Revisionist World Organization." Sioma's statement said that the Petition was not directed against the policy of the British government, but that it was the right of any group to petition a government to oppose a specific policy that was against the group's interests.

In the same month, Sioma wrote to Jabotinsky that

> Commencing last week, Miss Meyerheim is working for us only half a day. If you consider it advisable to engage Mr. Faber, about whom I wrote to you, at a small salary of let us say £2/10/ per a week to work on the Petition and the boycott,[5] then it is worth keeping the office going. Otherwise, I would close it down because the telephone expense and typist are just not justified at the present rate of work.

Another letter, dated February 7, 1934, discusses logistics:

> I do not know what Dr. Schwartzman[6] actually wants. I feel that he is publicity hungry and he would like to do something and fight somebody and as far as I am concerned he can have a free field. On Sunday week, there is a general meeting of all Revisionists in this country, which is being called on notice of invitation drafted by Schwartzman and a copy of which I enclose.
>
> I wish he would take over the office and the work in England, and leave me with just two things only – negotiations with our friend [Haskel] and the Arlosoroff business. If you wish you can offer it to him.

The next day Sioma wrote again:

> Under the influence of your letter of yesterday, and the accusation that I struck you a blow right on the temple,[7] I went to this morning to see our friend [Haskel] and told him the story exactly as it happened, and got him to give me another £150 which I instructed the bank to remit to you.

---

5   The boycott of trade with Germany.
6   Schwartzman had been a member of the Grossman group but later switched allegiance to Sioma.
7   A metaphor for strong criticism.

It was not exactly a pleasant task, but he is under a certain obligation to me in connection with some work that I have been doing for him in regard to his holdings in Palestine, hence I was in a position to influence him. However, I am not going to approach him again with regard to money matters. Please write to him and thank him for the £250 he has given for the case this month.

Chaim Weizmann sent the following letter to Harry Sacher[8] in London:

You will remember hearing from Shertok[9] a few weeks ago with regard to Landau's intention of transferring his 49 per cent of the shares in the *Palestine Post* to Michael Haskel, and thus [transferring the newspaper] to complete and intransigent Revisionist control.

There are one or two things which have recently been brought to my notice in the same connection. It appears that a determined effort is being made through the Haskel director in London, Mr. Jacoby [*sic*], to influence the policy of the JTA. He has lately, however, been making an effort to use the JTA for purposes of Revisionist propaganda and publicity and a similar tendency is visible from Jerusalem in the messages of the newly appointed correspondence of the JTA there. I thought I ought to pass on this information to you. I need hardly say that I shall very greatly appreciate any advice or suggestion. You may be good enough to offer as to the best way of handling it.

Jabotinsky advised Sioma on March 6, 1934, that the executive of the UZR, which sat in Paris, had selected him as one of six delegates to the

---

8   Harry Sacher (1881–1971) was an Englishman who became a journalist and author after studying law. He met Weizmann soon after his arrival in Manchester and they became close friends. In 1920 he settled in Palestine and practiced law, but returned to London in 1930. He had married one of the Marks family of the Marks and Spencer retail group and joined the company on his return. He was an influential figure in London Jewish circles.

9   Moshe Shertok (later Sharett, 1894–1965), Israel's second prime minister (1953–1955). In 1933 he was head of the Jewish Agency in Palestine. A staunch supporter of Ben-Gurion's faction, he was an antagonist of the Revisionists.

Zionist Executive Assembly in Palestine. The assembly, which was part of a ten-day meeting of the Zionist General Council in Jerusalem, was to be followed by a meeting of the Actions Committee of the Zionist Council. Sioma was asked to attend a meeting of the UZR executive committee in Paris on his way to Palestine. Jabotinsky wrote two letters to Sioma while he was in Paris, giving him instructions to follow at the assembly in Jerusalem. In particular, one letter contained the text of a statement prepared by the executive committee that he was to read to the conference as the UZR first speaker.

The reaction of the general council to the message delivered by Sioma was the subject of a report by the correspondent of the London *Jewish Chronicle* in Jerusalem.

A minor sensation during the outset of the general debate was the written statement on behalf all the Revisionist party, read out by Mr. S. Y. Jacobi of England. It met with a rebuke on the part of the Chairman, and the Prosecutor for the Court of Honour demanded a copy of the document. The Chairman said that parts of the statement showed disrespect to the General Council.

The statement started by picturing the present position within the Zionist Movement as having arisen from a decision of the Zionist Executive to close the gates of Palestine to the B'rith Trumpeldor [Betar] members, one of the largest of all Jewish youth organisations, accompanied by a second decision the meaning of which is the expulsion of the Betarim[10] from all posts within the Zionist organisation.

The statement hinted somewhat strongly that there was a sort of dictatorship over the Zionist organisation by the Labour Party, which was accused together with the Executive of having "endorsed class warfare and aspired towards class dictatorship, a political situation bristling with menace in connection with the legislative body to be created here on the basis of an anti-Zionist

---

10   Members of Betar.

majority," and which failed to fight those dangers adequately; and further accusing the Executive of undue measures in preventing "the political attack of the masses – a project of a world petition."

The report of the statement seemed to be an out and out flouting of the authority of the Zionist Organisation and of its Executive which, as was pointed out during the debate, had been elected by a Congress majority. Although the statement expresses the concerns of the Revisionists over the character which recent factional disputes have assumed, it does not hesitate to lay the blame entirely on the other party; and certainly the tone of the declaration was not conceived in any conciliatory spirit, if that were at all the intention.

The *Chronicle* reported on a subsequent meeting of the Actions Committee at which

> proceedings were initiated in the Congress Court against the Revisionists on the ground of a declaration read out there by Mr. Jacobi, the Chairman of the Revisionist Party Council, containing statements considered incompatible with membership of the Zionist Organization. The Court is to establish whether the declaration does not involve the self-expulsion of the Revisionist faction from the Zionist Organization.

The *Chronicle* also reported on a Revisionist meeting at the Eden Theatre which "was under heavy police guard." It was attended by 230 delegates and over a thousand guests. The meeting adopted resolutions for the compulsory arbitration of labor disputes with employers and the establishment of neutral labor exchanges because the left-wing bias of the present exchange denied jobs to workers who belonged to a Revisionist organization.

There are five letters from Jabotinsky addressed to Sioma in Tel Aviv dating from March 23 to April 9. Two refer directly to the developing situation in Palestine. One was an instruction to Sioma to inform the UZR Committee in Palestine that the executive committee in Paris had authorized Sioma to determine the resignation process from the congress, if that was the course to be followed. The other letter advised Sioma that the Paris office had received a report from their group in Palestine stating that, with only one exception, they did not wish to resign from the main Zionist body.

There is a gap of one month in Jabotinsky's letters to Sioma until May 2, when Sioma is back in London.

Sioma frequently engaged in public debate with opponents of the Revisionist movement through the medium of letters to the editor of Jewish newspapers. In the July 13, 1934, issue of the London-based *Jewish Chronicle*, he wrote an impassioned letter in response to an article published in that paper which put forward the view that Herzl did not believe in a Jewish state. In response, Sioma quoted several written comments by Herzl, taken from his diary and autobiographical notes, proving that Herzl did believe that in due course a Jewish state would be established as a result of the First Zionist Congress held in 1897. This question was one of the central points at issue among the Revisionists, who spoke loudly and fervently in favor of a Jewish state in Palestine. The Zionist Organization opted for the wording of the Balfour Declaration of a home for the Jews in Palestine in the belief that this would not antagonize the British mandatory authority or the Arabs as much as the demand for a state would do.

On August 8, 1934, Sioma wrote a densely typed six-page letter to the Glasgow Jewish newspaper, the *Jewish Echo*. The letter, more than sixteen hundred words in length, was in response to recent references in the paper concerning the conflict that had arisen in Palestine between the Jewish Agency and Betar over the issue of immigration certificates to Palestine. Sioma explained "the essence of the conflict" in these terms. The Jewish Agency as the tool of the Zionist executive was known to discriminate against applications for immigration certificates to Palestine from Betar members. In order to bypass this stranglehold on the issue of immigrations certificates, Revisionist settlers in Palestine had taken advantage of a little-known regulation in the Mandate that allowed them to apply as individual settlers for immigration permits for their potential workers. In a nasty response, the Jewish Agency was able to influence the mandatory authority to deprive Betar of all rights for immigration permits. The Jewish Court of Honor in Jerusalem rejected the Revisionist appeal against the Zionist executive's move. Sioma's letter finished by calling on the public to give its "closest attention to this misuse of an official function."

In early September 1934, Edna left England by ship with their two daughters to visit her family in Melbourne. The journey took a month. They stayed in Melbourne for five months. In a letter that Sioma wrote to Edna while she was in Melbourne, he complained about his problems dealing with Haskel.

> He is evasive and difficult, and sometimes impossible. Yesterday I had actually decided to resign and let him cook his own stew, but the thought came to me that it would be unfair to you and to the kiddies. And I held my hand. However, I did leave his flat abruptly and did not return until late in the evening, when we both were to go to the Samuels for supper. Over dinner Haskel was talking the whole time. I could have screamed. This morning I demonstratively did not call on him.
>
> We have moved into Haskel's new offices. They are quite nice, and will be very comfortable, after he has gone to South Africa.
>
> Anderson of the Royal Exchange telephoned to me and asked me to call. I did. He told me that there are renewed hopes to have the mortgage bank loan [on the Jacobi home] arranged. Let's hope there will be a favourable resolution. I will then not be dependent on Haskel's whimsy.
>
> I am kept busy by Haskel until late at night. On Friday I told him that you will need a new fur coat next winter, could he help in getting somebody to select it for you? He asked what price I was prepared to pay and I answered about £100. He said you could get a mink coat for that money and offered to select the skins for you to store them. Hal[11] did not think that storage was a good idea and then suggested that he had in Melbourne a made up mink coat of

---

11   Hal Saulwick, Edna's brother-in-law, who was married to Edna's sister Marjorie. Hal was a Melbourne furrier who often traveled to England and Europe to buy furs.

very good quality for about £180 Australian which is £140 English. He would write to you by airmail and you can inspect the coat and take it if you like it. I shall then send them a draft of the money. We left it at that.

Whatever happens I will make this year at least a £1,000 more than we need to cover the ordinary budget. We might as well take advantage of it and get you a coat that will serve you a lifetime. It is better than getting a car, and you will enjoy it more. Of course, the pity is you won't be able to show off in it in Melbourne.

On December 21, 1934, the *Chronicle* published yet another letter from Sioma. This one concerned the disagreement between the Revisionists and the general Zionists on the question of the Transfer agreement. The Revisionists were still fighting for the introduction of a worldwide boycott of German goods while the Zionists were prepared to deal with the Nazis. Sioma wrote that he had been a delegate representing the Revisionists to the World Jewish Economic Conference that was held in Amsterdam in July 1933 to discuss the boycott, but no decision was reached.

CHAPTER 15

JABOTINSKY, BEN-GURION, JACOBI, AND THE NEW ZIONIST ORGANIZATION

As an indication of the ill-will that existed on the part of Ben-Gurion toward Jabotinsky and the Revisionists in February 1933, Ben-Gurion delivered his most violent diatribe against them. He accused the Revisionists of strikebreaking and confusingly labeled their movement as both a "Hitlerist danger…and [like] the Communists in Moscow." He called Jabotinsky "Vladimir Hitler." Ben-Gurion spoke in terms of the struggle with both the Revisionists and with the "fascist" employers who gave work to members of Betar. After Arlosoroff's murder, Ben-Gurion was quick to condemn Stavsky as a loyal Revisionist "standing under the supreme and exclusive orders of Vladimir Jabotinsky."

Notwithstanding the failure of its purpose, the petition movement, measured in terms of the numbers supporting it, showed the depth of Revisionist support. Jabotinsky was buoyed by the result of the vote, and despite the enmity that had existed between the parties, he wrote to the Labor Party in Palestine in July 1934 suggesting a peace conference. The intention of the meeting, he suggested, would be to present a united front to the mandatory authority to ease its restrictions on Jewish immigration to Palestine in view of the growing threat to Jews in Europe.[1] Although Jabotinsky received no formal response to his letter, the Labor leaders initiated talks with all the other major political parties in Palestine – the General Zionists, Mizrachi, the new Jewish State Party, and the Revisionists. The Revisionists were represented by Sioma and Schwartzman, another member of the NZO London executive, at a meeting of all the parties that took place in October 1934.

Nothing concrete came out of the conference, but Pinhas Rutenberg, who as the head of the Palestine Electric Corporation was more interested in the peaceful development of the economy in Palestine, which was being hindered by the warring factions, arranged a meeting in London between Jabotinsky and Ben-Gurion. Rutenberg had known both men for twenty years and had remained on friendly terms with both.

The first meeting took place on October 10, 1934, in London. The talks lasted for more than three weeks. Ben-Gurion and Jabotinsky issued a statement on October 26 that was a pact to establish what might be described as normal adversarial relations between political adversaries. Each party was to refrain from "party warfare which is outside the limits of political and ideological discussion." Both men wanted to avoid the demeaning levels of violence that had taken place between the two groups, particularly in Palestine. Therefore, the statement continued that each party would "apply the most rigorous means to eradicate acts of terror and violence." The pact was intended to exclude the violent disruption of party meetings, the libel or slander of each other, and an agreement not to collaborate with governments against one's political opponents. The agreement was signed on November 11.

Some of these negotiations took place in the Jacobi home, which Jabotinsky, Jacobi, and Ben-Gurion shared while Edna and the children were in Australia. Jabotinsky wrote to Edna from there on November 4, 1934.

---

1   Gilbert, *Israel: A History*, 76. Here, Gilbert gives the number of Jews entering Palestine legally in 1934 at forty-two thousand – the largest number allowed in a single year since the beginning of the Mandate.

Dear Edna,

Please, when washing up teacups and other machinery, is it really indispensable to wash the outside of them too? Kindly cable expert advice.

Otherwise, there is no trouble. There is a distinct accent of youth. In this double bachelordom Sioma, being a mere kid, can't appreciate it quite fully, but I was 54 the other day. Every sardine tin opened without feminine assistance, and especially every saucer dried without disaster has the taste of glorious achievement, reminding me of my undergraduate days in Italy. There is not much else to remind one of Italy in this climate just now. And the big stove in the kitchen refused to burn this morning, so one wasn't obliged to have a bath, which is a relief. But Sioma has already provided for a scientist appropriately trained to call today to repair the infernal instrument. Youth is cruel.

Edna, your house is the historic stage of most of my conversations with the fire-eatingest of all Left Labour men of Palestine, Ben-Gurion. Our mutual friendliness and cordiality is a surprise to both of us, and when his party learns how he broiled eggs on your gas griller for me to eat he will be lynched. He still makes a feeble pretence to believe that Stavsky and Rosenblatt "did it," but Sioma and I have laughed it out from his innards I'm sure. As to whether these negotiations will prove any earthly use in the end is quite another question. But in any case in the name of both exalted parties I offer you my gratitude for your unconscious hospitality. Kiss the girls for me, and recommend me to your parents as a great and true admirer of their daughter.

Yours ever,

V. J.

The agreement between Jabotinsky and Ben-Gurion was greeted by Ben-Gurion's party with hostility. Despite his explanation of having signed it as a member of the World Zionist Organization and not as a member of the Histadrut, there was considerable opposition from his colleagues. Although Ben-Gurion vigorously defended his position on his return to

Palestine, the opposition that he encountered from his colleagues was so strong that on February 13, 1935, he announced the cancellation of further negotiations. However, it was agreed that whether the agreement should be put into effect would be decided by a referendum among members of the Histadrut. In the vote, which took place on March 24, 1935, it was rejected by 60 percent of the Histadrut membership.

The Revisionists then called on the Actions Committee of the World Zionist Organization to have round-table conference to resolve the issues. This was refused. To the Revisionists, who had already been rebuffed on a number of attempts to heal the breach, this was the final straw.

On April 22, 1935, the Executive Committee of the World Union of Revisionists accepted a motion from Jabotinsky that the Revisionists withdraw from the Zionist Organization. The executive issued a proclamation that it had formed an Independent Zionist Organization and that a meeting of the new organization would be convened in December that year. Confident of support for this move by the members, particularly in Poland, Jabotinsky persuaded the executive to hold a plebiscite of members to determine support for the move.

Even though the decision of the Revisionists to withdraw had been announced by proclamation and was thus common knowledge among the Zionists and the Jewish community generally, on May 2, Jabotinsky wrote to Sioma that he had received a friendly letter from Ben-Gurion and that he had replied in the same spirit. He told Sioma that Ben-Gurion would be in London on May 6 for several days and suggested that the two meet. Jabotinsky felt that Ben-Gurion's letter indicated that the Zionist Federation, as distinct from the Histadrut, would not force a position that was unacceptable to the Revisionists.

A central issue that concerned the Revisionists over the split would be the loss of any control that they exercised over the issue of immigration certificates to Betar members. It was Sioma's task to strike a deal with Ben-Gurion that despite a Revisionist withdrawal, they could still retain a position on the committee that determined the issue of certificates for migration to Palestine. Jabotinsky wrote two letters to Ben-Gurion arguing this position.

On May 8, 1935, Sioma wrote a letter to his colleagues on the Revisionist executive in Paris. A copy was sent to Jabotinsky, who was campaigning for the plebiscite in Poland. The letter reported his conversations with Ben-Gurion, who rejected the request for a position on the committee that determined immigration certificates on the basis that their argument was "pilpulistic."[2] Ben-Gurion took the straightforward line that if you withdrew from the World Zionist Organization to set up a rival group, then you could hardly expect to be able to retain membership of a sub-committee of the organization from which you had just withdrawn. However he would be prepared to recommend that we should maintain membership of the sub-committee but with no voting rights. He was critical of the proposed split and was certain that it would not advance the cause of Zionism. In spite of the failure of Sioma's objective in holding the meeting, his letter concluded that "On the whole the conversation was friendly.

On May 12, Jabotinsky wrote enthusiastically to Sioma from Poland forecasting that the vote in that country in favor of a split would be "a practically unanimous yes." Even a number of non-Revisionists in Poland were "in revolt against the present rulers of the Zionist Organization." Any adult Jew would be allowed to vote, subject to signing a declaration that "I support the demand for a Jewish State on both sides of the Jordan." He went on to cite a provision in the Mandate that in his view "explicitly sanctions the existence of pro-Palestinian bodies outside the Zionist Organization" and that "we should demand proportional representation on the Jewish Agency."

Despite the friendly relations established with Ben-Gurion, Sioma found it necessary to write to the office of the Jewish Agency in London on May 20. His letter protested that the Jewish Agency representative in Poland had advised the Revisionist representative there that because the Revisionists had left the Zionist Organization, he could not process any applications for permits from Betar members to enter Palestine. The

---

2   From the Hebrew word *pilpul,* a method of studying the Talmud through textual analysis, and more loosely described as an overly clever interpretation.

Jewish Agency representative said further that in the future any applications received from Betar members would be handled on a case-by-case basis rather than in groups, as had been the practice in the past. Sioma requested that the status quo be maintained. He signed his letter as "Member of the Executive, World Union of Zionist Revisionists."

The plebiscite was conducted on May 29, 1935. The results were that 167,000 voted in favor of the establishment of the New Zionist Organization (NZO) and only three thousand voted against it.

On July 28, Sioma formally opened the New Revisionist Club in Whitechapel Road in the East End of London. In his address, Sioma spoke of three main goals of the formation of the NZO. The first was to avert the threat of a proposed legislative council in Palestine that would be elected by a general franchise that would give control of the council, and thus an agenda for the country, to the Arabs.[3] The second goal was to reform the restrictive practices of the Jewish Agency in its regulation of immigration to Palestine that discriminated against Betar members. The third goal was to press for the opening of Transjordan to Jewish immigration because it held three times as much land and water as Palestine.

The first congress of the NZO was held in Vienna on September 12, 1935. The New York *Jewish Daily Bulletin* of the next day carried an extensive report of the meeting. It listed Sioma as a member of the elected executive and reported a speech by him at some length.

The first point that Sioma addressed related to the Transfer Agreement,[4] which has been referred to above, that had been made with Nazi Germany. It will be recalled that under the agreement, Jews who wished to immigrate to Palestine could deposit money in a trust account in Germany. The money was then to be used to pay Germans who exported goods to Palestine. The Germans who were now resident in Palestine were paid for their import of goods to Palestine in Palestine pounds. It appeared to be a workable

---

3   This was first proposed in the Churchill White Paper of 1922 and not put into effect, but it was revived in the Passfield White Paper of 1930. In 1934, the best estimate of the population of Palestine was 907,000 Arabs and 254,000 Jews, or 3.6 to 1.

4   Known in Hebrew as the Haavarah Agreement.

proposal. But in his speech, Sioma reported that although goods to the value of 34 million marks had been sent to Palestine, only the equivalent of 19 million marks had been paid to German Jews in Palestine. They were owed the equivalent 6 million marks, and 20 percent of the funds realized went to administrative expenses. A resolution was passed condemning the agreement, calling for its immediate termination and reverting to the position before the agreement was reached in which German Jews had been allowed to take $5,000 out of the country with them. Sioma moved a resolution condemning the barter pact. The resolution was carried.

The principal resolution carried at the congress was the adoption of a constitution that sought to establish a Jewish state in Palestine, with a Jewish majority on both sides of the Jordan.

The London *Jewish Chronicle* also reported on the congress in some detail, including several paragraphs on Sioma's address. Most significantly for Sioma's involvement in the new organization was the report in the *Chronicle* that the executive committee of the NZO would have its headquarters in London.

When he returned to London, he received a handwritten letter from Jabotinsky. "Here in Paris we are penniless…to be brief I have been in some tight corners but never yet in a corner like this." His letter went on that he expected to receive a share of royalties for a film script from New York which would amount to £133 which he intended to give to the NZO. He urged Sioma and other leaders of the NZO in London to follow his example. The letter continued, uncharacteristically, to seek Sioma's advice on how he should proceed to obtain a renewal of his visa to travel to England. He wanted to avoid being questioned by the authorities and asked whether someone in the NZO London office could approach the Home Office directly to obtain the visa for him. He felt that this was preferable because "our Zionist friends have been pouring and heaping calumny [on me] for years and years. Otherwise we face prospects which to me look unpleasant – several campaigns and fights with a decent chance to win. But I don't see how we can fight unless financed to bridge over December to March."

In a recorded interview with Sioma's wife Edna when she was ninety years old, she related that Sioma had often flown to France to meet an arms dealer on the Swiss border in order to buy weapons for the Revisionists. She recalled the arms dealer's name as Sir Basil Zaharoff.[5] There are no references in Revisionist literature to the purchase of weapons, although there can be no doubt that this must have occurred. In Sioma's files there is only one cryptic cable sent to him by Jabotinsky in June 1935 that may have referred to arms purchase. The cable read: "Gideon purchased merchandise Italy cheaply for 3,600 pounds there from 1,600 available here 1,000 needed immediately 1,000 September please help. Vladimir."

The background to this weapons purchase can be found in the dissatisfaction felt by a number of Jews in Palestine with the Haganah's inability to defend the Jewish population of the towns and the Jewish settlements during the 1929 "riots." Some members of the Haganah left to form new self-defense groups which in the early1930s developed into a new organization, the Irgun Zeva'i Le'umi. In August 1933 a supervisory committee for the Irgun was established that included representatives from most of the Zionist political parties. The members of this committee were Meir Grossman (Jewish State Party), Rabbi Meir Bar-Ilan (Mizrachi), either Immanuel Neumann or Yehoshua Supersky (General Zionists), and Jabotinsky or Eliyahu Ben-Horin for the Revisionists. The committee was in charge of the Irgun until 1937, when the group split yet again. From that point on, the Irgun was under Jabotinsky's sole command. At the same time it was agreed that Jabotinsky could delegate this command to Sioma.[6]

In August 1935, the London *Jewish World* published a column that reported the opening of a New Revisionist social club by Sioma in the Communal Centre in Whitechapel Road. At the opening, Sioma spoke of the fifty thousand Jews who had reached Palestine in 1934, but pointed out that only 8 percent of them had gone into farming because the mandatory authority was making it difficult for Jews to buy land. He went on to

---

5   Sir Basil Zaharoff (1849–1936) came from a Greek family that lived in Turkey. He moved to Europe and dealt in arms ranging from submarines to machine guns. He was very active during World War I and was decorated by the French government. He had met Lloyd George in England.

6   Schechtman, *Fighter and Prophet*, 448.

outline the major reasons for the establishment of the NZO. These were to open immigration to Palestine to those who belonged to organizations whose politics were not approved by the Jewish Agency and to open up Transjordan to Jewish settlement because of the larger area of land available for settlement and the comparative abundance of water.

The founding congress of the NZO was to be held in Vienna in September 1935. Three years before the *Anschluss*, Jabotinsky was sensitive to the heavily pro-Nazi feeling in Austria. In a letter to Sioma six weeks before the congress was due to open, Jabotinsky wrote that he had decided to ask the Austrian government whether their feelings would be hurt if the congress reacted strongly to the latest developments in Nazi Germany. His letter to the Austrian government went on that if this placed the Austrians in a difficult position, the congress would meet elsewhere. Since the Austrian government did not object, the congress in Vienna went ahead, although in a letter to Sioma before it commenced, Jabotinsky remarked on the regrettable "outburst [against the congress being held in Vienna] of the Viennese Catholic newspaper."

At the congress, Sioma was elected to the executive committee of the NZO, which was to have its headquarters in London. Sioma's speech at the congress was reported in some detail in the London *Jewish Chronicle*. In his speech, he attacked the Transfer Agreement and the Zionist body, Haavarah, that had been set up in Palestine to handle the agreement. He accused Haavarah of having taken 22 percent of the proceeds of the operation in administrative costs and failing to distribute 22 million marks to the German immigrants who had arrived under the agreement. He pointed out that people wanting to leave Germany at the time could do so if they left 66.6 percent of their capital behind them. Currently under the agreement, German immigrants had been able to retain only 39 percent of their capital, and for this small margin (an increase from 33.4 percent to 39 percent) the opportunity of boycotting trade with Germany had been lost. The congress passed a resolution that condemned the Transfer Agreement.

In order to relieve the NZO's financial crisis, Sioma flew to South Africa on October 7, 1935, to raise funds from its usually generous Jewish community. But on touchdown in the Ugandan airport at Kampala, the

Imperial Airways plane burst a tire and crashed. None of the twenty-four passengers was injured, but the plane was completely wrecked. The passengers had to wait for another plane to continue their journey. Sioma's delayed arrival meant that he was only in South Africa for a little more than a week.

The *Johannesburg Star* reported that Sioma addressed a "crowded hall" in a leading hotel on November 10. In the advertisement for the meeting, he was named as "Head of the Political Department of the NZO." He spoke about the recent elections at the Zionist Congress, "which gave a powerful mandate for the policy of the renowned leader of the organization Vladimir Jabotinsky." He accused the main Zionist body of having drifted away from the concept of a Jewish state in Palestine. It had failed to attract large-scale Jewish immigration, and he accused the Labor-dominated Histadrut of discrimination in allocating entry permits to the country. Economically, Palestine was in crisis. The last two years had seen an adverse balance of trade of over £70 million, and Sioma predicted that if this continued, it would mean disaster for the country.

The truncated trip failed to attract the financial support that Sioma had hoped for from South African Revisionists. The note from Jabotinsky that Sioma received on his return concerning the movement's financial position is the only angry letter on record that Jabotinsky wrote to Sioma. One of Jabotinsky's biographers noted that at this time Jabotinsky was upset by the petty squabbles that were erupting within the NZO movement. He particularly resented being asked to mediate in the disputes.[7] The letter that Jabotinsky wrote to Sioma also complained of being brought into a dispute between Sioma and Betar in Poland. Betar had complained of the content of a letter that Sioma had written to them, claiming that he was holding up some certificates of entry to Palestine. Jabotinsky's letter to Sioma said that he sided with Betar and asked Sioma to resolve the matter.

Paradoxically, Jabotinsky's letter went on to suggest to Sioma that the leadership of Betar would be given to Sioma if he wanted it. There is no further reference to this suggestion in later correspondence.

---

7   Schechtman, *Fighter and Prophet*, 224.

CHAPTER 16

BACK TO THE NZO

Jabotinsky was not deterred by the referendum of members of Histadrut that rejected the agreement for a rapprochement between the two Zionist groups in 1934. In a letter dated May 29, 1936, he wrote to Weizmann seeking to present a combined front to the world of the two Zionist bodies.[1] The proposal was for a ten-year plan that would aim for the immigration of 1.5 million Jews to Palestine over that period. This would establish a Jewish majority in Palestine. No response to Jabotinsky's fresh overture is recorded in the files.

The Jewish population in Palestine had increased from 235,000 in 1933 to 384,000 in 1936. In protest against this level of Jewish immigration, the Arab population began a national strike on April 15, 1936. That day, three Jews were killed on the road near Nablus. In a reprisal attack, an armed Jewish group killed several Arabs near Tel Aviv. What can best be described as a civil war followed these incidents. Jewish settlements were attacked, and Jewish shops, houses, orchards, and farms were destroyed. In the following months, the Jewish death toll numbered more than eighty. The British army in Palestine tried to restore order. British troops killed

---

1   Copy in Sioma's files.

more than 140 Arabs in the course of the battles that ensued, and more than thirty British soldiers died.

The response of the British government was to appoint yet another British Royal Commission in August 1936. Its purpose was to

> ascertain the underlying causes of the disturbances which broke out in Palestine in the middle of April; to enquire into the manner in which the Mandate for Palestine is being implemented in relation to the obligations of the Mandatory Authority towards the Arabs and the Jews respectively; and to ascertain whether, upon a proper construction of the terms of the Mandate, either the Arabs or the Jews have any legitimate grievances on account of the way in which the Mandate has been or is being implemented; and if the Commission is satisfied that any such grievances are well-founded, to make recommendation; for their removal and for the prevention of their recurrence.

It was known as the Peel Commission after its chairman, the Earl Peel.[2]

Despite this difficult period for the Zionist cause, on October 6, 1936, Jabotinsky wrote a letter from Warsaw to Sioma in London in which he acknowledged and understood Sioma's decision to cease his public activities and to dedicate his time to "personal matters." What these matters were is unclear. They may have involved Haskel's business affairs both in London and Palestine. Haskel's Kenya gold mine had been floated on the London Stock Exchange earlier that year, and as Haskel's London agent and a director of the company, Sioma was heavily involved with the management of the company's activities there. He was still a member of the executive of the Joint British Committee of ORT-OZE. Apart from another letter of the same date in which Jabotinsky gave Sioma a series

---

2   William Peel, the first Earl Peel (1867–1937), a distinguished jurist and member of cabinet, was the son of Viscount Peel and the grandson of Sir Robert Peel, who was famous for his creation of the English police force, the "bobbies." There are wonderful photographs of the members of the Peel Commission in Palestine, where they had gone "to see for themselves," wearing full morning dress and top hats.

of messages and requests, including putting off any discussions regarding the reorganization of the NZO office in London until Jabotinsky arrived there in two months' time, the volume of correspondence from Jabotinsky to Sioma was greatly diminished.

If it had been Sioma's intention to withdraw from all public activities, he does not seem to have been able to achieve this. Among Sioma's papers there is a fifteen-page speech on foolscap about the activities of ORT-OZE in 1936. It is dated in Sioma's handwriting "February 1937," but it is not known where the speech was delivered or whether it was Sioma who delivered it. The speech analyzes the plight of the Jews in Poland, Lithuania, Latvia, Romania, and Russia in Sioma's clear style and describes difficult situations with carefully detailed data. At the end of the paper is a table setting out the activities of ORT-OZE in five eastern European countries. There were 240 centers where services were offered to the Jews of Poland, including prenatal care, infant care, school hygiene clinics, ambulance services, and summer camps for children. In Lithuania there were forty-four such services, sixty-seven in Romania, and twenty-one in Latvia. In total, ORT-OZE provided a total of 384 service centers in Europe.

It is unlikely that Sioma was still employed by ORT-OZE for its fund-raising activities. In a brochure issued by the organization in November 1936, Sioma was listed as honorary secretary of the executive of the British office of the group. In the history of ORT-OZE outlined in the brochure, Sioma was mentioned in the section of their fund-raising campaigns overseas, particularly his successes in South Africa and Australia.

Jabotinsky appeared before the Peel Commission on February 11, 1937. The commission sat in the House of Lords, which seats only 120 people. Sioma had obtained a press pass for his wife, Edna, who heard Jabotinsky give an impressive address. Jabotinsky later told a friend that it was the best speech that he had ever made. Peel challenged Jabotinsky on the grounds that Jabotinsky's proposed level of Jewish immigration to Palestine could never be reconciled with Arab demands for its total prohibition. Jabotinsky responded that if a "colonizing regime" were allowed, the capacity of Palestine to absorb an increased population would create a country with room for both Jews and Arabs.

Churchill also appeared before the commission. In response to an assertion by one of its members that Jews in Palestine were a "foreign race" among the Arab population, Churchill responded that the Arabs were the foreigners. "In the time of Christ when Palestine was a Roman province the population [of the Jews] was much greater.... When the great hordes of Islam swept over these places they broke it all up.... You have seen the terraces on the hills which used to be cultivated, which under Arab rule are now deserts."[3]

Sioma could not forsake his Zionist commitment. It would seem that he had been supportive of Jabotinsky in his appearance before the Royal Commission, and by the end of February 1937 he was back in NZO harness. He accompanied Jabotinsky on a boat for the seventeen-day voyage to South Africa for a fund-raising tour of that country. The voyage provided relaxation for both men, who had agreed not to talk about Zionist business for the first four days. Each day they walked seven times around the exercise deck. On March 15, 1937, they arrived in Cape Town, where they were joined by Haskel. Their party was received by the prime minister, General J. B. M. Hertzog, and then they were welcomed at a lunch which was attended by several cabinet ministers. Six days later, the three men addressed a large meeting in Johannesburg. Sioma's speech at the meeting was reported in full in the local NZO journal, *The Eleventh Hour*.[4] The paper commented that the trio – Jabotinsky, Sioma, and Haskel – "were a very strong team." The essence of Sioma's reported speech was the fight between the main Zionist organization and the NZO. This had gone so far, he said, that the Histadrut in Palestine, as the agent of the main Zionist body, had a policy of denying membership to Revisionist workers and thus depriving them of the right to work. In addition, the Histadrut also attempted to prevent Revisionists from obtaining certificates of entry to Palestine.

While he was in South Africa, Sioma wrote a long article about Transjordan for *The Eleventh Hour*. The front cover of this issue was a

---

3   Gilbert, *Churchill and the Jews*, 115.

4   A platform to report their meetings and a vehicle for their writings, it started publication to coincide with the tour.

map showing the original Mandate of Palestine approved by the League of Nations for the whole of biblical Israel, and how it was now divided by the Jordan River to create Palestine as we now know it on one side and Jordan, or "Trans-Jordan" as it was then known, on the other. Underneath the map was a note that Palestine to the west of the Jordan was an area of twenty-six thousand square kilometers with a population of 1.2 million, while the area of Transjordan was ninety thousand square kilometers with a population of only 320,000. The article expounded the NZO view that Palestine should exist on both sides of the Jordan.

When word reached South Africa that the Peel Commission was proposing to formally recommend the partition of Palestine between Jews and Arabs on the western side of the Jordan, Jabotinsky asked Sioma to go back to London to rally support to oppose the idea. Before he left for London, Sioma was given written instructions on the matters to which he should give his attention on his return. These related to general housekeeping concerns, including the Tel Hai Foundation,[5] but Jabotinsky left to Sioma's discretion the task of establishing a lobby group to oppose the concept of partition. While the commission's final report recommended partition of Palestine between Jews and Arabs, it recognized that neither would be prepared to accept partition. The British government reserved its decision. As expected, both groups refused to accept partition, so the British government appointed another commission of inquiry, the Woodhead Commission, to examine the recommendation. Its advice was to reject partition, and this was accepted by the British government.

Shortly after his return to London, Sioma wrote to Jabotinsky that, to add to his workload, "Dr Klinger[6] has left London and I have had to

---

5   Tel Hai was the name of the kibbutz where Joseph Trumpeldor was killed during an attack by Arabs in 1919. Named in honor of Trumpeldor, the foundation was the central financial institution of the Revisionists. There is a substantial archive in the Jabotinsky Institute on the Tel Hai Foundation. The dates shown in the catalogue are from 1929 to 1968.

6   Dr. Stefan Klinger, a member of the London executive of the NZO, who had taken over running the office when Sioma withdrew from that role.

take over management of the office," an additional task that was intruding on his other work. Nevertheless, Sioma seems to have resumed an active involvement in NZO affairs.

In November 1937, renewed attacks on Jews by Arabs broke out in Palestine. Five members of the socialist Histadrut were killed while working in the fields near Jerusalem. The Jewish Agency favored a policy of *havlagah*, restraint, in the face of Arab violence. The NZO opposed restraint. Reprisals were carried out against Arabs in Jerusalem, and the Jewish Agency accused Revisionists of being responsible. The British authorities arrested a number of leading Revisionists.

Sioma wrote a long letter to the London *Jewish Chronicle* from the offices of the NZO on the arrests. It was published on December 3, 1937. His letter was written "to throw some light on the fact that the recent arrests of Jews in Palestine following reprisals against Arab terrorism were confined almost exclusively to members of the NZO...." Sioma's letter accused "the Jewish Agency of exploiting its official position for the purposes of wreaking vengeance on its political opponents...by making statements that amounted to a denunciation of members of the NZO as responsible for the reprisals." Sioma appealed for funds to help support the prisoners and their families. A week later, the *Chronicle* published a letter from Professor Brodetsky, a member of the executive of the World Zionist Organization, in which he rejected Sioma's allegations against the Jewish Agency. Further correspondence from Sioma and Brodetsky followed, the latter carrying a response from Moshe Shertok denying that he had ever accused the Revisionists. Seeking to be evenhanded, the *Chronicle* published two letters from the general public about the argument, one supporting Sioma and the other condemning the Revisionists. The argument lasted for five of the weekly issues of the *Chronicle*, during which Sioma wrote three long letters to the paper. He was not prepared to be browbeaten by the heavyweights of the Zionist establishment.

The first world assembly of the NZO opened in Prague on January 31, 1938. On February 9, Jabotinsky wrote a letter in longhand to Sioma's wife, Edna, who had now returned to London.

Dear Edna Albertovna,[7]

Please don't be cross with me for having contributed to increasing Sioma's burdens. Quite apart from his value to the Movement, and the Movement's importance to him, I have a perfectly distinct feeling that it is within the framework of the Movement that most of us will finally discover their own basis of settlement...but of this you may be sure. Should a serious conflict arise between the family's interests and Sioma's burden I will release him, and even to insist on his release.

This has been the best conference I [have] ever attended since Helsingfors[8] in 1906. It began excellently...but began to decline from the second day and was doomed to end in general dissatisfaction had not Sioma's arrival literally turned everything up side "up." The financial committee, from the moment he put his nose into the room, stopped babbling and decided to send out eight delegates to rob everybody robbable, to find the cash. The Nessiut,[9] which was to be composed of grumbling absentees, plus the undersigned, is now acclaimed as the solidest body we ever had. Everybody without exception is happy; as to myself, I feel like a million dollars. There is nothing I adore as much as friendship... we are going to be kings soon, Edna, and it's going to be together. Don't be afraid to back the horse I am riding – so far, my hunches have proved right, much more often than not.

Yours very affectionately,

V. J.

Jabotinsky returned to South Africa soon after the conference to resume the fund-raising he had been forced to abandon to attend the Peel Commission hearings. Sioma offered to accompany Jabotinsky, but

---

7   This was Jabotinsky's usual form of address to Edna Jacobi, using the Russian patronymic of her father's name, Albert, and adding the suffix "-ovna."

8   The Swedish name for Helsinki. In 1906 it was part of Russia. A Zionist conference, the first after Herzl's death, was held there in 1906.

9   Office of the presidency.

his offer was rejected by the executive committee of the South African NZO on the grounds that his presence was not required "while Jabo himself is here." The rejection was perhaps influenced by the very bad press that was accorded to Sioma by the organ of the main Zionist body in South Africa, the *Zionist Record*. The paper accused him of "recriminations and allegations…infused with bitterness and rancour" in a speech that Sioma made in Johannesburg during their last visit. It would be most uncharacteristic of Sioma to have used such language or to have spoken in such a manner. Other press reports throughout the world commented that he was calm, factual, and reasoned. The Zionist press in this case was indicative of the animosity that the main Zionist body bore toward the Revisionists.

Adding to the huge task of assisting Jews to escape persecution in eastern Europe was the new problem of helping Jews from Austria and Czechoslovakia when Germany annexed those countries in March 1938. Sioma was in Prague on Revisionist business with the Czech Tatra Bank when the German army invaded. On July 6, 1938, Jabotinsky wrote an urgent letter to the NZO organization in South Africa appealing for funds to assist 361 German and Austrian Jews, the majority of whom belonged to Betar, who had managed to reach Palestine. The English Council for German Jews had refused to help the group because they were "illegal immigrants." The Jewish Agency in Palestine had refused assistance because they were members of Betar.

The lack of financial backing for the NZO was now critical. In August 1938 Jabotinsky wrote to Sioma that Dr. Benjamin Akzin had resigned. Akzin had been an important member of the group since 1925. Jabotinsky was convinced that Azkin's resignation was because the NZO could not afford to pay him a salary, although the resignation was couched in terms of his disappointment that the NZO had chosen not to rejoin the main Zionist body. Later that month, Jabotinsky reported to Sioma that another stalwart of the NZO, Dr. Michael Schwartzman, had also resigned.

To add to Jabotinsky's problems, his letter to Sioma of August 22, 1938, acknowledged Sioma's decision to take his family to Australia. Jabotinsky agreed that he could see no possibility of the movement's financial situation improving to the point where it could pay Sioma, or anyone else, a reasonable salary, so he understood that Sioma had no choice but to resign. In Australia they would have the support of Edna's family, and it might be possible for Sioma to pursue his profession as an engineer. However, circumstances were to defeat the Jacobi family's planned move. A polio epidemic had broken out in Australia in 1937. Schools were closed and children did not go to cinemas or other public places where they might be exposed to infection. Although it was thought that the epidemic had peaked in 1937, the Australian winter months – June, July, and August 1938 – saw another outbreak of the disease. More than one thousand deaths were reported during the course of the epidemic and it was estimated that more than ten thousand were disabled by the disease, which caused paralysis and distortion of limbs and other bones in the body. Edna recalled during an interview that Sioma had already bought tickets for the voyage to Australia, but they heeded her Melbourne family's advice to delay the journey because of the fresh outbreak of the disease and the possibility of their daughters being infected. Sioma resumed his involvement with the NZO.

Following the Peel Commission report, Britain limited the number of Jews that were allowed to settle in Palestine to twelve thousand per year. The British mandatory government instituted a blockade to prevent any illegal immigration of Jews who were not officially admitted within that limit.

A Jewish group in Britain, the Council for German Jewry, had collected funds to help resettle German and Austrian Jews. The council was now torn between what it saw as its duty, as good British citizens, to obey the rules that restricted Jewish immigration to Palestine, or to help all Jews in need. In a letter that Jabotinsky wrote to NZO supporters in South Africa in July 1938 seeking their financial help, he reported that the Council for German Jewry had decided to refuse support for Jews who arrived in Palestine illegally. The council allocated sixty pounds per head to legal immigrants who arrived in Palestine to assist in their settlement, but not to others. To add to the hardships already endured by Revisionist "illegals" making their way to Palestine in unseaworthy ships, the money that the Council for German Jewry provided was distributed in Palestine by the Jewish Agency, who refused to pass it on to Revisionist and Betar members. When an NZO representative inquired from the Jewish Agency in London whether their members who managed to reach Palestine would be able to claim the sixty pounds, he was told that it was most likely that they would not receive anything.

Provoked by this intolerable position, Jabotinsky once again assigned Sioma to negotiate a rapprochement with the main Zionist organization. On October 7, 1938, Sioma wrote to Ben-Gurion suggesting that the two organizations should create a united front in an emergency committee "to deal with all matters relating to the future of Palestine." The two met the following day. There is no record of the meeting, but Ben-Gurion's letter to Sioma, dated October 10, 1938, summarized "what I told you at our conversation." Sioma had addressed the letter suggesting the meeting to Ben-Gurion as chairman of the Zionist executive and signed it as chairman of the Nessiut of the NZO. Although Ben-Gurion's reply was written on Jewish Agency letterhead, Ben-Gurion signed it as an individual without any title and addressed it to Sioma as an individual, with no reference to the NZO or to his position in the organization. It reduced their discussion to an informal chat between two individuals.

Sioma had not suggested establishing a combined party, but rather an emergency committee consisting of representatives of both parties. It was not long since the rank-and-file of Ben-Gurion's own party had rejected his attempt to reconcile the two groups. Ben-Gurion was not prepared to be put in a similar position again. He rejected Sioma's suggestion on two grounds. First, because it would not be a genuine consolidation of Zionist bodies, it would not impress either the British government or the League of Nations. Second, it would split the ranks of Ben-Gurion's own Zionist Organization and the Jewish Agency, as many members of both bodies would oppose the move. Ben-Gurion felt that the only way forward was that "we must have real unity – a single all embracing democratic disciplined Zionist Organization," and that if the NZO decided to abandon its separate activities, he would personally endeavor to secure the appointment of Revisionist representatives to the various organs of the

Zionist organization, even before the next congress. The letter concluded that, as Ben-Gurion had told Sioma during their discussion, these were his personal views, but if there was a genuine desire on the part of the NZO for "real unity, I will do everything in my power to achieve it."

The entire correspondence was leaked to the Johannesburg *Jewish Herald*, which printed it in full on December 9, 1938. The paper was clearly supportive of the NZO. The editorial comment on the correspondence was that while Ben-Gurion was having discussions with Sioma and exchanging the correspondence, he was, at the same time, instructing his party in Palestine to cancel any agreement that they might have reached with the NZO concerning self-defense in that country. The Jewish Telegraph Agency had reported that such an agreement between the parties had been signed. The *Jewish Herald* printed a copy of the cable that Ben-Gurion had sent to his office in Palestine on September 23, 1938: "If not yet signed, don't. If signed annul signature." That cable was sent before Sioma's meeting with Ben-Gurion.

Within the Revisionist groups, party unity was becoming a major problem for Jabotinsky. Letters that Jabotinsky wrote to Sioma from Bucharest and Warsaw in October 1938 include references to the internal problems within the NZO.

Abraham Stern[10] was proving difficult to control, and Jabotinsky's dismissal of some who had been in command of the Irgun was causing unrest. In addition, there were disputes within party ranks in Warsaw, where there was an unofficial NZO embassy. The NZO published a weekly newspaper in Yiddish in Warsaw. Tensions between the personalities in the party over the publication were so high that during a heated argument, one executive member physically assaulted another.

---

10   Abraham Stern (1907–1942), a brilliant graduate of the Hebrew University of Jerusalem, joined the Irgun in 1932. During the 1930s he was active in Poland, where he recruited for this NZO armed wing. He later became an urban revolutionary who declared war on what he saw as the British occupation of Palestine. His group was responsible for a number of physical acts of violence, including blowing up the King David Hotel in Jerusalem. A wanted man in Palestine, he was captured by officers of the British Palestine Police, who executed him on the spot.

Jabotinsky arrived in London in January 1939. In order to preserve unity within the party, he pressed Sioma to take over the leadership of the Nessiut. Sioma had discussions with a number of senior people in the movement in order to gauge the party's feelings about this proposal. After further discussions with Jabotinsky, Sioma accepted the position. In February 1939, Jabotinsky gave Sioma power of attorney to manage the movement's affairs. Specifically, Jabotinsky's letter to Sioma of February 4, 1939, gave him the authority to settle all matters relating to illegal immigration that arose within the ranks of the NZO, Betar, and the Irgun. Further, Sioma was given authority to hire and dismiss the personnel of these groups at his sole discretion. The letter went on to state that Sioma's decisions would have the validity of resolutions taken by the presidency of the NZO, Betar, and the Irgun.

CHAPTER 17

AF AL PI – CLANDESTINE IMMIGRATION IN SPITE OF THE BRITISH RESTRICTIONS

Jabotinsky had written several letters in mid-1934 to Sioma expressing the view that the Revisionists were lagging behind other Zionist groups in running illegal immigrants into Palestine. In a letter dated September 30 of that year, he wrote that currently some six hundred to eight hundred immigrants were being landed in Netanya[1] each month by the "leftists" and that the British succeeded in arresting only 10 percent of them. Unauthorized aliyah was important to the Revisionist movement, wrote Jabotinsky. It was "the best demonstration of a craving for Palestine: a personified petition."

A biographer documents the importance of aliyah to the Revisionists:

> During the second half of the 1930s, specifically during the years 1939–40, the Revisionists and affiliated elements brought in some

---

1   A settlement, founded in 1929 north of Tel Aviv, whose extensive beachfront made it ideal for landing immigrants.

15,000 immigrants in 25 ships, a number accounting for 40 per cent of the total number of illegal immigrants arriving by sea.[2]

Jabotinsky initiated the running of "illegals" for the Revisionists in 1934 with a group on the ship *Union,* which brought 117 Betar members to Palestine.[3] One hundred were successfully brought ashore but another seventeen were captured by Palestinian police. Although this was within the 10 percent of arrests encountered by other groups running "illegals" for the next several years, the Revisionists abandoned using ships to deliver this form of aliyah. Instead they obtained visas for Jewish "tourists" who had no intention of leaving Palestine once they had arrived. Official figures published by the Palestine Administration estimated that the number arriving as such "tourists" in the years 1932 to 1938 was between twenty-five and thirty thousand.

There have been a number of references in earlier chapters to the Revisionist youth movement, Betar, and to the armed force of the Revisionists, the Irgun. Jabotinsky had an overarching influence on these groups in his position as head of the Revisionist movement. Relationships between these three parties were complex. Although many of the youths trained in the essentially militaristic Betar group ended up in the Irgun or in the political wing of the Revisionists, there were many views within these groups of how the different sections of the same party should interrelate, and where responsibilities began and ended.

Even within Betar, there were three quite distinct organizational themes. The foundation of this movement was a considerable number of youth training groups that were still very active in Europe.[4] Betar also

---

2   Yaacov Shavit, *Jabotinsky and the Revisionist Movement, 1925–1948* (London: Frank Cass, 1988), 376. Two other writers, Epstein and Perl, have written about the ships in detail: their names, ports of origin, number of passengers, and the groups responsible for them.

3   Katz, *Lone Wolf,* 1638. However, Ludmilla Epstein, in *Before the Curtain Fell* (Tel Aviv: Misdar Jabotinsky, 1990), 73, lists two earlier voyages of Betar members in 1923 and 1928.

4   At the 1934 Revisionist Conference, the Betar delegates represented some forty thousand Polish members and seventy thousand members worldwide.

served as a recruiting ground for adult members of the party. In Palestine, the Betar movement consisted of labor pioneers working on kibbutzim, and those who were born in Palestine and lived mostly in the cities or towns. Finally, there were the older members who were working in the political milieu of the Revisionist movement.

It has been mentioned in an earlier chapter how the Irgun had grown out of dissatisfaction with the Jewish self-defense force in Palestine, the Haganah. Betar was also a recruiting ground for the Irgun.

Inevitably there were tensions between the three bodies – the Revisionist political arm, Betar, and the Irgun. Not all members of Betar or the Irgun believed in the politics of the Revisionists. They saw the parent body as a Zionist political party in conflict with the Zionists led by Ben-Gurion. Some believed that a political movement was not the way to establish a Jewish state and that direct military action was preferred. So there were ideological differences and personality conflicts. One writer has postulated that it was almost inevitable that a radicalization of the Betar movement would occur.[5] At the same time, the breakaway armed wing of the Irgun had developed. It believed that the British Mandate stood in the way of a Jewish independence and must be forced out of Palestine.

However, there was one activity on which all three sections of the Revisionist movement agreed. This was to evade the British limitation of Jewish immigration to Palestine by running illegal immigrants past the British army and the British Palestine Police Force. From 1936 the New Zionist Organization (NZO), Betar, and the Irgun began the ongoing operation. The NZO was responsible for negotiating with governments, Betar was responsible for bringing the "illegals" to the ports of embarkation and organizing the ships for them to board, and the Irgun was in charge of their safe landing in Palestine.

Jabotinsky had conceived of a plan to bring together the Zionist aim for Jews to immigrate to Palestine with the eagerness of the Polish population and government for Jews to leave Poland. Jabotinsky began his

---

5   Shavit, *Jabotinsky and the Revisionist Movement*, 56–57.

campaign in April 1936 by calling on the Polish ambassador in London. The first part of the plan was for the Polish government to pressure the British government to open the gates of Palestine to Jewish immigration. Sufficiently encouraged by his reception, Jabotinsky decided to open an NZO office in Warsaw. He went to Warsaw and was able to put his proposal on a more formal basis to the Polish foreign minister, Jozef Beck. Shortly afterwards, Jabotinsky met Beck again at a League of Nations conference in Geneva. This was followed by the Polish ambassador in London calling on British foreign secretary Anthony Eden in an endeavor to persuade the British government to play their part in the plan.

Jabotinsky's efforts over the next two years came to nothing. In 1988, Jerzy Tomaszewski published a number of documents that were found in the archives of the Polish Ministry of Foreign Affairs. These documents relate to the NZO's attempts to persuade the Polish government to assist in accelerated Polish Jewish migration to Palestine. While the Polish government supported the general concept, it felt that Britain had to be persuaded and that America was the only country that could exercise this influence. There was a telling comment in one official Polish report of a discussion with Jabotinsky in June 1939. "Mr. Jabotinsky gave the impression of being a very good person but disappointed and mentally broken."[6] Other factors that did not assist Jabotinsky's efforts were other Revisionists initiating their own plans to enlist Polish support. There was also outright hostility from within Zionist ranks over cooperation with the anti-Semitic Polish government. Sholem Asch wrote that Jabotinsky had "placed the most dangerous weapon in the hands of those who hate us most."[7] The plan ultimately failed because it was Britain that controlled entry to Palestine, and the influence that the Polish government could bring to bear on the British was very limited.

Inevitably, the Revisionist movement was short of the funds necessary

---

6   "Vladimir Jabotinsky's Talks with Representatives of the Polish Government," in Antony Polonsky, ed., *Polin: Studies in Polish Jewry*, vol. 3, *The Jews of Warsaw* (Oxford: Littman Library of Jewish Civilization, 2004), 289.

7   Chimen Abramsky, Maciej Jachimczyk, and Antony Polonsky, *The Jews in Poland* (Oxford: Basil Blackwell, 1986), 134.

even for their own more limited operation. Money was needed for transport to the embarkation points, and ships had to be chartered, fueled, and provisioned. There was a considerable expense involved in running a clandestine operation in Europe, chartering ships for the voyage, and then hiding and settling the immigrants.

Jabotinsky had asked the South African Revisionists for the funds needed for the task. They launched a campaign entitled Af Al Pi, which translates roughly as "in spite of," which was very successful. Jabotinsky was to write of this new "Jewish national sport...that was helping to win a country for a homeless rabble...other sports are games...but ours is sacredly serious." He devoted himself to this task. His letters to Sioma, who was still in London, were sent from various parts of Europe reporting on developments and frustrations of the planned evacuations to Palestine. One of Jabotinsky's biographers wrote that "there had emerged across Eastern and Central Europe a team of local Betar leaders and Irgun emissaries – under Jacobi's overall direction from London.... They organized the groups, shepherded them from countries of origin, across frontiers, to the ports."[8]

The internal Revisionist situation that Jabotinsky and Sioma faced was the attraction that the armed wing of the movement, Irgun, had for the militarily trained members of Betar. As one writer expressed it, "Between September 1938 and August 1940 Jabotinsky's authority underwent a process of Betar's loyalty moving from the Revisionists to Irgun."[9]

Perhaps in order to rectify this situation, in March 1939 Jabotinsky instructed Sioma to move to Warsaw to take over all the affairs of the NZO and its affiliated bodies in eastern Europe.[10]

Jabotinsky continued to send Sioma instructions from London. In a series of telegrams and letters, all dated March 16, Jabotinsky reinforced Sioma's position in Warsaw by giving him specific powers of attorney to investigate the Irgun's press conferences, control the NZO's local

---

8   Katz, *Lone Wolf*, 1698.

9   Colin Shindler, *The Triumph of Military Zionism* (London: Taurus, 2006), 169.

10   Katz, *Lone Wolf*, 1644.

newspaper, and finally to attend, without any restrictions, to all matters pertaining to the movement, making decisions as he saw fit.

These short and succinct telegrams and letters were supported by two long letters. One was primarily concerned with the fate of a group of Austrian Jews who were incarcerated in a cellar in Constanza, the Romanian port on the Black Sea that was used to embark "illegals" on ships to Palestine. The British government representative in Romania had used his influence to prevent these and other Jews from leaving by ship from Constanza.

A second long letter instructed Sioma to sort out the personality problems that beset the NZO personnel in Warsaw. Specifically, Jabotinsky warned Sioma to be "in no way influenced by Joseph Boris Schechtman's vendetta moods." It is not known what may have passed between Sioma and Schechtman, but in 1961 Schechtman published a two-volume biography of Jabotinsky[11] that failed to mention Sioma, and referred only to his correspondence with Jabotinsky in footnotes where this could not be avoided. It can only be assumed that this was one of Schechtman's vendettas.

Sioma was not in Warsaw on March 16. He had gone to Prague for discussions with the head office of the Tatra Bank. Sioma was managing director of the Aliyah Bank Limited, which was registered in London on April 28, 1939. Its offices were in the City of London. The Aliyah Bank was a branch, or perhaps a subsidiary, of the old established Tatra Bank.[12] The directors of the Aliyah Bank were Jabotinsky, Sioma, and another London-based Revisionist, Dr. Simon Klinger. The company listed its purposes as assisting the emigration of Jews from Germany and other eastern European countries, promoting economic development in Palestine, and conducting general banking business. While the Aliyah Bank is not mentioned in either of the Jabotinsky biographies or in other literature relating to the NZO, correspondence between Sioma and his

---

11 Joseph B. Schechtman, *Fighter and Prophet: The Vladimir Jabotinsky Story; The Last Years* (New York: Thomas Yoseloff, 1961).

12 Surviving documentation does not disclose the exact nature of the relationship.

South African contacts seeking funds shows quite clearly that the bank was the vehicle used to finance Af Al Pi. Sioma wrote from London to Haskel in Johannesburg on July 22, 1939, seeking the funds that would enable Af Al Pi to purchase a ship. The letter is headed "Re Aliyah Bank."

Sioma was still in Prague for discussions with the Tatra Bank on March 15, 1939, when the German army marched into the city. His wife, Edna, knew that he was there and recounted that she was sick with worry when the news of the German invasion reached London. She was particularly concerned when Sioma would not leave Prague immediately but stayed on for several days until he had completed his business negotiations.

In the meantime Jabotinsky had written another letter to Sioma in Warsaw, dated March 16, asking Sioma to investigate and report on the bad feeling and destructive arguments within the NZO group in Warsaw and a strike by the staff of the NZO's local newspaper. On the same day, he wrote Sioma another long letter asking him to bring the representatives of the Irgun in Warsaw into line. The Irgun had called a press conference in Warsaw during which they had made statements that were related to both political and military issues. The Irgun, wrote an angry Jabotinsky, "can only act in Palestine…and outside of Palestine all its activities can only be conducted under the authority of the *Shilton*."[13] He finished this long letter by expressing the hope that Sioma would be able to "report to me that formal and sufficient moral guarantees have been given precluding the repetition of *any* action purporting to emanate from the Irgun outside of Palestine."

Sioma is rarely mentioned in the books that have been written about the illegal immigration of the time. Several of the people involved in organizing ships do not recall meeting him, or if they did it was in London. They assumed that he was engaged in arranging matters from London rather than being involved on a practical level in Europe.

However, an analysis of letters to and from Sioma, more than twenty-five in total, indicates quite clearly that Sioma was in Europe almost continuously from March 1939 until his death. He flew between London,

---

13   The world leadership.

Paris, Warsaw, Budapest, Athens, Bucharest, and Bratislava. His wife Edna recalled that in those days, he worked by day and flew by night.

His function in Warsaw included both administrative duties and acting as a troubleshooter when immigration activities ran into difficulty anywhere in eastern Europe. On May 14, 1939, he wrote to Edna from Bratislava, which had been declared the capital of the first independent Slovak republic only two months before. He had hoped to arrange for Jews from there to go to Palestine, only to find that this was no longer possible. He wrote that he would return to Budapest the following day and from there he would make phone calls to determine whether he should go to Yugoslavia or back to Warsaw.

In the particularly hectic month of May 1939, he wrote postcards to his daughters from Stockholm, Riga, Cracow (from two different trips), Athens, Rome, and Budapest in addition to Bratislava. He stayed in Athens for nearly a week in an attempt to charter Greek ships. Edna recounted that Sioma told her that his negotiations in Athens included meetings with Aristotle Onassis (the Greek shipping magnate).

In June 1939, he was briefly back in London before he flew to Paris to meet with Weizmann and Baron Robert de Rothschild, a member of the French Rothschild family. Rothschild had initiated the meeting in order to create a unified fund-raising effort of the NZO and the main Zionist body. Baron Robert de Rothschild was not a Zionist. His aim, he wrote, was to "get most of the Jewish refugees [from Germany, Poland and other eastern European countries] in France out of the country under the best possible circumstances, and then to see what can be done for others elsewhere…but my motto is France before all else." It was the story that had been played out in the United States, Britain, and Germany, in which Western, acculturated Jews were anxious to get the "foreign Jews" from eastern Europe out of the way.

Neither Sioma nor Weizmann would have cared about Rothschild's motivation as long as he agreed to provide the funds that would enable more Jews to reach Palestine. However, negotiations petered out because the two Zionist organizations could not agree. Weizmann's June 19 letter to Rothschild reported that his representatives, "men of wide sympathies and most moderate views," met with Sioma and his colleague for discussions, but that no agreement could be reached on the question of who should control the joint operation and administer its funds. Weizmann insisted that control should remain with the Jewish Agency and the Va'ad Leumi.[14] As the NZO was not represented on either body, there was an impasse.

The correspondence that followed this meeting provokes a wry smile. Sioma's letters to Rothschild were in French, and Rothschild's replies were in English.

While Sioma was in London, he was in almost daily communication with a firm of London ship brokers for either the purchase or the charter of ships to run the blockade of Palestine. The purchase of a five-hundred-ton ship was available for £1,500. The cost of chartering an eighteen-hundred-ton vessel was £900 per month. From these figures of the relative costs of ship charter or purchase, the latter was clearly a better commercial proposition. There were other advantages. Ship owners could choose their own captain and crew, who would obey the owner's instructions. The ship could also be fueled and provisioned where directed by the owners. The ship brokers responded to an inquiry from Sioma about registering a ship in Panama, but funds were not forthcoming for either a purchase or a time charter despite Sioma's constant, urgent cabled appeals to South African Jewry.

On July 9, he wrote to Edna from Athens. He intended that his letter reach her on the day of their wedding anniversary, July 11. It was a moving love letter on the occasion of their tenth wedding anniversary.

> Need I tell you how sorry I am not to be with you on that day? The gods have willed it that we should be apart so often, and be thousands of miles away from each other on the days when we most desire to be together. I should have perhaps defied them on this particular day, forgotten all other duties and obligations and stayed at home, but I couldn't, honey: it would have broken me morally. True that more often than not, things have gone wrong

---

14   The National Council, a representative body of the Jewish community in Palestine.

with my business arrangements, but this was never due to lack of trying on my part, nor to a desire to take things easy, or to please my own convenience. I would have never forgiven myself if the arrangements that I now have in hand failed because I did not give them the necessary attention on the spot. Besides, they affect so many human lives.

Now on the threshold of a new decade in our life together, what shall we wish for? Good health and financial security is all I need for complete happiness. Everything else I have. As for you, you should also wish that your husband shall be less *meshugah*.[15]

I am off tomorrow, to Bucharest Hotel Majestic, shall stay there until the end of the week. Then to Budapest, Warsaw, Paris and home. I should be able to return to London well before the end of July. All my love, my own.

Yours always,

Sioma

The reference to his business arrangements having failed related to the collapse of the Jordania insurance enterprise and, according to a letter that Edna wrote to Haskel after Sioma's death, the stock market slump in 1937. He had taken up a small parcel of shares in Michael Haskel's latest gold-mining enterprise, which was unsuccessful. It would appear that Sioma's engagement with ORT-OZE was no longer in force.

A letter on the Aliyah Bank's letterhead addressed to Edna Jacobi after Sioma's death survived in her records. Dated December 7, 1939, the letter lists Sioma's salary paid by the bank for the four months preceding September 30, 1939, at sixty British pounds sterling per month. The directors of the bank listed on its letterhead were Jabotinsky, Klinger, and Sioma. It would seem that his salary was his only source of income at the time.

Sioma was back in Europe again at the end of July. During the first week of August, he was in Hungary and Romania. His files from those

---

15　"Crazy," in Yiddish.

months were full of correspondence and cables about the difficulties that he encountered with shipping agents, charterers, and ship owners about money. He reported about one ship that arrived off the Palestinian coast with some seven hundred Jews aboard that was not met as promised. Unable to discharge its passengers, it eventually docked in Beirut, where the Jews were interned and the ship detained.

On August 20, 1939, Sioma was in the Hotel Ambassador in Paris. There he wrote a handwritten letter to Michael Haskel in Johannesburg.

The letter is headed "Private and very confidential."

> My dear Haskel,
> It is a long time since I have written to you. You must forgive me. In all my life as a Zionist and a communal worker, I have never been driven so hard, nor felt responsibility so heavily. In my desire to do all I can I deny myself rest and leisure, I don't see my family, I have no time to write to friends, not excluding you and Jabo.
>
> The last six weeks I have been rushing about Europe in an effort to speed up our Aliyah work, which is meeting with great difficulties and obstacles right now. It has become a fight between us with our small resources and Great Britain with her vast power. At every step we are being blocked and have to battle our way through.
>
> To give you two examples: After a lot of trouble and preparation we got for some thousand refugees from Poland a permit to proceed to Peru. The Romanian government had issued the necessary transit visas, so we arranged for a Romanian train to take over the refugees at the Polish frontier. We chartered a boat and brought it to Constanza at the cost of £3000. We had made all the preparations. The refugees sold and liquidated all their possessions, took the train to Constanza. The boat was already there with food for a thousand people for a month. All of a sudden, an order was issued by the Romanian government not to allow the refugees to pass the frontier and cancelled the Romanian train which was waiting for them. I flew to Bucharest, visited every minister and

official, who had any influence in the matter, but was informed that the order could not be rescinded because it was issued at the expressed demand of the British Foreign Office made direct to the Romanian Prime Minister on the grounds that the British had information from their Criminal Investigation Department that the refugees intended to go to Palestine, and not to Peru. All our protests were in vain: the visas had been issued with the express consent of the Romanian Prime Minister himself. The refugees sold everything that they possessed to charter the ship, etc. It was inhumane – but it did not help. We ordered the refugees to remain at the frontier in the fields. They spent two weeks there. Now the Polish authorities will not allow them to remain at the frontier any longer, and we are compelled to take them someplace near Warsaw and arrange to them to camp there until – as we still hope – our interventions with the Romanian authorities succeed – we are trying every possible way.

(I have been informed by important people that the British Government threatened not to grant the Romanians loan facilities, if they allowed these emigrants through!)[16]

Another case of British intervention is in Switzerland. There 200 refugees from Austria have been forced by the government to make arrangements for departure from Switzerland. They asked us to help. For months, we tried to secure the transit visas through France. This was very difficult. Finally, after we satisfied all demands and regulations of the French authorities we secured a passenger steamer which is terribly costly. After we got individual Chinese visas for the refugees, and from the Swiss government

---

16 William R. Perl, *The Four-Front War* (New York: Crown, 1979), 178, cites the minutes of a meeting convened on July 7, 1939, by the secretary of the colonies to discuss ways to stop the flow of Jewish immigrants to Palestine at the source. On page 180, Perl cites a directive issued by the British secretary of state, Lord Halifax, dated July 21, 1939, that was sent to British representatives in Bucharest, Budapest, Warsaw, Belgrade, and Sofia, instructing them to use their influence to prevent Jews from leaving from those countries.

return visas valid for a long period of time, etc., we managed to arrange the trip. All of a sudden, the manager of our office in Zurich was called to Police Headquarters and ordered to close down his office and to cease work. The refugees' passports were withdrawn, and they were forbidden to leave. The reason given was that the British authorities suspect that the refugees intended to land in Palestine, and have asked the Swiss government to prevent them from leaving.

I suppose the above two cases are sufficient to show you with what difficulty emigration work is faced with nowadays.

A steamer with refugees which was delayed on the way due to some needed repairs wished to enter a port on the Mediterranean to have provisions and coal for the journey. It was driven out of all the ports it entered because of the intervention of the British consuls, and not allowed to stay the two or three days necessary to bunker and buy food. At last in Smyrna the passengers revolted and threatened to throw the captain and crew overboard if they leave the port before taking coal and food. We rushed money and supplies and managed to provision the ship before she sailed away.

I need not tell you that the work continues and will not stop while we have any means at all. Every ounce of energy and every available pound is going into this work. Our employees are starving. Our press is suffering because we cannot send out this kind of news without endangering the emigrants, and we have no other activity right now which is as important.

Your colleague asked me for details of the interview at Baron Rothschild's [place] with Weizmann. I am sorry that this was reported to your Executive. I had promised Rothschild not to make it public, and I should not like to lose his confidence.

Your private information, (please destroy this letter) Rothschild arranged the interview with the view of having us work together in this particular line. We both agreed but Weizmann suggested that details should be worked out in London. There after some delay, for which I was not to blame, a meeting took place between four of us, two of the London Zionist office and two of us. I suggested the joint committee, which should conduct the whole work, and agreed that on that committee they should have a majority and we the minority. They were not satisfied with such an arrangement and demanded that this committee shall be subordinated to the Jewish Agency, and to receive its instructions from it. I declined categorically and negotiations broke down. *There is no hope to work with them in any sphere of activity.*

As to the ship which we wish to buy I could write a book on our efforts and disappointments. We missed the opportunity with the first ship because we hadn't the money, then, we negotiated another under the French flag (I wrote to you about it) but the French government intervened and banned the sale if the flag was to be changed (which was indispensable). We then started to look for a boat in the Baltic ports of Scandinavian countries. I have now received a report from our agent that he found a suitable vessel in Stockholm and is negotiating terms. If it is in any way near our means we shall try to buy it and I shall cable once again to South Africa. You will have to help. If we had our own ship, we would have saved thousands of pounds during the last six weeks alone. I can't explain in a letter why we find it so difficult to get a ship suitable for our purposes, nor can I deal even slightly with many other things.

Forgive if this letter is not quite clear, I am very tired. I have been in the air for nine hours and had [a] number of conversations with the various parts of the globe until the early hours of the morning and in two hours time I leave again. Only I thought I would not leave you without a letter any longer and since I can't write from Romania or Greece, I have to write here and now.

Kind regards.

Through all of these difficulties, the exhausting travel and fighting with various authorities in a number of countries, all to save Jewish lives, Sioma was, as one of Jabotinsky's biographers wrote, "a sick man assailed by headaches, and though he insisted on carrying on, his suffering reached a climax in Bucharest."[17]

Edna recalled that Sioma had suffered headaches for many years, certainly since she had known him in Australia and probably before that. They were diagnosed as migraines, for which he was prescribed a strong painkiller. More recently, a diagnosis had been made that his headaches were due to dental problems and he had teeth removed, but to no avail.

An unknown author wrote a description of Sioma's "office" in Bucharest that was published in the London *Jewish Standard* on November 21, 1941, as a tribute to Sioma two years after his death.

> I found Jacobi installed in one of the largest hotels. There was a whole suite of rooms at his disposal. There were offices, typists and telephonists. The head porter at the door of the hotel, when I asked for Jacobi, said quite perfunctorily and with obvious respect for someone with power and authority, "Oh you mean the Palestine Immigration Department."
>
> I was shown into a large room. Jacobi sat at the head of a long table at which were four other men, all known to me for their involvement in the illegal immigration movement. The whole machine worked like H.Q. staff of an army. I took my seat and delivered my report.
>
> Jacobi was obviously unwell. I put it down to the usual English ailment of a bad cold. He agreed but kept rubbing his head as if in great pain. He worked all through that day and into the night. He was loaded up with this work of organizing what was taking place in four or five countries and in addition he carried the financial responsibility of the organization.

Nothing ever went according to plan. Transit visas would be revoked; shipping companies with signed contracts would demand more money; food and supplies for the journey would not be delivered or were stolen.

---

17   Katz, *Lone Wolf*, 1741.

On October 27, 1939, Sioma wrote to Edna from Bucharest. He had arrived there four days before. In his letter, he told her how he had collapsed in the foyer of the hotel. He was assisted to his room by a doctor who was with the Revisionist Party in the hotel. A physician was called in who made a diagnosis that Sioma's symptoms indicated a problem with his sinuses, a common diagnosis of the cause of severe headaches. A nasal spray was prescribed and a specialist in sinuses who had trained in Vienna was called in. The specialist confirmed the diagnosis and proceeded, in Sioma's words, to "rough handle me." The rough handling was trying to drain the sinuses by inserting needles through his nose and cheeks, bombarding his head with ultra-short-wave radiotherapy from two lamps, one on each side of his face, and finally with another needle breaking off some sinus bone. Sioma's letter went on, "The doctor was quite happy about the result, but I wasn't, it hurt like hell."

Sioma wrote that he had not been able to continue to conduct his business in Bucharest and had been forbidden to travel. However, he hoped to be able to finish there in a few days, then go to Budapest and then on to Paris. But the treatment was not successful and his symptoms continued.

Eventually, Sioma was referred to another physician at a leading Bucharest hospital. There he was diagnosed with a swelling of the optic nerves in both eyes, a sign of pressure on the brain. A specialist in Paris who was consulted by phone advised surgery. The original incorrect diagnosis had delayed the possibility of treatment for two weeks. The Bucharest doctor's letter of referral was dated November 6, two weeks after Sioma had collapsed. Sioma was rushed to Paris on the Simplon Express accompanied by a doctor. He arrived there on November 9 and moved into his usual Paris hotel, the Ambassador.

Sioma's family, his mother, his sister and his two brothers were living in Paris. They had left Tel Aviv after Sioma's father had died. Edna flew to Paris. Further examinations in Paris diagnosed a tumor on the brain. Surgery was essential. Sioma wrote a letter to the prefect of police in Paris on November 15 that he "had to undergo an operation as certified by Dr. Rappoport." That night he was able to speak to his daughters in

England by telephone. Surgery was performed in Paris the following day by Professor Clovis Vincent,[18] who had the reputation of being the best neurological surgeon in Europe. Sioma died twenty minutes after the operation.

He was forty-two years old. He was survived by his widow and two little girls aged nine and seven.

One history of the "illegal immigration" of Jews from Europe covering the period from March 1937, when the illegal movements became more pressing and active, until the time of Sioma's death in November 1939, lists a total of forty-two ships that sailed for Palestine with "illegals." The groups that organized these ships are listed. The Revisionists are named as the organizers of twenty-three (55 percent) of those ships.[19] The British Criminal Investigation Department in Jerusalem reported that the Revisionists were bringing illegal immigrants "on by far the biggest scale."[20]

18 Professor Vincent (1879–1947) had just been elected the first professor of neurosurgery in France.
19 Perl, *The Four-Front War*, 367–70.
20 Shavit, *Jabotinsky and the Revisionist Movement*, vol. 2, 424.

CHAPTER 18

POSTSCRIPT

Sioma's body was sent from Paris to London by ship. There were delays due to the wartime shortage of shipping and to bureaucratic procedures on both sides of the Channel. The requirements of both French and British authorities in France were particularly onerous. A number of documents, all duly "legalized," had to be obtained before shipping could be arranged. The coffin left Paris by train draped in a blue and white flag that would later become the flag of the State of Israel. It had been escorted to the station by a group of his colleagues, who placed a bunch of flowers on the coffin. When the casket finally reached London it was taken to the Revisionist offices, where a guard of honor was posted by members of the Executive Committee of the World Union of Zionist Revisionists, the Nessiut, of which Sioma had been chairman. Lighted candles were placed around the coffin in the manner that was used for English lying-in-state funerals of important persons. The funeral took place on the following day. The *Jewish Chronicle* of London carried the following notice on November 24, 1939:

Funeral Notice.

Mr. S. Y. Jacobi

ORT-OZE and Zionist Worker

> We regret to announce the death, which occurred in Paris, following an operation, of Mr. Solomon Y. Jacobi, a member of the executive of the New Zionist Organization and an Executive Member of the Joint British Committee of ORT-OZE.
>
> The funeral will proceed from the Head Office of the New Zionist Organization, 47 Finchley Road, NW8, to the Willesden Cemetery today, Friday (November 24th) at 11 o'clock.

Photographs show a crowded graveside at the cemetery, but there are no press descriptions of the service. One photograph taken at the graveside showed Edna in the place of the chief mourner. At the time, it was not an Anglo custom for women to attend Jewish funerals, although in most European countries they did so.

Jabotinsky delivered the graveside oration, part of which has been quoted in the opening chapter of this book. This is the rest of his speech.

> There is no other example in my memory of a life so completely dedicated to duty; at least of no other masculine life, for the phenomenon is perhaps a little less rare among women. I only met Jacobi when he was twenty-one, but it was evidently years before that, in his early adolescence, that he had fixed for himself a standard of conduct and service to which he adhered to the end. To describe this standard, one must use solid old formulas: staunch loyalty, chivalry, fearless courage; formulas we usually avoid because too seldom are they really deserved. They were in Jacobi's case.
>
> Some day, I hope, a complete history of our military renaissance – the rebirth of Israel as one of the fighting races of this earth – will be written; among its volumes Jacobi's Druzhina[1] will be awarded a special place of honour. In a sense, it was more than a "legion," i.e., than a part of some other nation's army: it was a purely Jewish unit, not only commanded by Jews but obeying a purely Jewish "general staff."
>
> Once more Jacobi returned to Russia: it was about 1921 or

---

1   Russian/Ukrainian, a detachment of select troops.

1922 when he went there to smuggle out of that forbidden walled-in territory his parents, brothers, and sister – and succeeded. Here I report it in a couple of lines: those who knew Russia during the first years of Leninism realize what an epic of adventure, ingenuity, and gallantry such a feat represents.

After that he had a few quiet years in England while finishing at Loughborough his engineer's education begun in Odessa. He graduated in 1924. I think he really loved engineering: it answered so completely two of the dominant strains of his character – the urge for logical clarity and the urge for concrete and tangible achievement. And it was a time of reawakening industrial enterprise, not only in England and all over Europe but – in miniature – also in Palestine: everywhere there were promising openings for a gifted and vigorous young scientist with an English diploma. It was perhaps utterly wrong of me, at such a moment, to offer him the post of secretary-general to the Revisionist Executive in Paris – a gloriously and unsafely underpaid function in the front rank of a dissident party persecuted and maligned by all the ghetto in Zionism. But what matters for a sketch of Jacobi's personality is that he accepted.

This is not a biography, nor is it a history of the Revisionist and New-Zionist movement: I am only trying to sketch a character. In this short note I can no more than touch, and even that superficially, upon a few selected episodes typical of the role Solomon Jacobi has played in our movement.

Let one episode be the Stavsky affair. It was by far not a simple matter to organize the proper defence of the two youths charged with the murder of Arlosoroff. There were, at the time, only four prominent Jewish lawyers in Palestine with any experience in criminal defence; and the Jewish Agency immediately "retained" all those big four to represent interests hostile to Stavsky and Rosenblatt. A criminalist of adequate calibre had to be found in London. This fact is only one illustration of the hundred and one difficulties inherent in this enterprise which had to be conducted in the face of two hostile bureaucracies, one British and one Jewish, of a press lustily reveling in calumny, and of a police system and a judiciary singularly different from Western standards. The fight lasted for over a year and resulted in Rosenblatt's acquittal by the first court and in Stavsky's acquittal by the Court of Appeal after the first court had sentenced him to death. It demanded a great deal of money, and still more of organizing ability.

That was in 1934; the second episode belongs to early 1938, when the first "Konvent"[2] of the N.Z.O. assembled in Prague. All those who were present will bear me out: at that assembly, representing an extremely complicated movement with a range from religious orthodoxy to the Gideonic[3] tradition, and facing as usual a fight on three external fronts, the rallying figure was Jacobi. He had been delayed in coming and only arrived by plane in the third morning of the proceedings: and immediately a feeling of assurance and confidence spread throughout all the building, assembly hall and committee rooms – that special unforgettable feeling which only appears in the presence of the right man in the right place. When I called his attention to the fact he was astonished and asked: "How could that be possible? How can they know me? I hardly even speak at our conventions." True: he hardly ever spoke from a conventional tribune, and he certainly never went on any of those lecturing tours through eastern Europe which for most of us were the ordinary means of getting in touch with our masses. Yet all knew that here is a man on whom you can rely, true, strong, efficient, fair and selfless: they knew it by the wireless telegraphy of personality.

It is a strange, uncanny word, "personality," so mysterious that perhaps its truest Hebrew translation would be "shekhina."[4] This was a big and noble shekhina that has been taken away so untimely

---

2   Convention.
3   Biblical warrior tradition.
4   The Talmud suggests that the Shekhinah is that which created the spirit within the prophets to prophesy, and within King David to compose his Psalms.

and cruelly: a shekhina woven of courage both physical and civic, loyalty, modesty; of clear-sighted intelligence far and high above even what is called best in the average; of cool judgment and cool speech covering a rare talent for friendship and love; and of that inexpressible patrician quality in act and thought and gesture which is the summit of the Betar's vision of the Jew, prince among the nations. Something of great and rare value has been taken away from all of us: from his home where a gentlewoman mourns who had followed him into this Jewish wilderness from happy Australia, a silhouette in which both are blended the steel and the velvet that belong to the nature of Jewish womanhood; and from us – a movement so young yet with so crowded a cemetery.

My thoughts are bitter. A string of names is dragging across my memory, names of comrades in arms or of pupils – Trumpeldor, Vladimir Tiomkin, Jacques Segal, Shlomo Ben Josef,[5] and who knows how many more now throughout Poland; and today this name, both a comrade and a pupil. So many, so uncommonly, so senselessly many... My thoughts are bitter; but, as I have always done and I advise you all to do. The only right thing and the only proud thing to do before the grave is to follow the lesson of the Kaddish.[6] Not a word of the sorrow: speak only of the pride, our pride and our resolve, unbending, unconquerable *"yitgadal."*[7]

The documents that Edna retained relating to the period of her life after Sioma's death indicate that the financial position of the family was extremely difficult. In the last years of his life, Sioma had devoted himself almost entirely to NZO affairs. Any funds raised by the group went toward the rescue of those Jews who were not yet engulfed by Germany and arranging for their transport to Palestine. Michael Haskel had been the generous benefactor of the Revisionist movement since 1934, but five

---

5   Friends and members of the Revisionist movement who had died.

6   A blessing, used here as the mourner's prayer.

7   The opening word of the Kaddish, meaning "Let [the Name of God] be made great."

years later his wealth had declined and he was unable to afford his earlier levels of assistance. The other major source of NZO income, Jabotinsky's speaking tours of eastern Europe, had ceased to exist. This lack of resources meant that the NZO was even less able to pay a reasonable salary to their members who worked full-time for the cause. Sioma had sacrificed any other sources of income to devote himself to the task of rescue. Gone were the days when he could write to Edna and tell her that his earnings for the year would allow her to buy a mink coat, or allow him to purchase antique furnishings and other beautiful pieces for their home.

On December 26, 1939, a month after Sioma's funeral, Jabotinsky wrote to Haskel from London.

> My dear Haskel,
>
> Forgive my very long silence. With me it is as with you – Jacobi's death "has taken the heart out of me." Strangely enough, not at first. Perhaps, I was relieved to know that at least he would not be left a cripple. But as time goes on, the loss grows on me. Every day, there are places or situations which suddenly remind me of where he stood and what he did or said, a year ago or two years, or just almost yesterday. I confess I feel pretty helpless. Nothing done since 1931 was done without him. I feel like climbing steep stairs with out a banister. But worse than that is the monstrous absurdity of his end.
>
> I wonder if you know the details? It seems he had been ill for many years. A growth under the skull. This was the reason of his headaches. In September they suddenly grew intolerable, but the doctor he went to (after much pressure by Edna and us), found it was sinusitis. So he went to Bucharest on Aliyah and Bank business. And from there, one morning we got a cable, giving the right diagnosis and announcing that he would go to Paris, accompanied by a doctor friend, for surgery.
>
> He died 20 minutes after the operation. The surgeon (probably the best in Europe, Vincent) said he had never seen a tumor of such size. It was better for Jacobi not to have survived. A lady who

saw a lot of him in Bucharest was here last week. She is the wife of a co-director of the Aliyah Bank. From her story, it appears that during his stay there, although half paralyzed by considerable pain, he carried on with a great deal of lucidity.

Edna is very brave and sweet; she won't let the disaster crush her and the children. She has decided to stay on in England and has returned to Hodford Road from the country, where she had gone when evacuation was the rule. She told me that you wrote to her, and asking what you can do for her, and was evidently moved to the very depths of her being. But one can guess by simply imagining how one would feel in her shoes at her age and not surrounded by her family and friendly antipodeans. My wife loves her and the children very much and I think Edna reciprocates the feeling. But somehow I feel that of all of us you were the one she feels at home with most, and your letter has been a great comfort to her.

Does she need anything specifically? I cannot tell. It is not clear yet, at least to me, whether she will have to pay death duties on various insurances, and how much will be left. The Aliyah Bank owes her under the contract, a year's salary, i.e. £720, and I hope we will be able to pay it in a few short term installments. But for the moment, the Bank's assets and cash are mostly represented by sums deposited at one of the Big Five banks, and these are likely to be released only after the war, although of course we are trying hard to get it now. But I don't feel like talking business today.

God bless you,

V. Jabotinsky

Edna did not stay in England. She believed that the Aliyah Bank owed Sioma a year's salary, but the real situation was that he was owed for only two months. She liquidated the few assets that there were in Sioma's estate and was able to find a ship, during the difficult wartime period of early 1940, that would take her and her two little girls, aged nine and seven, to Australia.

Vladimir Jabotinsky died of a heart attack in the United States on

August 4, 1940. He was sixty years old. A report of his death included the information that the only personal effects found in his pockets were four dollars and a tobacco pipe.

Michael Haskel was hit by a car in Johannesburg on February 1, 1942. He died in the hospital the following day without recovering consciousness. He was sixty-one. His estate was valued at £30,000, a considerable sum for those days, but a commentary on his life reported that by then his fortune had diminished considerably from its peak some ten years earlier.

SELECTED BIBLIOGRAPHY

Abramsky, Chimen, Maciej Jachimczyk, and Antony Polonsky. *The Jews in Poland.* Oxford: Basil Blackwell, 1986.

Abramson, Henry. *A Prayer for Government: Ukrainian Jews in Revolutionary Times, 1917–1920.* Cambridge: Harvard University Press, 1999.

Applebaum, Anne. *Between East and West: Across the Borderlands of Europe.* New York: Pantheon, 1994.

Babel, Isaac. *The Collected Stories.* Harmondsworth, Middlesex: Penguin, 1961.

Brenner, Lenni. *The Iron Wall: Zionist Revisionism from Jabotinsky to Shamir.* London: Zed Books, 1984.

Bunin, Ivan. *Cursed Days: A Diary of Revolution.* Chicago: Ivan R. Dee, 1998.

Eban, Abba. *My People: The Story of the Jews.* New York: Behrman House, 1968.

Floud, Roderick, and Seán Glynn, eds. *London Higher: The Establishment of Higher Education.* London: Athlone Press, 1988.

Garrard, John, and Carol Garrard. *The Bones of Berdichev: The Life and Fate of Vasily Grossman.* New York: The Free Press, 1990.

Gilbert, Martin. *Churchill and the Jews: A Lifelong Friendship.* London: Simon and Schuster, 2007.

———. *Israel: A History.* London: Black Swan, 1998.

———. *Winston S. Churchill.* Vol. 5, *The Prophet of Truth, 1922–1939.* London: Heinemann, 1976.

———. *Winston S. Churchill.* Companion vol. 5, part 3, *Documents: The Coming of War, 1936–1939.* London: Heinemann, 1982.

Grossman, Vasily Semyonovich. *Everything Flows.* New York: New York Review of Books, 2009.

Heller, Celia Stopnicka. *On the Edge of Destruction: Jews of Poland between the Two World Wars.* Detroit: Wayne State University, 1994.

Herlihy, Patricia. *Odessa: A History, 1794–1914*. Cambridge: Harvard University Press, 1968.

Honig, Eliyahu. *Zionism in Australia, 1920–1939: The Formative Years*. Sydney: Mandelbaum Trust, 1997.

Hyams, Bernard K. *The History of the Australian Zionist Movement*. Melbourne: Zionist Federation of Australia, 1988.

Jabotinsky, Ze'ev (Vladimir). *The Five: A Novel of Jewish Life in Turn-of-the-Century Odessa*. New York: Cornell University Press, 2005.

——. *The Jewish War Front*. London: George Allen and Unwin, 1940.

James, Lawrence. *The Golden Warrior: The Life and Legend of Lawrence of Arabia*. London: Abacus, 1996.

Karsh, Efraim. *Palestine Betrayed*. New Haven: Yale University Press, 2010.

Katz, Shmuel. *Lone Wolf: A Biography of Vladimir (Ze'ev) Jabotinsky*. New York: Barricade Books, 1996.

——. *Days of Fire*. London: W. H. Allen, 1968.

King, Charles. *Odessa: Genius and Death in a City of Dreams*. New York: W. W. Norton and Company, 2011.

Klier, John, and Shlomo Lambroza. *Pogroms: Anti-Jewish Violence in Modern Russian History*. New York: Cambridge University Press, 1992.

Lawrence, T. E. *Seven Pillars of Wisdom*. London: Jonathan Cape, 1935.

Lipman, V. D. *A Century of Social Service: 1859–1959*. London: Routledge and Kegan Paul, 1959.

Medoff, Rafael. *Militant Zionism in America: The Rise and Impact of the Jabotinsky Movement in the United States, 1926–1948*. Tuscaloosa, AL: University of Alabama Press, 2002.

Morris, Benny. *Righteous Victims: A History of the Zionist Arab Conflict, 1881–2001*. New York: Knopf, 1999.

Oz, Amos. *A Tale of Love and Darkness*. London: Chatto and Windus, 2003.

Perl, William R. *The Four-Front War*. New York: Crown, 1979.

Polonsky, Antony. *The Jews in Poland and Russia*. Vol. 2, *1881–1914*. Oxford: Littman Library of Jewish Civilization, 2010.

——, ed. *Polin: Studies in Polish Jewry*. Vol. 3, *The Jews of Warsaw*. Oxford: Littman Library of Jewish Civilization, 2004.

Polonsky, Antony, Ezra Mendelson, and Jerzy Tomaszewski, eds. *Jews in Independent Poland, 1918–1939*. London: Littman, 1994.

Rabinowitch, Alexander. *The Bolsheviks in Power*. Bloomington, IN: Indiana University Press, 2008.

Rubinstein, H. L. *The Jews in Australia, 1788–1945*. Melbourne: William Heinemann, 1991.

———. *The Jews in Victoria*. North Sydney: Allen and Unwin, 1986.

Rutland, S.D. *Edge of the Diaspora*. Sydney: William Collins, 1988.

Sachar, Howard M. *The Course of Modern Jewish History*. New York: Vintage, 1997.

Samuel, Horace B. *Beneath the Whitewash: A Critical Analysis of the Report of the Commission on the Palestine Disturbances of August 1928*. London: The Hogarth Press, 1930.

———. *Unholy Memories of the Holy Land*. London: The Hogarth Press, 1930.

Scammell, Michael. *Koestler: The Literary and Political Odyssey of a Twentieth-Century Skeptic*. New York: Random House, 2009.

Schneer, Jonathan. *The Balfour Declaration: The Origins of the Arab-Israeli Conflict*. New York: Random House, 2010.

Schama, Simon. *Two Rothschilds and the Land of Israel*. New York: Knopf, 1978.

Schechtman, Joseph B. *Fighter and Prophet: The Vladimir Jabotinsky Story; The Last Years*. New York: Thomas Yoseloff, 1961.

Shavit, Yaacov. *Jabotinsky and the Revisionist Movement, 1925–1948*. London: Frank Cass, 1988.

Shimoni, Gideon. *Jews and Zionism: The South African Experience, 1910–1967*. Cape Town: Oxford University Press, 1980.

Shindler, Colin. *The Triumph of Military Zionism*. London: Taurus, 2006.

Toynbee, Arnold, and Kenneth P. Kirkwood. *Turkey*. London: E. Benn, 1926.

Tuchman, Barbara W. *Bible and Sword: How the British Came to Palestine*. London: Macmillan, 1989.

Weinbaum, Laurence. *A Marriage of Convenience: The New Zionist Organization and the Polish Government*. New York: Columbia University Press, 1993.

Weinberg, Robert. "The Pogrom of 1905 in Odessa: A Case Study." In *Pogroms: Anti-Jewish Violence in Modern Russian History*, edited by John D. Klier and Shlomo Lambroza, 248–289. New York: Cambridge, 1992.

Zipperstein, Steven J. *The Jews of Odessa: A Cultural History, 1794–1881*. Palo Alto, CA: Stanford University Press, 1985.

Abdullah 51, 52, 53
Aboriginals 87
acetone, Weizmann's process
    for 46
Acre 43
    prison 50
Actions Committee (AC; World
    Zionist Organization) 55, 74,
    153, 160–63, 167, 168, 176
Adelaide 118
    Jacobi fund-raising in 94, 95
Af Al Pi campaign 199–203,
    205–9
Agra 86
Ahimeir, Abba 141–43
Akzin, Benjamin 190
Albu, Sir George 122
Alexander II 80
Alexander III 17
Alexandria, Jacobi fund-raising
    in 82
Aliyah Bank Limited, Jacobi
    managing director of 5, 200–
    201, 204, 219
Aliyah Bet 4
Allenby, Lord 158
Allied Powers 41

Supreme Council and the Balfour
    Declaration 49
Allies 34, 41, 44
Almaz (ship), as euphemism
    for murder of Revolution
    opponents 29
Altalena (ship) 154
America. *See* Canada; United States
American Jewish Year Book
    1919 1
    1929 106
American Joint Distribution
    Committee 106, 107, 123
American Society for Jewish Farm
    Settlement in Russia 106
Amsterdam 171
Anarchists 30
Anderson (of the Royal
    Exchange) 170
Anglo-Jewry 48
Antioch 43
Antwerp 152
Arabia 45
Arabs 48, 162, 178, 186
    attacks on Jews 50, 183, 188
    and cessation of Jewish
    immigration 50

hostility to Jews in Palestine   51
national strike (1936)   183–84
nationalism   45
natural increase   115–16
skirmishes with the French in
  Syria   51
Argus (Melbourne newsp.), report
  on meeting in Montefiore
  Hall   91
Arlosoroff, Haim   139–42
  murder of   142, 143, 145, 147,
  148–49, 154, 165
Arlosoroff, Mrs.   139, 145, 146,
  154
Armenians   16
arms purchases   180
Asch, Sholem   198
Ashkenazi Jews   75
Asquith, Herbert Henry   45
Athens   4, 202
Auckland   95
Australia   4, 5, 39, 97 n. 4, 100,
  103, 107, 132, 156, 160, 209
  British Jews in Australia   122
  effect of Passfield White Paper
  on Zionist movement in   120
  Jacobi decision to take family
  to   190–91
  Jacobi's fund-raising in   85–96,
  185
  Jewish population of   95, 122
  Zionist movement in   108
Australian Jewish Chronicle (Sydney
  Jewish newsp.), report on Jacobi's
  Sydney meetings   94, 117
Australian Jewish Herald (AJH;
  Melbourne)   89
  Jacobi's articles in   108–111, 115,
  118

report on Jacobi's Melbourne
  meeting and text of address   90
Australian Zionist Federation   91
Australian Mutual Provident Society
  (AMP)   156
Australian Zionist Federation   117
Austria   44, 69
  plight of Jews from   190, 200,
  206

Babel, Isaac   17
"Babi Yar" (Yevtushenko)   10
Babi Yar massacre   9–10
Baghdad   86, 113
Bakst, Nikolai   80
Balfour, Arthur James   42, 42 n. 2,
  46, 48
Balfour Declaration   41–42, 47, 53,
  54, 67, 109, 111, 135, 137, 169
  text   49
  Arab request to impudiate   52
  and the Passfield White
  Paper   119
Baltic countries   69, 70
  Jewish emigration to Australia
  from   123
Bar-Ilan, Meir   180
Basel   133, 136
Batavia   87, 114
Beck, Jozef   198
Begin, Menachem   6 n. 8, 146
Beirut   205
Belarus, Jewish unemployment
  in   123
Belgrade   206n
Ben-Gurion, David   50–51 n. 8,
  139, 141–42, 197
  and the *Altalena*   154
  attitude toward Revisionists   173

and Jabotinsky 174–77
–Jabotinsky pact 174–76
Jacobi's negotiations with 5–6
on possible rapprochement with
the NZO 192–93
and the Stavsky Affair 145
Ben-Horin, Eliyahu 180
Ben Josef, Shlomo 216
Ben-Yehuda, Eliezer 75
Ben-Zvi, Itzhak 51 n. 8
Benares 86
Bene Israel 86
Beneath the Whitewash (Horace
Samuel) 148
Berdichev 1, 7, 8, 11–13
Jewish population of 11–12
plaque commemorating Jews
of 12
Berlin 68, 76, 81, 85, 97, 100, 104,
105, 152
Emigdirect office in 89
ORT office in 80
Bessarabia 81
Betar 4, 4 n. 6, 70, 141,142, 160 n.
1, 167, 173, 196–97, 196 nn. 3, 4,
190, 217
dispute with Jacobi 182
members' entry to Palestine
168, 169–70, 176–78, 190, 192,
194, 199
Birmingham (England) 65
Black Hundred 37, 37 n. 15
Black Sea 45
"Black Tuesday" 107
Blackpool 65
blockade of Palestine, British 4, 4
n. 7, 154, 191, 203
Bloemfontein 123
Jacobi at Community Hall
in 127
B'nai B'rith lodges (Egypt) 82
B'nai B'rith Messenger, on Jacobi's
spring 1929 trip to USA 97
Bolsheviks 2, 23, 25–26, 25 n. 4,
29, 31, 32, 33, 33n, 34, 37–38, 39,
57, 61, 64, 66
Bombay 85, 86
Boulogne Agreement 136, 137
Bradford 65
Bratislava 202
Brindisi, Jabotinsky and Rutenberg
meeting in 58
Brisbane 93, 94, 114, 118
Jacobi fund-raising in 95
Britain 3, 44–45, 46, 47, 51, 58–60,
61, 62–66, 80, 93, 103, 134, 202,
211
fund-raising in 65, 130, 159
interest in the "Holy Land" 43
and Jabotinsky's "Petition
Movement" 163–65
Jabotinsky seeking visa to 179
Jacobi becoming citizen of 132
Jacobi publicizing Jordania
in 157–58
Revisionist view of relations
with 73
British administration in
Palestine 58, 73, 110
personnel's anti-Zionist
stance 55
British Admiralty Laboratory 46
British Colonial Office 120
British Criminal Investigation
Department (Jerusalem),
on Revisionists and illegal
immigration 211

British high commissioner in
    Palestine   50, 53
Broadhurst, Major   150
Brodetsky, Selig   160, 160 n. 2, 161,
    162–63, 188
Brodie, Israel   112, 117, 118
Brussels   81
Bucharest   4, 193, 202, 205, 206n,
    210, 218, 219
    Betar   4, 4 n. 6
    Jacobi's "office" in   209–10
Budapest   202, 206n
Bulawayo   123
Bulgaria   81
Bund   12, 12 n. 3, 22, 22 n. 2, 26

Cairo   51, 52, 101
    Jacobi fund-raising in   82
Calais, "Calais Agreement"   138
Calcutta   86
Canada   81, 107
Canton (China)   114
Cape Town   123, 126, 186
    Thirteenth Zionist Conference
    held in   125
Cardiff   65
Catherine the Great   11, 14
Central Council of the Zionist
    Federation of Odessa   18, 24
central Europe reconstructive
    relief   106
Central Revisionist Office
    (Paris)   73
Cheka   61
chief rabbi of the British
    Empire   5, 81, 89
China   4, 5, 43, 112
    Jewish community of   113–14
Chmielnicki, Bogdan   21, 21 n. 1

cholera   35
Christchurch   95
Churchill, Winston   5, 49–50, 52,
    53n, 151, 163, 164
    appearance before Peel
    Commission   186
    and Lawrence   51
    and Weizmann   54
    White Paper (1922)   53, 67, 178
    n. 3
Club of Revisionist-
    Maximalists   142–43
Cologne   81
Committee for Jewish Migration. See
    Emigdirect
Constantinople   45
Constanza   62, 200, 205
Copenhagen   104, 134
correspondence Jabotinsky-
    Jacobi   3, 65, 66, 79, 80, 82,
    93–94, 102 n. 3, 132
    on birth of Jacobi's second
    daughter   130
    Jabotinsky on Jacobi's 1935 South
    African trip   182
    Jabotinksy's instructions to
    Jacobi for Zionist Executive
    assembly   167
    on Jabotinsky's intention to form
    new party   71
    on illegal immigrants to
    Palestine   195
    Jacobi given authority to settle
    illegal immigration matters   194
    Jacobi on Actions
    Committee   163
    on Jacobi's decision to take his
    family to Australia   190–91
    on Jacobi's employment   83

on Jacobi's work with ORT-OZE 82
on Jordania 158
on London Revisionist office 165
on negotiations with British life insurance company 78–79
and the partition plan 187
on rift in Revisionist movement 137
re Stavsky Affair 146–47, 149, 150–51
on UZR 139
on UZR resignation from Zionist Congress 169
when Jacobi head of London office 147–48
Cossacks 21, 24
Council for German Jewry 191–92
Council of Jewish Women: functions for Jacobi 92, 94
Council of the League of Nations 53
Cracow 202
Crimean Peninsula 13, 18, 29, 38
Czechoslovakia 69
plight of Jews in 190

Damascus 51
Danzig 81
Danziger, Dr. 149
David Wolfsohn Zionist Lodge (Whitechapel) 60
death, Jacobi's 4, 5, 147, 201, 210–11, 213–14
Delhi 86
DeMille, Cecil B. 96, 96n
Denikin, General 39, 39n

Department of Immigration and Travel of British Expeditionary Force (Egypt), Jacobi's *laissez passer* from 59
Di Tribune (Yiddish newsp., Copenhagen) 134
Doyle, Conan, in Hebrew translation 76
Dreyfus, Charles 46
Dunedin 95
Durban 120, 123, 126
Dutch East Indies 85, 87
Dvinsk 105

Eagle Star life assurance company 158
East Indies 4
East London College 59–60, 59 n. 2, 62–63
eastern Europe 3, 4, 11, 54, 70, 114, 140, 163–64, 185, 199, 200, 216, 218
Jabotinsky electioneering in 136
Jews' health in 81
Jews' situation 65, 80–81, 90, 91, 124, 190, 202
Eban, Abba 24
Eden, Anthony 198
education
Jacobi's 13, 14, 19, 30–31, 35–36, 58
in Palestine 116–17
Egypt 4, 43, 51, 58, 80, 85, 86
Jacobi fund-raising in 82
Einstein, Albert 5, 76, 81, 89, 114, 131
letter of introduction by 96, 122
Ekaterinoslav 61

Eleventh Hour, The (S. Africa NZO
    journal)
    Jacobi article on Transjordan
    for   186–87
    report on Jacobi speech   186
Emigdirect   3, 3 n. 5, 80, 81, 83, 89,
    91, 97, 100, 104, 119, 124
    Australian request to cancel
    Jacobi trip   89
    and HIAS   106
    Jacobi working for   82
    Jacobi's fund-raising for   95, 127
emigration from eastern Europe
    and Russia, Jewish   81
employment bureau (Sydney),
    Jewish   94
engineering   1, 3, 4, 19, 30, 31, 35,
    57, 58–60, 62, 64, 66, 72, 112, 215
England. *See* Britain
English (language)   3, 101, 103–4,
    203
English Council for German
    Jews   190
Epstein, Jacob   50 n. 8
Epstein, Ludmilla   196 nn. 2, 3
Eshkol, Levi   51 n. 8
Ettinger, Mark   91
"The Exile," article by Jacobi   31,
    31 n. 9

Faber, Mr.   165
Falk, L. A.   118, 118 n. 3
Far-East, fund-raising for ORT-
    OZE   112, 113–14
Federation of Ukrainian Jews
    (England)   60
Feisal, Sherif   51, 109
First Aliyah   18

First Russian Revolution
    (1905)   14, 22
Five, The (Jabotinsky)   16, 16 n. 7
Foreign Office, British: blocking
    refugees from Europe   206
France, French   14, 16, 23, 36, 38,
    44–45, 47, 103, 122, 202, 206
    skirmishes with Arabs   51
French (language)   3, 60, 65, 153,
    203
fund-raising   3–4, 39, 69, 79, 82,
    83, 85, 87, 95–96, 97, 104, 112,
    113–14, 127
    American groups   106
    in Australia   85–96, 185
    in Britain   65, 130–31, 159
    for emigration of Jews from
    Europe (1939)   202
    Jabotinsky   69, 189
    for ORT-OZE   80, 82–83, 95,
    97, 118, 127–28, 130, 159, 185
    pamphlets for   125, 131
    in South Africa   4, 5, 39, 121–25,
    181–82, 185, 186
    1928 trip   85–86

Galilee   50, 58
Galperin, Eliyahu   102, 102 n. 3
Gaza Strip   52
General Zionists   147, 174, 180
Genoa   81
George (South Africa)   123
German Jews in Australia   122
German Jews   111
German (language)   3, 59, 60, 65,
    69, 75, 103, 65
Germany   44, 69, 76, 78, 88, 122,
    142, 200, 202

control of Odessa (1917–
1918)   33–34, 33n
Gilbert, Martin   119, 151, 174n
Glasgow   38, 158
Gomel   22
Gorky, Maxim   17 n. 9
Grauman, Sir Harry   122
Great Depression, the   118–19,
127–28
Greeks   16
Greenberg, Leopold   122
Grishin-Almazov, Colonel   36–37,
36 n. 14
Grossman, Meir   71, 83n, 104, 148,
180
administrator of Revisionist
movement   134–35, 137–38
split with Jabotinsky   135–38
Grossman, Vasily   12
Gruzenberg, Oscar   28
Gunsberg, Horace de   80

Hadassah   115
Hadera   18
Haganah   50, 180, 197
Haifa   119, 161
attacks on Revisionists in   161
n. 4
Halifax, Lord   206n
Hamburg   133
Ha-olam (news magazine; Palestine),
obituary on Jacobi in   60–62
Hardoon (family)   113
Harrington, Lord   93
Hasefer [Limited] (publishing
house)   75–76, 77
Hashemite Kingdom   53
Hasidism   11, 11 n. 2

Haskalah ("Enlightenment")   12,
12 n. 4
Haskel, Michael   131, 132–34, 133
nn. 6, 7, 160, 186, 204
and Af Al Pi campaign   201
death of   220
financial support for Revisionist
movement   5, 121, 133, 146–47,
165–66, 218–19
Jacobi letter about Aliyah
work   205–6
Jacobi London representative
for   132, 151, 160, 164
problems with   170
havlagah (restraint) in face of Arab
violence   188
Haydemakes   32–33
Hazit ha-Am (Revisionist newsp.,
Pal.), attack on Arlosoroff
in   141–42
health
of Jews in Eastern Europe and
Russia   81, 123
of Palestine population   116
Hebrew
adopted as common language at
Eleventh Zionist Congress   75
classical   65, 75, 86
modern   3, 24, 59, 65, 68, 75, 76
recognition as an official language
of Palestine   75
Hebrew Geographical Atlas, The   76,
77
Hebrew Sheltering and Immigrant
Aid Society   106
Hebrew Standard (Sydney), report on
Jacobi's visit   94
Hebrew University of Jerusalem
52, 75

Hebron   105, 119
Hehaver (Zionist youth group)   26
Herut (newsp.), tribute to Jacobi   6,
    6 n. 8
Herzl, Theodor   44, 67, 111, 169
Hertzog, J. B. M.   121, 186
hevra kadisha (Jewish burial society),
    Odessa   14
HIAS. *See* Hebrew Sheltering and
    Immigrant Aid Society
Histadrut of Zionist Activist Youth
    in the name of Trumpeldor. *See*
    Betar
Histadrut   50, 141, 188
    denying membership to
    Revisionist workers   186
    members invading
    synagogue   154
    rejection of Jabotinsky–Ben-
    Gurion pact   176, 183
Hitler, Adolf   12, 141, 142
Hoffman, Jacob   160, 160 n. 1
"homeland for the Jews"   44, 58,
    109, 111
Hong Kong   114
Honig (Sydney Zionist)   118
Horowitz (National JNF Fund
    Committee member)   163
Hungary   204
hydroelectric station, Palestine   50,
    58, 66

"illegal" immigration to
    Palestine   154n, 162, 190, 195,
    197
    Jacobi activity for   199–202
    Revisionist's role in   211
Immigration Department, Palestine
    government   156

immigration to Palestine,
    Jewish   53, 93, 174, 180
    Betar members'   168, 169, 176–
    77, 196
    cessation of   50
    control of   73
    Histadrut allocating entry permits
    for   182, 186
    limitation on   54, 119, 125,
    173–74, 191
Imperial Airways plane crash   182
"In the Days of the Pogroms"
    (Jacobi speech)   127
Independent Zionist Organization.
    See New Zionist Organization
India   4, 5, 43, 44, 85
Institute of Railway Engineers
    (Petersburg)   19, 30, 31
international defense force, proposal
    for Jewish   65
Iraq   41, 51
Ireland   65
Irgun Zeva'i Le'umi   154, 180, 193,
    194, 196–97, 199, 201
"The Iron Wall" (Jabotinsky)   69
Israel, biblical   54, 55, 71
Israel Defense Forces (IDF)   154
Israel's Messenger (Shanghai Jewish
    newsp.)   114
Istanbul   62
Italian   153
Italy   58
Ivri (Johannesburg Jewish newsp.)
    interview with Jacobi   123
    report on mass meeting in
    Johannesburg   124

Jabotinsky, Joanna   78, 121

Jabotinsky, Vladimir   43, 102 n. 3,
   50–51, 54, 104, 109, 134, 137,
   141n, 204
   and Ahimeir   142–43
   articles critical of left-wing
   parties   140
   asking Jacobi to work with
   UZR   72
   attitude to strikes   141
   barred from Palestine   120
   and Ben-Gurion   173, 174–77
   best man at Jacobi's
   wedding   102
   call for cancellation of
   White Paper (after Shaw
   Commission)   135
   death of   219–220
   decision to move to
   Palestine   94, 94 n. 2
   exchange of letters with Jacobi
   See correspondence Jabotinsky-
   Jacobi
   first meeting with Jacobi   58
   friendship with Jacobi   2–3, 65,
   66
   fund-raising tours   69, 189
   graveside oration for Jacobi   2,
   214–16
   and Hasefer   75–76
   high regard for Jacobi   127
   influence on Betar and the
   Irgun   196
   and the Irgun   180
   "The Iron Wall"   69
   Jacobi working with   74–75
   on Jacobi's fund-raising   130
   and Jewish emigration from
   Poland   197–98
   and Jewish Legion   47–48, 50,
   50 n. 8
   and Judea Life Insurance
   Company   155–56
   and the Labor Party in
   Palestine   173
   and leave of absence from
   chairmanship of Executive
   Committee of WUZR   137
   letter to Haskel after Jacobi's
   death   218–19
   meetings with Ben-Gurion   6,
   174
   and Palestine work visa   156
   and the "Petition
   Movement"   163–165
   lecture at Manhattan Opera
   House   77
   move to Paris   69
   and peace conference between
   Palestine parties   173–74
   proposal for Jewish Agency
   Executive   54
   reaction to 1905 pogrom in
   Odessa   23
   resignation from the Zionist
   Organization   55, 67–68
   reviving *Rasswyet*   69
   and Rutenberg   58
   Samson the Nazarite   96
   seeking rapprochement with main
   Zionist organization   192
   at Seventeenth Zionist
   Congress   137
   and the Seventh Dominion
   League   93
   South Africa trip (1930)   121
   speeches difficult for   152–53

split with Weizmann   55, 104
USA trip (1926)   77, 78
The Five   16, 16 n. 7
"We the Bourgeois"   140
Jabotinsky–Ben-Gurion pact   174–76
Jacobi, Carmel   130, 153 n. 5
Jacobi, Edna Jones   5, 6, 107, 112, 132, 133 n. 6, 191, 201, 202, 209, 219
  anniversary letter from Sioma   203–4
  at Jacobi's funeral   214
  engagement to Jacobi   91–92
  financial situation   204, 217–18
  first marriage and divorce   99, 101
  hearing Jabotinsky's speech before the Peel Commission   185
  on Jacobi meeting with Zaharoff   179–80
  letters from Jabotinsky   3, 130, 152n, 175, 188–89
  marriage to Jacobi   100–105
  move to Australia after Jacobi's death   219
  visit to South Africa   126–27
  visits to Melbourne   108, 120, 160, 170–71, 174
Jacobi, Naomi   114–15, 120, 127, 152n
Jaffa   119
Jerusalem   43, 102, 103, 109, 156, 167
  Arab attack on   50
  Government House   52
  Jacobi surveyor in   57

Seventh Dominion League in   93
Jewish Agency   73, 111, 126, 177, 181, 203, 208
  accusing Revisionists of reprisals against Arabs   188
  and Betar immigration certificates   169, 177–78
  Council of the League of Nations call for   54
  directing political work   110
  Executive   54, 103
  non-Zionist members   103–4, 109, 110–11
  policy of restraint   188
  refusal to assist German and Austrian Revisionists and Betar members   190, 192
  retaining lawyers in Stavsky Affair   215
Jewish Battalion   68
Jewish Chronicle (London)
  ad for JNF Assurance Department   157
  ads for Jordania in   158
  on Jacobi's activities for JBC   130
  Jacobi's funeral notice   213–14
  letters on responsibility of NZO for reprisals against Arabs in Palestine   188
  letters to the editor by Jacobi   169, 171
  report on fund-raising campaign for Ukrainian Jews   65
  report on Jacobi's message to Zionist General Council   167–68
  report on NZO Vienna congress   179, 181

Jewish Court of Honor, Betar
members' requests for
immigration certificates and
the   170
Jewish Daily Bulletin (New York)
on Jacobi's visit to USA
(1926)   77
on Jacobi's meeting with OZE in
New York   107
on Jacobi's speech at NZO
Vienna congress   178, 181
Jewish Defence Corps   2
Jewish Democratic Party   26
Jewish Echo (Glasgow), Jacobi letter
to the editor in   169
Jewish Guardian, article on misery of
Ukrainian Jews   65
Jewish Health Organisation of
Great Britain. *See* OZE
Jewish Health Society. *See* OZE
Jewish Herald (Melbourne)   95
Jewish Herald (South Africa)   153
n. 6
Jacobi–Ben-Gurion
correspondence leaked in   193
Jewish Legion   47–48, 58, 104, 134
Jewish life insurance companies,
Jacobi's call for   79
Jewish National Fund   110, 111,
115, 163
Jewish People's Party   26
Jewish regiment in British army. *See*
Jewish Legion
Jewish Settlement Treasury   78
Jewish Standard (London),
description of Jacobi's Bucharest
"office"   209
Jewish State Party   138, 174, 180

Jewish Telegraph Agency   132 n.
5, 163
on agreement on self-defense in
Palestine   193
on Jacobi's fundraising in
Melbourne   93
interview with Weizmann   137
on "Petition Movement"   164–
65
Jewish Times (New Zealand), on
Jacobi's 1928 visit   95
Jewish World (London), on opening
of New Revisionist club   180–81
"Jews in Eastern Europe: Story
of Post War Plight" (article in
Argus)   91
Jews of India, The (unfinished
Jacobi article)   86
Johannesburg Star, report on Jacobi
speech   182
Johannesburg   123, 126, 127, 201,
206
Jabotinsky speech in   121
report on mass meeting in
Standard Theatre   124
Joint British Committee (JBC)
for the Reconstruction of East
European Jewry   130, 184. *See
also* ORT-OZE
Jones, Albert   88, 91, 92, 117, 120
Jones, Edna. *See* Jacobi, Edna
Jordan River   42, 51, 136
Jordan   51
Jordania Society Limited   156–58,
163, 204
Jacobi managing director for   5,
157–58, 160, 164
Judaism   103

Judea Industrial Corporation   78, 97, 155

Judea Life Insurance Company   79, 94, 94 n. 2, 97 n. 4, 126, 155–56

Kadoori (family)   113

Kampala   181–82

Keidany   105

Kenworthy, Joseph   93

Kenya   160

Kenya Consolidated Goldfields Limited   160

Keren Hayesod   79

Kerensky government   25 n. 4, 57

Khadzhi-Be. *See* Odessa

Kiesling, Barrett C.   96n

Kiev   9

Kimberley   123

King of Kings (film)   96

Kishiniev pogrom   22

Klausner, J.   63

Klinger, Simon   200, 204

Klinger, Stefan   187, 187 n. 6

Koestler, Arthur   69, 70

Kook, Rabbi Abraham Isaac   102, 102 n. 2

Kovno   104

L'Aurore (Cairo newsp.)   82

La Bourse Egyptienne (Cairo newsp.)   82

La Liberté (Cairo newsp.)   82

Labor Party (Zionist)   167
attitude toward Revisionists   140, 147, 148, 173–74, 182
See also left-wing Zionist movement

Land of Israel   41

land sales to Jews in Palestine, British approval for   119, 125

Landau (*Palestine Post* shareholder)   166

Landau, J. L   122

Lasky, Neville   81, 105

Latvia   185

Lawrence, T. E.   45, 52, 52–53 n. 9

lawyers for Stavsky Affair defendants, Jacobi engaging   146, 148

League for the Revision of Zionist Policies – Provisional Organizational Bureau (letterhead)   72

League of Nations   42, 132
Mandate for Palestine   53, 67, 73

Lebanon   45

left-wing Zionist movement   6
and the Revisionist right   74, 103, 140, 141, 145, 168
See also Labor Party

letters to the editor in Jewish newspapers, Jacobi's   169

Levant Fair   130, 130 n. 1

Levey, J. H.   81, 130, 157

Levi Yitzhak of Berdichev   11–12

Levinson Estate   91

Limit, The (Loughborough College magazine)   31 n. 9, 79

Lipsky, Louis   77–78

Literary and Debating Society (Loughborough College)   64

Lithuania
condition of Jews in   125, 185
Jewish emigrants in South Africa   122–23

Liverpool   65, 81

Lloyd George, David 42, 46, 48, 49, 50
Locker, Berl 160, 160 n. 3, 161, 163
London 46, 58, 61, 71, 72, 77, 78, 85, 93, 100, 105, 127, 152, 176, 187, 200, 207
Emigdirect office in 81–82
Golders Green 129
Jacobi in 4, 5, 6, 19. 59, 62–65, 79, 129, 199
Jacobi publicizing Jordania in 158
Jacobi Revisionist bureau chief in 139, 158
NZO headquarters in 179
ORT ball at Dorechester Hotel in 132
Revisionist office in 4, 134, 136, 213
Zionist office in 208
London Employment Exchange 59
London Federation of Ukrainian Jews, Council of the 65
London Jewish Cemetery (Willesden) 5
London Relief Federation 95
London Stock Exchange 160
Los Angeles 96
Loughborough College (Leicestershire) 63–64, 66, 79, 215
Oratory Night 65–65
reference from 130
Lytton, Lord 158

Maan 51

Macassa 114
Maccabean Hall (Sydney) 94
Maccabi (sports group) 26
MacDonald, Ramsay 119, 135
Manchester 46, 158
Mandate, British Palestine 51, 53, 70, 73, 116, 153, 162, 188
blockade against illegal immigration of Jews 191
Irgun attitude to 197
map recording his journey to India (1928) 86
Marley, Lord 5, 131, 131n
Marseilles 85
Masel, Alec 118
"May Laws" 18
McMahon letter 45
Mediterranean Sea 45
Mehmet Ali 43, 43 n. 6
Melbourne 94, 95, 99, 100, 104, 108, 111, 112, 114–15, 120, 170–71
attempt to establish Revisionist movement 117
Carlton Hall meeting against Passfield White Paper 120
East Melbourne synagogue 118
immigrant problem of Jewish community 88–89
Jacobi's fund-raising mission to 87–93
Toorak Road Synagogue 117
Melbourne Hebrew Congregation 88
Melbourne Jewish Advisory Board 88
Mesopotamia 41, 45
Meyerheim, Miss 165

Michelson, Prof.   96
Middle East Department   49, 51
Ministry of Foreign Affairs,
    documents on the NZO in
    Poland's   198
Mirls, Roy   99
Mizrachi   174
Monash, General Sir John Monash,
    letter of support to Jacobi   92,
    118
Monash House (Melbourne)   92
Montagu, Edwin   47, 48
Montefiore Hall (Melbourne)   91
Montefiore Home (Melbourne)   90
monument commerating Babi Yar
    massacre   10
Morocco   75
Moscow   35
Motza   119
My People: The History of the Jews
    (Eban)   24

Nansen Passport   132
Napoleon   43
national home for the Jewish
    people   41, 47, 48, 52, 53, 136
Nessiut. *See* Union of Zionist-
    Revisionists: Executive
    Committee
Netanya   195
Neumann, Immanuel   180
New Palestine, on Jabotinsky's
    speech to Fifteenth Zionist
    Congress   74
New Revisionist Club
    (London)   178, 180
New South Wales, immigration of
    Jews to   94

New York City   72, 96–97, 97 n. 4,
    105, 107, 122
New York Times, article on pogroms
    against Ukranian Jews   60
New Zealand   85, 100
    Jacobi fund-raising in   95
New Zionist Organization
    (NZO)   5, 176, 178, 197, 202,
    203
    first world assembly   188
    finances   179, 181, 190, 191,
    217–18
    internal problems   182, 193
    Jacobi involvement in   186–87,
    190–92, 216–18
    Jacobi's speech at Vienna
    congress   178–79, 181
    London office   213–14
    and the *Jewish Herald*   193
    office in Warsaw   198, 199–200
    reasons for establishing   178,
    181
    supporting Palestine on both
    sides of the Jordan   187
    See also Revisionist movement,
    Revisionists; World Union of
    Zionist Revisionists
Newcastle   158
newspapers, Jewish
    NZO Yiddish Warsaw
    weekly   193
    reports on Jacobi's 1930 South
    African trip in   123
    support of mainstream Zionist
    Organization   70
    See also by individual names
Nikitin   39
Nobel (explosives
    manufacturer)   82–83

Novograd-Volinks 7

occupations of Jews in the East 86
October Revolution (1917) 25
Odessa 1, 2, 9, 12, 13–17, 23, 25,
   30, 32, 36–40, 57, 61, 62, 63
   commission to keep order in 37
   first synagogue in 14
   Jacobi bringing family out of 60,
   61–62, 64, 215
   Jacobi's birthplace in
   documents 13
   Jacobi's speeches on experiences
   in 66
   Jewish self-defense in 21–40,
   66, 127
   Jewish population 15–16
   pogroms in 13–14, 21, 22
Odessa Committee 17
Odessa military hospital 19
Odessa News 38
Odessa Polytechnic Institute, Civil
   Engineering Faculty 35–36
Odessa Zionist Histadrut 24
Odessa Zionist Organization 57
Okoyed 26–30, 31, 32–33, 34, 36,
   37
   dismantling by Red Army 39
   photos described 27, 31–32
Onassis, Aristotle 202
Order of the Sons of Zion 78
Organizational Committee of
   Jewish Self-Defense Forces of
   the City of Odessa 24
ORT 3, 3 nn. 4, 5, 80
   ball (1933) 132
ORT-OZE 5, 39, 62, 91, 97, 100,
   104, 105–6

advance announcement of
   Jacobi's arrival 114
Berlin office 105, 122, 127
board 89
British branch 105
cancelling fund-raising in
   Australia 119
Central Committee 130
Jacobi text for speech 185
Jacobi's employment by 3, 80,
   82, 83, 100, 159, 185, 204
Jacobi's fund-raising for 80,
   82–83, 95, 112, 118, 127–28, 130,
   133, 159, 185
Jacobi's spring 1929 fund-raising
   trip to America 96–97
Jacobi's letters of introduction
   from 121–22, 130
Joint British Committee
   (JBC) 130, 184
London office 81
United Committee 81
ORT Reconstruction Fund,
   American 106
Ottoman Empire 41
overseas aid for Jews,
   American 106. *See also*
   Emigdirect; ORT
OZE 81, 97, 104, 106
   American National
   Committee 107
   Berlin 85, 107
   Central Committee of 122
   Jacobi as representative in U.S.
   and Canada 107
   Jacobi fund-raising for 97
   Jacobi's letters of
   introduction 85

summer camp   105
   See also ORT-OZE

Pale of Settlement   11, 11 n. 1, 18
   emigration from   18–19
Palestine Police Force, British   197
Palestine Post
   and Haskel   132 n. 5, 134, 166
   reports on Stavsky Affair   150
Palestine   2, 4, 18, 41, 45, 49, 51,
   71, 81, 88, 134, 162
   Arab "riots" in   50, 109, 119,
   180
   borders   52, 54
   British administration in   120
   call for Jewish self-defense
   in   126
   cessation of Jewish immigration
   to   50
   dissension between Revisionists
   and Labor in   140
   economics of   116
   First Aliyah   18
   French-Arab skirmishes in
   northern   51
   funds for education and health
   in   116
   geopolitical importance   43, 110
   goal of Jewish majority in   93,
   115, 126, 136, 183
   Haskel as South Africa's honorary
   commissioner in   134
   hatred between Jewish left and
   Revisionist right   141
   as home for the Jewish
   people   41, 47, 48, 52, 53, 67
   idea of Jewish state in   48, 67,
   71, 109, 136, 169, 182

idea of Jews return to   41–42, 44
insurance companies investments
   in   155, 157
Jacobi in   57, 101–2, 167
Jacobi's family in   60, 62, 82,
   101–2, 127
Jacobi's request for *laissez-passer* to
   (1922)   63
Jacobi's request for travel permit
   to   19, 40
the Jacobis' marriage in   100
Jewish opposition to idea of a
   state   103
Jewish population of   44
Jewish settlement in   115
Jews' emigration to
   Australia   122
and Jordania Society Limited   5
and Judea Life Insurance
   Company   155–56
land requirements for Jews
   in   116
limitation on Jewish immigration
   to   54, 153, 197
need for Jewish middle class
   in   140–41
planned evacuations from Europe
   to   199
possible settlement of Jews
   in   45, 47
secondary industry in   116
Stavsky Affair in   145–50, 154
Palmerston, Lord   44
pamphlets for fund-raising
   campaigns   125, 131
Paris   42, 69, 76, 152
   Jabotinsky in   3, 66, 71, 74, 79,
   130, 134, 135, 137, 179

Jabotinsky-Jacobi meetings
in 151, 159, 164
Jacobi in 3, 4, 73, 74, 77, 79, 83,
85, 100, 105, 151, 159, 164, 167,
202, 204, 205, 206, 210, 211, 214
Jacobi's death in 1, 4, 5, 210–11
Jacobi's family in 210
foundation of Revisionist Party
in 42, 71
Revisionist office in 72, 73, 74,
76, 82, 104, 105, 136, 169
Weizmann, Jacobi, Baron Robert
de Rothschild meeting in 202
UZR executive in 166, 167, 168,
177
Parliament, Chuchill's White Paper
and 53
Passage of a Life: An
Appreciation from Palestine" (S.
Ussishkin) 60–62
Passfield, Lord 119
Passfield White Paper (1930) 119–
20, 125–26, 178 n. 3
Patterson, J. H. 149
Peel Commission 184, 191
Jabotinsky appearing before 185
partition proposal 187
Peel, William 184, 184n
Penang 86
Perl, William 196 n. 2, 206n
Persia 75
Perth 93, 95
Jewish community 87
Peru 205
Petition movement 163–65, 173
Petlura, Symon 36–37, 36 n. 13
Petrograd 32
Poalei Zion 26

pogroms
eastern Europe 124
Odessa 13–14, 21
Palestine. *See* "riots," Arab
Ukraine 1, 17, 21–23, 25, 31,
60, 61
Poland 11, 54, 81, 88, 123, 152,
164, 202
and Betar members' applications
to enter Palestine 177–78
condition of Jews in 124, 125,
185
Jabotinsky's plan for Jewish
emigration from 197–98
Jewish refugees from 205
Jews' emigration to
Australia 122
and plebiscite on withdrawal from
Zionist Organization 176, 177
Poliakov, Samuel 80
Polish 75
Ponevezh 105
Port Said 100, 101, 103, 127
Prague 4, 81, 147, 200–201
first NZO world assembly
in 188, 216
Preserving the Health of the Jews
in Eastern Europe. *See* OZE:
American National Committee
Prisoner of Zenda (Hope), Hebrew
translation 76
"Projected Campaign in Provinces"
(*Jewish Guardian*) 65
Prudential Assurance
Company 157
Prussia 44
Pushkin, Alexander 14–15

Rachel's Tomb   102–3
Radical Poalei Zion party   26
Railway University. *See* Institute of
    Railway Engineers
Rangoon   86
Rappoport, Dr.   210
Rappoport, I. R   13, 61
Rasswyet (weekly Zionist
    journal)   69, 70
    "Insurance and Markets" (Jacobi
    article)   78–79
    "Revisionism in America (Letter
    from New York)" (Jacobi
    article)   77
    transfer to Paris   140
"Reconstructing European Jewry:
    Distinguished Visitor Arrives"
    (headline about Jacobi)   89
"Reconstructing Jewish Life
    in Eastern Europe" (Jacobi
    article)   114
Red Army   2, 23, 35, 36, 38
    arrest of Jacobi by   38–39
Refugee Secures Second Place"
    (report on Oratory Night in
    Nottingham Evening Post)   64
Rehovot   18
Relief of German Jewry
    (conference, London)   150
restraint. See *havlagah*
Revisionist movement, Revisionist
    Party, Revisionists   3, 27, 42, 62,
    85, 90, 91, 108–11, 138–39, 109,
    162, 174, 197
    administrative world
    headquarters   134
    and arms purchases   180
    articles in *Zionist Record*
    about   125

attacked at Sixteenth Zionist
    Conference   103
Australia   117, 120
and Betar   70, 196–97, 196 n. 4
and boycott of German
    trade   147, 165, 171, 181
Central Committee   42, 71, 74,
    77
on class domination   74
Conference (1934)   196 n. 4
and the Eighteenth Zionist
    Congress   147
finances of   5, 78, 121, 134,
    139, 146, 150–51, 179, 181–82,
    198–99, 201
formation of Party   71
hatred of Jewish left   141
and illegal immigration   195–96,
    211
internal dissension   135–38, 176
Jabotinsky's USA trip to attract
    members   77
Jacobi London bureau chief
    of   146, 147
Jacobi's salary   159
and Judea Life Insurance
    Company   155–56
and Labor Party   140, 147, 148,
    167, 173–74, 182
London office   4, 104, 137, 147
on Jewish majority in
    Palestine   71, 93, 110, 126,
    136–37
meeting at Eden Theatre   168
message to Zionist General
    Council (1934)   167–68
and Palestine on both sides of
    the Jordan   42, 43, 70, 177, 179,
    187

Paris office 72, 76, 77, 82, 83,
104, 105
platform declaration 73–74
plebiscite on who should lead the
party 138
plebiscite on support for
withdrawal from the Zionist
Organization 176, 177–78
Political Commission 5
and resignation from
WZO 168–69
represented at Thirteenth South
African Zionist Conference 125
represented at Zionist
Conferences 136
rift with left-wing Zionist
movement 6
seen as fascists by left-wing
parties 140, 141
South African 182, 199
Stavsky Affair and the 145–50,
154
and the Transfer
Agreement 139, 171, 178–79,
181
Warsaw 4
and Wedgwood's idea for
Transjordan 93
World Conference (1932) 142
and the Zionist Federation 94
See also New Zionist
Organization; World Union of
Zionist Revisionists
Revisionist Provisonal Committee
(South Africa) 118
Revisionist Zionist Alliance (RZA).
See Union of Zionist-Revisionists
Ribas, José de 14

Richelieu, Duc 14
Riga 4 n. 6, 70, 71, 105, 202
"riots," Arab 50, 109, 119, 180
Rockefeller, John D. 106
Rogashev 7
Roman Catholic Church 45
Romania 152, 185, 204, 205–6
Rome 47, 202
Rosenberg (Roseby), David 117,
120
Rosenblatt, Zevi 142, 143, 145–46,
154, 175, 216
Rosenthal, Newman 95, 108, 117,
120
Rotary Club, Jacobi speaking at 65
Rothschild, Baron Robert de 202,
203, 207
Rothschild, Lord 5, 42, 42 n. 3, 48,
81, 89, 105, 114, 122, 130
Rotorua 95
Royal Exchange Assurance 157
Rumcherod 25, 25 n. 5
Ruslan (ship) 40, 40 n. 18
Russia 44, 45, 62, 81, 88, 106, 128
condition of Jews in 123–24,
125, 185
unemployed Jews in 90–91
Russian (language) 3, 60, 65, 75,
103, 153
Russian army service, reserves 19
Rutenberg, Pinhas 50, 57–58, 63,
66, 174
and Jabotinsky 58

Sacher, Harry 166, 166 n. 8
Safed 119
Saigon 114
Salonika 71

Salzman, S. D.   75
Samarang   87, 114
Samson the Nazarite (Jabotinsky)   96
Samuel family (London)   96
Samuel, Sir Herbert   50, 52, 76
Samuel, Horace   163, 170
   on Jabotinsky   68
   as defendant's lawyer in Stavsky
     Affair   148–51
San Francisco   95–96
San Remo   41
Sassoon (family)   86, 113
Saulwick, Hal   170–71, 170n
Saulwick, Marjorie   170n
Savoy Hotel (London), JBC fund-
   raising dinner at   130–31
Schechtman, Joseph Boris   200
Schwartz, Mark   126–27
Schwartzman, M.   165, 165 n. 6, ,
   174, 190
Scotland   65
   fund-raising for ORT-OZE
   in   130
   Jacobi publicizing Jordania
   in   157–58
Segal, Jacques   216
self-defense in Odessa, Jewish   21–
   40, 89–90, 114, 127
   dismantling by Red Army   39
   Jabotinsky on   23
   Jacobi's involvement in   24, 61
Sephardi Jews   75
   referring to Bene Israel as "the
    colored"   86
Seventh Dominion, The
   (Wedgwood)   92–93
Seventh Dominion League   93
Shanghai   114

Shaw, George Bernard   131
Shaw Commission of Inquiry   119
   White Paper following   135
Shechtman, J. B., description of
   Revisionist Paris office   74
Shepherd Hotel (Cairo)   100
Shepparton (Australia)   88
Shertok, Moshe   166, 166 n. 9, 188
ships, sought for illegal
   immigration   203, 205, 208
Simferopoltses   29–30
Singapore   5, 86, 114
Slobodka   104–5
Smuts, General   121
Smyrna   207
Snitovka   7
Society for Trades and Agricultural
   Labor. *See* ORT
Sofia   206n
Sokolow, Nahum   46
South Africa   5, 97 n. 4, 132, 133,
   134, 170
   and Af Al Pi campaign   199,
   203, 208
   and Aliyah Bank Limited   201
   composition of Jewish
   population   122–23
   Jabotinsky speaking tour in   121,
   156, 188–89
   Jacobi's fund-raising in   4, 5, 39,
   121–25, 126, 181–82, 185, 186
   Jewish population   123
   NZO in   190, 191
   Revisionists   182, 199
"South African Campaign for the
   Reconstruction of East European
   Jewry"   122
South African Jewish Board of
   Deputies   122

South African Jewish Chronicle, article
  about the Thirteenth South
  African Zionist Conference   125
South African Jewish World,
  report on mass meeting in
  Johannesburg   124
South African Life Assurance
  Company   126
South America   81
Southern India   86
St. Kilda (suburb of
  Melbourne)   92
St. Petersburg   1, 25, 30, 31, 35, 57
"The Stalin-Ben-Gurion-Hitler
  Axis" (article in *Hazit ha-
  Am*)   141–42
Stavsky, Abraham   142, 143, 145–
  46, 154, 173, 175, 216
Stavsky Affair   145–54, 215–16
Stern, Abraham   193, 193n
Stockholm   202, 208
strikes, Jabotinsky's attitude to   141
students, limitations on numbers
  of   18
Suez (port)   100
Suez Canal   45, 85, 100–101
Sun (newp., Melbourne), report on
  meeting in Montefiore Hall   91
Sunday Mail (Glasgow), interview
  with Jacobi   38
Super, Newton   120
Supersky, Yehoshua   180
Surabaya   87, 114
Switzerland   17, 103
  and British intervention against
  Jew refugees   206
Sydney   93, 95, 114, 118
  fund-raising campaign in   94

Sykes, Mark   46, 47
Sykes-Picot Agreement   45
Syria   41, 43, 45, 51, 52

Tales of Odessa (Babel)   17
Tamar (Jabotinsky's sister)   82
Tatra Bank (Prague)   190, 200
teacher of Hebrew and Jewish
  history, Jacobi as   60
Tel Aviv   62, 82, 101, 102, 119, 126,
  127, 139, 153 n. 7, 168, 183
  and the *Altalena*   154
  international fair   129–30
  Jabotinsky address in   120
Tel Hai Foundation   187
Third Australian Zionist
  Conference   118
Time Magazine, report on Seventh
  Dominion League in   93
Times (London)
  on Jews in land of their
  forefathers   44
  on Jordania Society Limited   157
Tiomkin brothers   83n
Tiomkin, Vladimir   216
"Tired of Giving?"   82, 114, 122,
  125
Tog (newsp.), article by Jacobi on
  Odessa and pogroms   25, 27,
  32–34
Tomaszewski, Jerzy   198
tourists
  "illegal"   154n
  Revisionists entering Palestine
  as   196
trade unions, American Jewish   106
Transfer Agreement   139–40, 171,
  178–79, 181

Transjordan 42, 51–52, 54, 71, 73, 93
  Jacobi speech on 186–87
  Jewish settlement barred in 52, 53, 67, 126, 178, 181
Treaty of Brest-Litovsk 33–34n
Trivus (signatory to Revisionist manifesto) 83n
Trumpeldor, Joseph 70n, 217
tuberculosis 123
Turkey 44–45
  Balfour Declaration in peace treaty with 49
Turks 16
Twain, Mark 14
Tyre 43

Ukraine 3, 18, 25, 31, 65
  Babi Yar massacre 10
  Jewish unemployment in 123
  and Jews' plight 60, 65
  pogroms 1, 2, 17, 21–24, 25, 31, 60, 61
Ukrainian (language) 60
Ukrainian Communist Party 23
"Ukranian Jews Aim to Stop Pogroms" (*New York Times*) 60
Union (ship) 196
Union of Sydney Zionists 118
United Committee of Jewish Democratic Organizations to Fight the Pogroms. See *Okoyed*
United Jewish Socialist party 26
United Kingdom 4
United States 4, 5, 18, 58, 80, 81, 85, 95, 97, 100, 103, 106, 122, 202
  Jabotinsky trip (1926) 3, 77–78
University of Novorossiysk (Odessa campus) 14, 16, 19, 36, 57

Ussishkin, Menachem 60, 60–61 n. 4
Ussishkin, Samuel 60–62

Va'ad Leumi, the 203
Victorian Jewish Immigration Questions Committee 89
Victorian Jewish Welfare Society (VJWS) 88
Vienna 69, 71, 142
  first NZO congress held in 178, 181
Vilnius 105
Vincent, Clovis 211, 211 n. 18
"Vladimir Hitler," Ben-Gurion term for Jabotinsky 173
Volksrust 123
"Volunteer Army" 36, 36–37 n. 14

Wailing Wall incident 119, 135
Waitomo 95
Wales 65
Wall Street crash (1929) 107
War Cabinet, British 48
Warsaw 4, 12, 105, 124, 138, 148, 149, 152, 193, 202, 206, 206n
  Irgun representatives in 199, 201
  NZO in 198, 201, 202
"The Way Towards a Jewish Majority in Palestine" (Jacobi article) 115
"We Must Have a Jewish Majority" (AJH article) 111
"We the Bourgeois" (Jabotinsky) 140
Webb, Sidney. *See* Lord Passfield
wedding, the Jacobis' 8, 102

Wedgwood, Josiah Clement
Wedgwood 5, 92–93
Weizmann, Chaim 46, 51, 67, 103,
108, 132, 132 n. 5, 202–3
and the British Mandate 55,
109–10, 137, 153, 161–62
and Churchill 54
description of Jabotinsky 68
and Jabotinsky letter to unite
Zionist bodies 183
on Jewish majority in
Palestine 137
with Jacobi and Baron Robert de
Rothschild in 202
proposing Palestine as Jewish
national home 47–48
resignation from presidency of
World Zionist Organization 137
split with Jabotinsky 104
Weizmann, Vera 104
Wellington 95
West Bank, the 51, 52
western Europe 80
"What of the Jewish Agency? A
Jewish National Home or a
New Jewish Ghetto?" (Jacobi
article) 110–111
White Army 2, 23, 36, 39
Jacobi's arrest by 40
White Paper
Churchill (1922) 53, 67, 71, 178
n. 3
Passfield (1930) 119–20, 125–
26, 178 n. 3
White Russia 123
Wilson, Woodrow 48
Women's Zionist League
(Johannesburg) 126

Woodhead Commission 187
World Jewish Economic
Conference 171
World Union of General
Zionists 164
World Union of Zionist Revisionists
(UZR) 71–72, 78, 139, 159, 167
Committee in Palestine 168–69
Declaration of the Central
Committee of 42, 71
Executive Committee of 135–
36, 137, 176, 178, 189, 192, 213
finances 78
Jacobi as secretary-general of
Central Committee of the 74,
215
Jacobi's coffin brought to London
office of 213
Jacobi's resignation from position
in 78
and Jabotinsky-Grossman
conflict 135–36, 137–38
Jacobi's title as secretary-general
of Central Committee of the 74
and withdrawal from the Zionist
Organization 176, 177–78
World War I, end of 33–34
World Zionist Organization 18,
47, 54, 72, 115, 139, 168
acceptance of Balfour
Declaration 169
acceptance of Mandate
terms 67
attitude to Revisionists 190
Actions Committee 55, 74, 153,
160–63, 167, 168, 176
Executive committee 54, 167–
68

internal politics 139, 160
Revisionists' withdrawal
from 137, 176–77
Wynn, Samuel 111

Yankelevitch family 60, 101, 210
Yankelevitch, Ira-Asaya 9
Yankelevitch, Leib Alterovich 7–8,
62
Yankelevitch, Mamuya-Dina
(Manya) 9, 102
Yankelevitch, Mordechai 9
Yankelevitch, Simha 9
Yankelevitch, Suria-Genia (Sarah)
Berovna 7, 101
Yemen 75
Yevtushenko, Yevgeni 10
Yiddish 3, 60, 65, 75, 103

Zaharoff, Sir Basil 180, 180n
Zangwill, Israel 76
Zeirei Zion 26
Zionism 2, 18, 42, 44, 46, 77, 90
Zionist, The, article by Jacobi about
Petlura in 36 n. 13
Zionist Congresses
Court 168
First 169
Sixth 44
Eleventh (1913) 75
Fifteenth (1927) 72
Sixteenth (1929) 103, 111, 136,
156
Seventeenth (1931) 133, 136
Eighteenth (1933) 147
Zionist Executive Assembly (1934),
Jacobi delegate to 166–67
Zionist Federation 94, 157, 176
Zionist General Council, Jacobi's
statement to 167–68
"The Zionist Leadership Has
Failed" (Jacobi article) 108–9
Zionist movement 104, 109
Australia 108, 117, 118
British 46, 48, 59
Jewish self-defense and the 22
Rasswyet articles on new platform
for 70
Zionist Organization of America
(ZOA) 77–78
Zionist Record (South African
paper) 190
articles by Jacobi in 125
report on Jacobi's 1931 South
African fund-raising 127
text of Jacobi speech in 127
Zohar. *See* Union of Zionist-
Revisionists
Zurich 4, 100, 103, 207

Sioma, five years old, in Berdichev ◥

◥ Sioma's mother, Suria-Genia, known as Sarah (b. 1873, Rogashov, Ukraine)

Sioma's father, Leib Alterovitch Yankelevich (b. 1872, Snitovka, Ukraine)

Sioma wearing the uniform of a student at the Odessa campus of the Novorossiysk University, 1917

Sioma wearing the uniform of ◥
the Institute of Railway
Engineers, Petersburg, 1917

▲ Sioma in the center of the seated row of the Organizational Committee of the
Odessa Self-Defense Force, 1917. He wears the uniform of a student of the
Institute of Railway Engineers. Clearly one of the youngest in photograph, he
had just been elected chairman of the group. Vladimir Tiomkin is second from
Sioma's left.

▲ The heavily armed Odessa Jewish self-defense force, 1918. Sioma, as commander, is seated at the center. He wears the uniform and cap of a student of the Institute of Railway Engineers.

▼ A surveying field trip as an engineering student at Loughborough College, 1924

▲ Another field trip as a student at Loughborough College, 1924

Sioma's graduation photograph
at Loughborough College, where
he earned his civil engineering
diploma in 1925

Meeting in Paris, 1925. Vladimir Tiomkin is on Sioma's left.

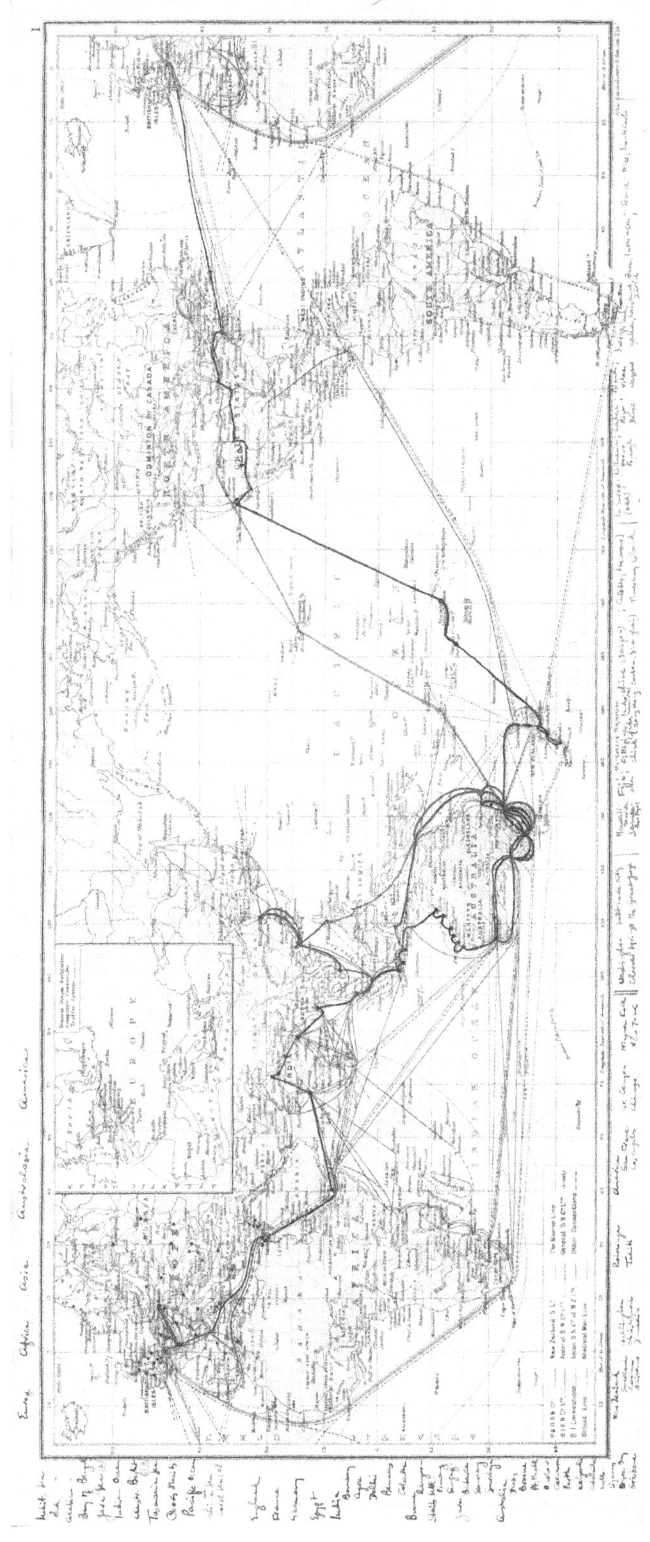

◀ Map from Sioma's scrapbook on which he marked his sea voyages for ORT and OZE from 1928 to 1932

▼ In tropical gear in Bombay,
February 1928

▲ With a Jewish community in Calcutta, March 1928

Sioma with Edna Jones, ◤
his fiancée, at the Melbourne
Botanical Gardens, May 1928

▲ Visiting the Jewish agricultural settlement in Shepparton, Victoria, Australia,
May 1928

▲ Sioma and Edna in their wedding photograph, Jerusalem, July 11, 1929. Edna is seated second from the right. Vladimir Jabotinsky, who acted as best man, stands next to Sioma in the back row, third from the right. The others in the group are Sioma's family, who were living in Palestine at the time.

▼ Sioma and Edna on their honeymoon, Rheinfall, Switzerland, 1929

The Sixteenth Zionist Conference, Zurich, August 13, 1929. Sioma and Edna are at the center between the two arms of the tables. Sioma's menu from the conference dinner, which is still in his family's possession, was autographed by Albert Einstein.

Edna, during a tour of ORT-OZE's work in Eastern Europe, Slobodka, Lithuania, August 1929

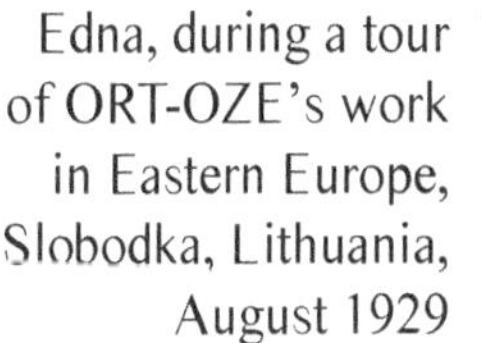

ORT-OZE summer camp for children outside Vilna, Lithuania, August 1929

Sioma and Edna visiting Sioma's family with Naomi, their first-born daughter, Tel Aviv, 1932

▲ Edna with their two daughters, Naomi and Carmel, 1934

▲ Edna, Sioma, Naomi, and Carmel boarding an aircraft for a holiday in France,
1935

▼ Jacobi family picnic with Joanna (Anya) Jabotinsky in Kew Gardens, London, 1935

▲ Edna with Naomi and Carmel, London, 1938

Sioma and Michael Haskel at the pyramids in Egypt, 1938

Sioma and Jabotinsky, 1937

Sioma and Jabotinsky, 1937 ◥

▲ Sioma's funeral at Willesden Cemetery, London, November 24, 1939.
Vladimir and Joanna Jabotinsky are standing with Edna.

www.ingramcontent.com/pod-product-compliance
Lightning Source LLC
Chambersburg PA
CBHW081357130726
47998CB00011B/2996